Saving the Text

Geoffrey H. Hartman is Karl Young Professor of English and Comparative Literature at Yale University.

Books

The Unmediated Vision. An Interpretation of Wordsworth, Hopkins, Rilke and Valéry   1954

André Malraux   1960

Wordsworth's Poetry 1787–1814   1964

Beyond Formalism: Literary Essays 1958–1970   1970

The Fate of Reading and Other Essays   1975

Akiba's Children   1978

Criticism in the Wilderness: The Study of Literature Today   1980

Editions

Hopkins: A Selection of Critical Essays   1966

Wordsworth: Selected Poetry and Prose   1970

New Perspectives on Coleridge and Wordsworth. English Institute Essays   1972

Romanticism: Vistas, Instances, Continuities. With D. Thorburn   1973

Psychoanalysis and the Question of the Text. English Institute Essays   1978

Saving the Text

Literature/Derrida/Philosophy

Geoffrey H. Hartman

The Johns Hopkins University Press
Baltimore and London

The Johns Hopkins University Press, Baltimore, Maryland 21218
The Johns Hopkins Press Ltd., London

Library of Congress Cataloging in Publication Data

Hartman, Geoffrey H
    Saving the text.

    Bibliography: p. 168
    Includes index.
    1. Criticism.   2. Derrida, Jacques.   Glas.
I.   Title.
PN81.H285   801'.95   80-21748
ISBN 0-8018-2452-4

For the Subject

Was aber bleibet, stiften die Dichter.

(That which remains is founded by poets.)

Friedrich Hölderlin

So wenig der Geist das Absolute ist, so wenig geht er auf in Seiendem. Nur dann wird er erkennen was ist, wenn er nicht sich durchstreicht. Die Kraft solchen Widerstandes ist das einzige Mass von Philosophie heute.

(Spirit is not the Absolute any more than it is something that disappears into being without a remainder. It will only recognize the nature of things if it does not cancel itself out. That force of resistance constitutes the sole measure of philosophy today.)

Theodor Adorno

Riechen wir noch Nichts von der göttlichen Verwesung?— auch Götter verwesen!... Mit welchen Wasser könnten wir uns reinigen? Welche Sühnfeiern, welche heiligen Spiele werden wir erfinden müssen?

(Do we not yet smell anything of the divine putrefaction? Gods, too, putrefy!... With what water could we purify ourselves? What festivals of atonement, what sacred games shall we have to invent?)

Friedrich Nietzsche

Contents

List of Figures   xi

Acknowledgments   xiii

Introduction   xv

1 *Monsieur Texte*   1

2 *Epiphony in Echoland*   33

3 *How to Reap a Page*   67

4 *Psychoanalysis: The French Connection*   96

5 *Words and Wounds*   118

Notes   158

Bibliography of Cited Works   168

Index of Names   176

Index of Subjects   181

List of Figures

1 Jacques Derrida, *Glas*, p. 7   10–11
2 Jacques Derrida, *Glas*, p. 8   12–13
3 Valerio Adami, *Ich*, signature painting   34
4 René Magritte, *L'île au trésor*   36
5 René Magritte, *La légende des siècles*   37
6 René Magritte, *Le domaine d'Arnheim*   38
7 Claes Oldenburg, *Proposed Colossal Monument to Replace the Washington Monument: Scissors in Movement*   39
8 Bill Lombardo, *Monument Sculpture*   40
9 Etienne-Louis Boullée, *Tour en cône tronqué*   41
10 Etienne-Louis Boullée, *Pyramide sous ciel gris*   42
11 *Top*, Thomas Bewick, Ass; *bottom*, Thomas Bewick, Thumbprint (signature)   43
12 Jacques Derrida, *Glas*, p. 251 (part)   53
13 Jost Ammann, *Aus dem Geschlechterbuch der Familie Tucker*   54
14 Johann Kaspar Hiltensperger, *Logocentric Labyrinth*   55
15 Jacques Derrida, *Glas*, p. 290   68–69
16 Jacques Derrida, *Glas*, p. 291   70–71
17 Jacques Derrida, *Glas*, p. 290 (part)   76
18 Jacques Derrida, *Glas*, p. 113b   88
19 Alberto Giacometti, *La main*   91
20 William Blake, signature painting from *Milton*   114
21 Victor Hugo, signature painting   115
22 Guillaume Apollinaire, signature poem from *Calligrammes*   116
23 William Blake, signature from title page to *Milton* (detail)   116

Acknowledgments

I have had the assistance, at various points, of Barbara Johnson, Lise Davis, and Claudia Brodsky. Jim di Loreto was indispensable in helping to prepare both the final manuscript and the index. Jacques Derrida generously facilitated permission to reproduce some pages of *Glas*. I thank him, the Editions Galilée, Valerio Adami, the Galerie Maeght, the Bibliothèque Nationale, and the Musée Victor Hugo for photographs or reproductions whose copyrights they hold. Also Mme. René Magritte and Harry Torczyner for generously allowing me to reproduce the works of Magritte on the cover and in the book.

Chapters 1 and 2 were originally published in the *Georgia Review* while under the editorship of John Irwin. Chapter 4 was an English Institute essay in *Psychoanalysis and the Question of the Text*, edited by me and published by the Johns Hopkins University Press. An early version of the opening pages of chapter 5 appeared in *Medicine and Literature*, ed. Enid R. Peschel (New York: Neale Watson, 1980).

Introduction

PHILOSOPHY, though it has its own classics, has rarely been content with the dependence of mind on text. It has wished to liberate thought from a grammar imposed either by language or by those special and influential closetings of language which every "great book" fosters. (Sometimes it has tried, instead, to find an ideal grammar occulted by too mutable a language.) The conflict of dialectic with rhetoric, of *ratio* with *oratio*, or, as Vico would say, in reaction to Descartes and taking up a distinction made by Aristotle, of topical truths leading to the *certum* and of scientific truths leading to more than verisimilitude, to the *verum* itself—these are but symptoms of a division in the world of thought that has lasted so long that it begins to seem fated. By calling this book *Saving the Text* I do not imply a religious effort in the ordinary sense: the allusion is to the well-known concept of "saving the appearances" (*sozein ta phainomena*), and my title suggests that we are still endeavoring to convert thinking to the fact that texts exist.

How can mind accept rather than subvert or overlook (by sophisticated scanning techniques, which are the opposites of close reading) the language of great writers, both in philosophy and literature? That struggle is intense and productive in Jacques Derrida. He is a philosopher who for many is not a philosopher at all but a strange philologist; students of literature often react to him with resentful admiration. His *discours de la folie* blurs genres or engages in so interminable a mode of analysis that the sanity of writing—its indebtedness to evolved conventions, as well as its apparent realism—is threatened. My book has Derrida as its focus, but it is not an exposition of his work. I am concerned chiefly with Derrida's place in the history of commentary, and with *Glas* as an event in that history.

It was *Glas* that helped me, a nonphilosopher, to approach Derrida and forgo the scruple that I had too small a knowledge of technical philosophy. For I was always thinking about the status of commentary, and what the history of interpretation, in the form of commentary, could teach. Derrida's *Glas* presented a challenge. It seemed to substantiate what Valéry had foreseen in his famous essay of 1919, "The Crisis of the European Mind," namely, that modern European culture would end up as an "infinitely rich nothing" ("*rien infiniment riche*") once diffusion of knowledge had advanced to the point where "no luminous inequality would remain and permit distinctive foci to merge," or where this spreading equalization would result in a "perfection of disorder" through the "free coexistence, in all cultivated minds, of the most dissimilar ideas." It also seemed to restate and revive a problem too neatly resolved by T. S. Eliot in *his* essay of 1919, "Tradition and the Individual Talent."

Eliot there raised the question of the new and emerging talent's relation to the mighty dead, to the *maiores* who shadowed about—more intensely in the modern period, because historical knowledge had kept more books alive—the individual artist. Given these conditions of modernity, in what form should the works of the great writers be preserved? Was Derrida's kind of exegesis, demonstrated so powerfully in *Glas*, a "solution," at least in the sense that the Barbarians, in Cavafy's famous poem, were a "kind of solution" during the Roman decadence? Derrida's commentary is a lens that gathers in the most varied texts *and* focuses them *and* burns through until we fear for them once again. It is so radical that, despite its reference to our dependence on the words of others, the contained (language) breaks the container (encyclopedic book, concept, meaning) and forces upon the reader a sense of the mortality of every code, of every covenanted meaning.

But what can it mean to place mind on its own axis and free it from books—to make mind its own text, as it were? Can we transcend telling toward, more simply, showing? Would that bring about (as both Husserl and Wittgenstein once hoped) a return to things themselves? Yet does not the very existence of words indicate a breach with the phenomenality of things, or with an ideal of showing, of evidentiality, taken from that sphere?

Perhaps the very notion of *totality* (words-and-things, the Speaking of Being, a telling that is a showing or vice-versa) is illusory. As a wish for total intelligibility it is not limited to philosophy, of course. Stanley Cavell sees it emanating from the silence of the silent movies, made conscious when the talkie appears. "It is the talkie itself that is now exploring the silence of movies. . . . With talkies we got back the clumsiness of speech, the dumbness and duplicities and concealments of assertion, the bafflement of soul and body by their inarticulateness and their terror of articulateness. Technical improvements will not overcome these ontological facts; they only magnify them. These ontological facts are tasks of art, as of existence. The advent of sound broke the spell of immediate intelligibility . . . " (*The World Viewed*).

Thus silence reasserts itself, in the sense that "words are out of reach, that there will never be the right time for them." The synchronization of voice and image or, ultimately, of time of saying and time of meaning, is recessed rather than advanced. Derrida too, in his way, dispels the "spell of voice." He associates the silence of things with the written word, as if it had always been of the word. For him, the technical change from speech to writing or print merely discloses an ontological fact that is more than ever the task both of art and of philosophy.

In the past, religion had often deferred, by various types of negative theology, total intelligibility: what Hegel called "absolute knowledge." Or it had allowed a methodical *memento mori* to disrupt that knowledge. The problem of religious thought, therefore, was finding a positive beyond the positivity of the negative (death). So Franz Rosenzweig, who is recalled by Levinas in *Totality and Infinity* (which tries to save "infinity" at the expense of "totality"), opens his major work, *The Star of Redemption*, with a meditation that challenges the philosophers. It asks them to recognize what they have denied: that their wish to know the All takes off from a fear of death. Rosenzweig's first pages are a relentless indictment of philosophy's pretensions, based on such denial. He evokes the falseness of the affirmations on which even negative or dialectical philosophies are founded. Philosophy's attempt to have "nothing" as its presupposition merely veils the reality of death as the something that always precedes. In a passage of extraordinary pathos, which I give in my own translation, Rosenzweig suggests that philosophy, rather than religion, has mystified nonbeing:

> Philosophy travels on over the grave that gapes before our feet at every step. It lets the body fall into the abyss, but the soul floats on high and away. That the fear of death knows nothing of such separation of body and soul, that it roars out, "I, I, I," and will not hear of such separation of body and soul—what does philosophy care for that? Let mortal man crawl to hide himself like a worm in the crevices of the naked earth before the hissing missiles of blind, implacable death, let him feel ineluctably and violently what he never feels otherwise: that his "I" is only an "It" when it dies, and let him, therefore, with every cry yet in his throat cry out his "I" against blind, implacable death that threatens him with such unthinkable annihilation—philosophy smiles its smile upon his need and with extended finger points out to this creature, as its limbs quake in fear for its worldly existence, a world beyond, which it does not want to know about. . . . But though philosophy denies [*leugnet*] the dark presupposition of all life, though it refuses to consider death as something but makes it into nothing [*Nichts*], it evokes for its own sake the semblance of presuppositionlessness. Thus, now, all knowledge of the All has for its presupposition—nothing.

What relevance does such a passage have to Derrida? How would one suggest a debt that may not exist? Does it come through Levinas, does it matter if it comes that way or through no one textual source? Derrida provokes such questions and allows them to gather without a resolution, like storm clouds that keep threatening. Often when we read him (especially in *Glas*) an image or quotation breaks its frame (it is split off, in Walter Benjamin's words, from homogeneous time) and catches the historian-interpreter. Rosenzweig's passage caught me while I was trying to understand the relation of philosophy to totality, and it took me back, beyond the Second World War, to the horror of the First (the *Star of Redemption*, completed in 1919, was published in 1921), when existentialism was not yet a name.

Derrida, carefully read, is a powerful "medium" who has absorbed and evolved ideas in their generic and mobile, rather than academic-rotarian, character. Take the French fascination with Poe and the mystery story. In Poe, death and nonbeing are everywhere, together with a mind mad enough to deny their evidence or to make scientific speculation in the face of death its triumph—a triumph of mind over death. Poe's stories animate the part, not the whole—or else the missing part that may link all the parts. Thus, clues or traces achieve an extraordinary *material* resonance: they become, despite conventional endings that give them their quietus, floating signifiers or ghostly *things* (furniture, vestments, teeth); their reality is in being these part-wholes that cannot be fully placed, attributed, humanized. Mallarmé's *Igitur* incandesces and formalizes the genre; and Derrida turns even psychoanalysis into a modern Gothic affair. Is not psychoanalysis, too, a quest for totality, or for the Monumental Institution, though carved out of the tremors and travails of family life and theorized into solid, scientific forms of ghostliness? Does it not repeople the mind with dead persons and dread voices: intimations of mortality in the form of dream or text fragments that break the frame of rational thought and bring back "immortal longings"?

Yet nonbeing and death need not be left to religious mysticism or the modern Gothic or science fiction. Heidegger's analysis of nonbeing also reverses what Rosenzweig had called the lie of philosophy. The second part of Heidegger's *Being and Time*, concerned with being-for-death (*Sein zum Tode*), debt or guilt (*Schuld*), calling (*Ruf*), inheritance (*Erbe*), and destiny (*Geschick*), may have shown Derrida how deeply ordinary and specifically temporal in their complexity, how near in their very distance, these concepts are. Yet Derrida's mind is so assimilative (*"reprosuctive,"* he puns, benefiting from a slip of the pen) that neither literature nor philosophy nor the sciences of man or of the mind can be identified as exclusive sources. Indeed, his very understanding of writing (*"écriture"*) rejects such source-hunting in favor of a more comprehensive haunting.

IT IS necessary to say something about the relation of commentary to *écriture*. Writing, as Derrida conceives it, is always "littérature et philosophie mêlées." Writing surpasses its starting point in these two major genres. So *Glas*, which figures largely in this book, is recognizably a commentary on Hegel and Genet, yet it does not remain subordinate to them—other texts also crisscross through the free play of a new, nonnarrative art form. As an art form, moreover, Derrida's commentary undermines both spatial and temporal perspectives, until we are left with no single unifying theme or structure but with the "ghosts of all things that are." These ghosts are shadows cast by the future as much as by the past: writing is their reality, as its massive oblique makes us inhabit the spectral core of things, "the dead whose names are in our lips" (Keats).

To avoid the charge of mystification, let me explain this linkage, in Derrida, of writing and nonbeing. His position is that what Heidegger calls the forgetting of Being is simply the forgetting of Writing; and that this forgetting goes together with a privileging of spoken speech or of mimesis or of the entire "Greek" realm of luminosity (whether attributed to phenomena or numina). Western tradition has been marked, Derrida claims, by a metaphysics of light, by the *violence* of light itself, from Apollonian cults to Cartesian philosophies. In the light of this emphatic light everything else appears obscure; especially the Hebraic development of aniconic writing and self-effacing commentary—of *textuality*.

When Heidegger, then, thinks he is thinking Greek (ur-Greek), he is thinking Hebrew. And, symbolically, the blackness of ink or print suggests that *écriture* is a hymn to the Spirit of Night, though it still wants itself Apollonian rather than Dionysian. ("Light perhaps has no opposite," writes Derrida, "if it does, it is certainly not night.") The passion for light, for absolute knowledge (Hegel), or for the translucence of the universal in the concrete (Coleridge's formula, taken from Schelling) is displaced by the passion of signifiers without a transcendental signified.

The Hebrew-Hellene distinction may be as fallible as Joyce suggests: "Jewgreek is greekjew. Extremes meet." The desire for totality, or even for unmediated vision—weaning oneself from book-culture in order to speak Being, or turning a book into a bible whose truth is revealed rather than read—cannot be confined by historicist categories, however fascinating they may be. Yet the distinction serves to reveal how the idea of a "reading *at sight*" or of "the immediate transparency . . . of the discourse of voice" has settled in our culture. I quote from Althusser's first chapter in *Reading Capital*; he notes there not only the "religious complicity between *Logos* and *Being*" but also Hegel's Eucharistic strengthening of it by including history itself as the substantial subject of "absolute knowledge." It is no accident, Althusser writes, "that when we turn the thin sheet of the theory of reading, we discover beneath it a theory of *expression*, and that we discover this theory of the expressive totality (in which each part is *pars totalis*, immediately expressing the whole that it inhabits in person) to be the theory which, in Hegel, for the last time and on the terrain of history itself, assembled all the complementary religious myths of the voice (the Logos)." It is no accident, similarly, that Derrida's *Glas* contains a reading of Hegel starting from the concept of absolute knowledge; that his reading makes us ask, with Althusser, What is it to read? and What is it to write?—but also delivers Hegel from Althusser's own residual historicism.

With so much historical knowledge, how can we avoid historicism, or the staging of history as a drama in which epiphanic raptures are replaced by epistemic ruptures, *coupures* as decisive as Hellene and Hebrew, or Hegel and Marx? Can a history be written that does not turn into something monumental and preemptive? In *The Unmediated Vision* I described Romantic and post-Romantic poets in their struggle against mediatedness, in their desire for the kind of vision denounced by Althusser and deconstructed by Derrida, but I was unable to formulate a theory of reading that would be historical rather than historicist. Such a theory is only less important than the realization that writing is an act with its own *conjuncture* whose properties do not coincide with present motives and ideologies.

AND YET: is not writing too much with us? There is today a writing mentality, as there is a push-button mentality; indeed, it might be argued that conversation and recitation are presently endangered. In Derrida himself one feels a barely veiled disgust at a *Teufelsdröckhean* excess of words. But to conceive of writing as a mode of silent speech, which might be converted back to voice by some magical or ethical transformer (releasing us from the black debt), is the mistake at issue. To see writing as silent speech is already to misunderstand it and to reduce its force. Writing, Derrida believes, undoes the illusion of the simple location of meaning or self-presence: an illusion fostered by what is nearest ourselves, our body (as Bergson had remarked) but particularly our voice, or the affective voice of others when it haunts us with their likeness.

There are two questions, then, raised by Derrida's emphasis on writing as more than an extension of voice. The first is, What complexity have we overlooked or surpressed—perhaps what threat have we warded off—by "forgetting" writing, a forgetting that includes its reduction to the status of mere technique, to a function of voiced and prior thought? Has *mimesis*, when it comes to writing, usurped *poesis*?

But correlatively, writing destroys simplicity of voice, an idea as vulnerable as the metaphysical doctrine of the substantial unity of the soul, attacked by T. S. Eliot in his "impersonal theory of poetry." Eliot said that a poet had a medium rather than a personality to express (see "Tradition and the Individual Talent"). There are, of course, many such impersonality theories in the modern period, and they all, like Eliot's, have trouble guarding themselves against an older mysticism. For they raise an issue too easily shunted aside by New Critical or persona poetics: Whose voice speaks when I speak, and in whose name do I speak? This question is also pursued by psychoanalytic investigation: into the multiple personality, the precariousness of integration, and the difficulty of synthesizing an ego ("creating one's own voice," as the current expression goes).

I take up the second issue first. We tend to suppose that every act of speech, spoken or written, has a specifiable frame of reference. Speech is *signed* by or *assigned* to a particular person (a "speaker" or "persona") and *addressed* to a particular person or assemblage. Yet when we look more closely at this frame of reference, we become aware how much is presupposed. The frame of reference is often a frame-up. It allows us to economize words or their resonances: to synthesize or disambiguate them. Should the frame be lost, so that speaker or addressee become indeterminate, then the meaning also becomes less settled. The "ghostly" question arises of who is speaking, to whom, from where, as a basic structure of orientation—everything we subsume under the concept of "intention"—is put in doubt. Obversely, whenever the content of a statement is too peculiar, then it has difficulty in finding an addressee, or is not "received." And if we do find it attributed to someone whose intention we think we know, we suspect that the deviant statement is not his or hers, but interpolated or corrupt.

We can apply this reflection to literature. Is not *literary* language the name we give to a diction whose frame of reference is such that words stand out as words (even as sounds) rather than being, at once, assimilable meanings? The meaning of words is not unimportant, of course; it is deviation from normal use that suggests that something is wrong with speaker or hearer, with the source or the receiver. For instance, two persons (voices) may be trying to get through at the same time; or perhaps we have come in at the wrong point, and cannot follow. To call a text literary is to *trust* that it will make sense eventually, even though its quality of reference may be complex, disturbed, unclear. It is a way of "saving the phenomena" of words that are out of the ordinary or bordering the nonsensical—that have no stabilized reference.

Referential meaning is tied to this matter of framing; where we draw the line becomes as important as what is delimited. To "forget" writing, then, is to mistake or underestimate the question of framing: yet only writing itself can reverse the forgetfulness we show to writing. Where writing is, something without properties appears. That something is qualified by being framed: think of the elusive figure in the endlessly enlarged photos of Antonioni's *Blow Up*, or of photographic traces of atomic particles, or of the Loch Ness monster. Or, to leave the realm of quasi-images, think of rhythms and words that come unbidden, or voices that enter through dreams and psychotic states.

Writing destabilizes words, in the sense that it makes us aware at one and the same time of their alien frame of reference (they are words of the other or

come to us already interpreted, trailing clouds of meaning, each one a repre-
sentamen) and of the active power of forgetfulness (a kind of silencing) which
it enables and which, in turn, enables us to write. Yet to talk about writing as
such or about language as such is too abstract, just as to talk about literary
language per se is too isolating. At some point the affective power of voice, as
well as the relation of particular words to that resonating field we call the
psyche, must be considered. Semiotic analysis of the word in the word, even
when as penetrating as Derrida's, with his method of putting statements *en
abyme*, cannot reach that field of pathos or power. The interpreter, at least,
has also to understand the wound in the word. In "Words and Wounds," my
last chapter, I try to do precisely that.

Yet Derrida knows perfectly well that words are dangerous gifts, to be
assimilated, purged, lived through. "In the question of style," he writes,
recalling etymologies, "there is always the exam, the weight of a pointed
object." That point may not exist save in the way that Shakespeare puts it,
when a jealousy-maddened Leontes says in *The Winter's Tale*: "Affection, thy
intention stabs the center." Language seeks and flees that stabbing point,
which is at once what wounds and what may suffer the wound. We don't
always know what we mean, and the speech that echoes our speech—the
interpreter's—need not lay the "haunting melody" of words to rest. In *Spurs*
(on the style of Nietzsche, and aware of overtones of hunting and injury)
Derrida writes: 'Il faut écrire entre plusieurs styles." "Two spurs at least," he
continues, associating *spur* also with *spoor*, "such is the debt that falls due.
Between them the abyss in which to throw, risk—lose perhaps—the anchor."
Glas, quite literally, is written and risked "between" Hegel and Genet.

This woven language ("several languages," in this kind of writing, "must
be spoken and several texts produced at the same time") is disconcerting
enough to recall us to our first question: What threat does writing pose that we
should try and reduce it to a function of voice? Or rather, of voice considered
as a simple substance? The answer, of course, is that writing simplified into
image of voice is no danger: it merely reinstates the "Greek" desire for
visibility. The metaphysics of light maintains itself. What Nietzsche called
the Great Noon triumphs in the doctrine of the logos as rational, visible word.
"What is there more mysterious than clarity," Valéry has Socrates say in
Eupalinos. "Certain people lose themselves in their thoughts; but for us
Greeks all things are forms." Only when writing discloses an echo rather than
an image, so that the sounding word has reverberations that transcend the
economy of clarity and form, do contradictions arise that shake the "temples
of wisdom and science" in Valéry's logocentric vision. "This great art requires
of us an admirably exact language. The very word that signifies language [i.e.,
logos] is also the name, with us, for reason and calculation; a single word says
these three things." There is one word for three things because they are a

single thing. But the use of one word for three things could suggest an equivocal and disquieting, rather than appropriate, economy.

I am not going to choose between Valéry (his desire for clarity, often self-subverted) and Derrida. But Derrida's style, so didactic and deliberate—so removed from irony or the reserve of dialogue or essays that retain a link to that form—Derrida's style has indeed passed beyond the premise and promise of at-one-ment. So the word for anchor, *ancre*, sounding like the word for ink, *encre*, at once closes the sentence from *Spurs* quoted above and opens the abyss mentioned within it. What gymnastics or abysmatics! "Spurs" is also made to suggest the circumflex on the word *être* (Being), and shows its "forgotten" *s* through that angular trace. That spur-spoor rides the *e*. If we substitute the *s* and write out *estre*, we can then reconstruct a link between *estre* and *reste*, as if they were anagrams of each other. Being is what remains, not what is. Poetry, as the perfection of writing, is the house of Being, but equally its remains, the disclosure of nonbeing or *Seinsvergessenheit*. Yet this "forgetfulness" does not happen to (*befällt, tomber sur*) Being, in the manner of accident or secondary quality. It is of the essence. In Heidegger's even less readable style: "Sie gehört zur Sache des Seins." Translated: "It belongs hearingly [*gehört*] to the case [*Sache*, Latin *causa*, French *cas*] Being has, to the thing or house [*causa, cas, casa, chose*] of Being." "La chose est oublique," we might say, imitating Derrida.

AT A CRUCIAL point in his *Biographia Literaria* Coleridge invents a commonsensical friend who writes a letter asking him to desist from involved speculations in the German mode. Your book will never sell, he cautions, and will certainly not be read in England, should you go on this way. I can imagine the contemporary Anglo-American reader asking similarly whether Derrida's *style* of speculation is necessary and, more pointedly, whether such licensed puns may not cheapen and weaken an argument of importance. For the verbal prestidigitation can create an apparently ordinary, yet totally *constructed*, prose that would be hypocritical (since it has nothing ordinary about it) if it did not expose itself continually as resolutely overdetermined words that slip the leash of meaning without escaping meaning. Our delight in the virtuoso linguist easily turns into a "seasickness on land" as this condition of writing "between styles" and constructing sentences by *bricolage* becomes apparent. But whether we feel nostalgia for the old, grounded style, or simply nausea, the question arises: Why is there such writing? Or, Why does it go on?

The separation of writing from the search for (ultimate) meaning is so counterintuitive that a new question emerges: Could we ever get used to this point of view and its shock to humanistic thinking? The answer, Time will tell, is more appropriate than may at first appear because, to a great extent, the search for meaning has been that for the meaning—or mastery—of time. This is Nietzsche's view in the *Genealogy of Morals*, where—except for the "ascetic ideal"—man is said to have had no meaning. For Nietzsche, the "Nothing" of asceticism served to reveal, by taking meanings away, the only meaning the human animal has, which is this very *will* to wish Nothingness rather than not wish at all.

The gaze of the thinker, especially the historical thinker, is therefore bleak. It is "a sad, hard but determined gaze—an eye that looks out (perhaps so as not to look inwards? not to look back?). Here is snow, here life falls silent; the last crows that are heard are named 'Why?' 'In vain!' 'Nada!' " (*Genealogy of Morals*). A snowman's vision this, as cold as that of Wallace Stevens, and as luxurious in its expressive strength.

For what survives in this graveyard of meanings is not simply a will, but specifically the *will to write*. The surprising power, even richness, of language in Nietzsche, Stevens, or Derrida betrays the inner relation of what is now called "deconstruction" to the very activity of writing. And that is Derrida's point, *his* understanding of Nietzsche's yea-saying within a suicidal nihilism. Language itself, nothing else, or the Nothing that is language, is the motivating residue. Despite obsolete and atrophied words, and falsified, disputable, or undecidable meanings, the will to write persists. But why is there this something, that is, discourse, rather than nothing?

Metaphysics deconstructs itself when it asks its leading question in this or a related form: What remains, and what of the remains, of writing? Does what remains have a tincture of immortality? Or is it merely the by-product, even waste product, of a self-consuming activity that has not managed to purify itself out of existence? The contemporary Hamlet, surrounded by corpses of ideas, by mouldering systems, still speaks his piece. Even when we can't laugh any more, Beckett says at the end of *Waiting for Godot*, there is still the will to laugh.

I WILL spend some time on Derrida's style in this book, both because I approach Derrida from a literary point of view, asking what his value may be to literary thinking, and because his style is, within philosophy itself, a remarkable and eccentric event, despite identifiable debts to Heidegger. The question of style, literary or philosophical, is crucial, for there are many who still insist that the best philosophers have no style or that style is simply a matter of craft or accommodation. It is not my purpose to decipher Derrida by means of stylistic analysis. But the style does trouble and fascinate; it is, as I have said, deliberate and even exhibitionistic, both in itself and in the way it conceives philosophy as intertextual commentary. It tends to thicken its *démarche* by multiplying citations and texts, framing them in unexpected ways, and creating quasi-new sentences out of *bricolage*. Derrida strives for elegant opacity rather than for translucence, and his prose moves often on a set of phantom limbs (intertextual echoes) that are the equivalent of "inspiration." Yet that inspiration, as in Valéry, is so tightly organized that it becomes unmysterious, and a fatality only in the sense that we live and write in a *second nature* of circumambient texts—texts we must come to repossess. "I have lost my mystery," the Pythian priestess laments in Valéry's poem. "An adulterous intelligence maneuvers a body it has understood."

If Derrida has an influence among both French- and English-speaking students of literature, it is certainly because of his totally nonmystical, professional understanding of style as the personal appropriation (Heidegger's *Ereignis*) of the impersonal medium of language, together with the way language purifies the attempt and illuminates the hold of words. "A Wisdom talks," Valéry's poem ends, "and sounds forth that august Voice, which knows itself when it resounds as no longer the voice of anyone. . . ."

Moreover, if predecessors are regarded as capable of interacting with successors through texts or reliques, then they are, to that extent, contemporaries or consociates; and the concept of "person" or "individual" becomes socialized into a complicated blend of symbolic—and sometimes negative or depersonalizing—properties. (Cf. Clifford Geertz, *The Interpretation of Cultures*, especially chap. 14.) The opening of *Glas*, "quoi du reste . . . d'un Hegel," would then be symptomatic of all attempts to understand those involved in our biography and who make it, equally, a "thanatography."

The relation of *techne* and *thanatopsis* in this most acute of impersonality theories is as strong as in Valéry or Mallarmé. Derrida prefers the word *thanatopraxis* because books like *Glas* raise the question of praxis, or of the practical value of a commentary style that eschews all allegoresis, all ideologizing moves. Yet the Pythian priestess did serve a god; and it remains an open question whether Derrida's "*discours prophétique et paré*," however decentralized or disseminating, can resist being in the service of political power.

The question would need an analysis of the idea of power itself: its curious, unending investment by metaphors of possession, appropriation, originality, breakthrough, penetration, centeredness, immediacy. Derrida tends to make them dependent on another term, *presence*, although purity (as in Valéry) might have been equally apt. In thinking about textuality as an antibody to body-images of power and presence, or revising the relation of textuality to re-presentation, or responding to modern philosophies of materialism, Derrida joins himself to a peer group consisting of Levinas, Blanchot, Lacan, Bataille, Althusser, Barthes, Sollers, Deleuze, and Foucault. This may raise, of course, the issue of priority or, more exactly, of correspondence. *Priority* remains a concept in the sphere of influence, temporal magic, and cryptomnesia. *Correspondence* is a word still open, with a historical aura that is not fully available, yet certainly includes notions of harmony and adequacy, the mysticism of Baudelaire's famous sonnet, the idea of the new and of the transmission of news, and the idea of both exchange and interchange, especially of personal letters (*correspondance intime*).

Is it an accident that Derrida's latest book, *La carte postale*, chooses its organizing metaphor from the sphere of telecommunications, within which "correspondence" does or does not take place? "Calling is always long distance" is how one might translate, in the light of Derrida's book, Heidegger's "Gerufen wird aus der Ferne in die Ferne" (*Being and Time*, sect. 74). The relations between *techne, mimesis*, and *thanatopraxis* amount now to a "*dessin funeste*" that is no less than an endgame vision. The play with words, one that associates, for instance, "dessein" and "destin" (exploring an error of Lacan's, as if a slip of tongue or pen were fated) and links them both to Heidegger's overburdened use of "*Geschick*" (*destiny*, what is "destinated" or sent through the mails, and *technique*), this overcoding creates death sentences that we dare not understand except as play—sentences that are like cards as well as on cards (including the Joker). One does not, after all—or does one not?—use post cards to send what often read like farewell notes, even suicide notes.

Nor is it possible, any longer, to distinguish in this writing between the personal and the collective: both inhabit exactly the same language, in the way a post card is at once public and private. Thus, the ideal of classification (already an important focus in *Glas*) or the ideal of embracing everything as a single system or network, without exclusions, is associated here not only with the very concept of *book* (a fortune-telling book, made of omens or presemiotic codes) but also with the way postal technology operates to give everything an *address*. Yet the stronger the reality-effect of this placement, equivalent to some ultimate, eschatological desire for presence or embodiment, the stronger too a sense of ghostliness, of "atrocious exclusion," depersonalization, of an otherness that is too intimate.

The first part of *La carte postale* elides specific texts and so divests itself of the comfort of commentary, of reposing on texts even if they are merely words within and upon words. We move nearer to the hollow of the mind as it reads itself. Derrida is a correspondent to himself in this mock journal and epistolary novel, which simulates the punctuality of dates and, with affection, the "I" and "Thou" needed for an interminable *nouvelle*, a speculation *sans terme*, that evokes couples or doubles, from Socrates and Plato on. A shrouded book, this, made of a collage of philo-sophemes: the fragments, undecidably *fiche* and fetish, of a death story that is equally a love story. If Don Quixote, if Emma Bovary, die into the world of the Romance, if Freud dies into the world of the Dream (making it as textual as life itself), then this quixotic, romantic, and Freudian thinker dies into the world of Philosophy. He returns it, as in *Glas,* to the status of a *coup de dés* (Mallarmé), of *Gerede* (Heidegger), of *remarques* or *Zettel* (Wittgenstein). Between these lapsed forms of a still rigorous discourse, his language teeters, as extraordinary as it is ordinary.

Saving the Text

I *Monsieur Texte*

"Thing": id est, thinking or think'd. Think, Thank, Tank—
Reservoir of what has been thinged—Denken, Danken—I
forget the German for Tank/The, Them, This, These, Thence,
Thick, Think, Thong, Thou

Coleridge, Notebooks[1]

CARTESIAN doubt is described by Coleridge as a "self-determined indetermination." A verbal root common to both adjective and noun here is
term, and thought seems always to be extending or delimiting "terms" or "boundaries," though the method of so doing varies greatly. The concepts of point
and line, or of word and sentence, or finer part-whole distinctions; the attempt
to classify and to reconstitute classes into a model of the whole—these are
exercises that the mind performs repeatedly, exhaustingly, beyond the possibility of immediate benefit of an obvious kind. There must be some pleasure
in this exercise of mind; and the simplest guess is that the pleasure is in mind
itself: in the deliberate act of perceiving/situating/understanding what is given,
the self-determination, or "self-constitution" (Husserl's word) of what is. This
provisional act of mastery is not merely tyrannous or selfish if it involves less a
subjection of nature to mind than what Wordsworth called a "mutual domi-
nation" or "interchangeable supremacy." Of this self-determination, in any
case, numbers and the symbolic system we call language are especially crucial
instances; but their relation to the world is, as has been said, one of provisional mastery only, and often so enormously involuted that what was
considered a helpful, prosthetic device may claim attention as a world in
itself, a secondary system which is closer to reality than reality. These remarks
are intended to suggest only that the boundary between nature and art or
primary and secondary, or even text and commentary—event and
interpretation—is highly fluid. Even were it fixed by the nature of things (a
phrase whose boundaries are also not secure: are we to understand the "nature
of things," *natura rerum*, or the nature of "things," reification?), it would still

1

be subject to either a passionate or a methodical doubt: some "self-determined indetermination."

And lately (a suitably vague term) we have been accustomed to bypass the peculiar entity "self" and say that things are subject to language, or a language-determined indetermination. Even the self, that is, has its boundaries fixed or unsettled by language. The seeming impotence of traditional humanistic philosophies, together with the obvious success science has had in turning its provisional mastery of the world into a real imposition, may have encouraged this turn to a symbolic system, which, though open to abuse and technological alienation, is so old, ongoing, and polyglot, and so inherent if not coherent in a biological sense, that it has a better chance of resisting the exploitative or marketing closures of science, or of ideologies that claim to be scientific. For what goes under the name, for instance, of a science of language is more like a methodical miscellany, a pleasingly ordered chaos like most literature, including Jacques Derrida's *Glas*.

The house that Jack has built, while not a pack of cards, will infuriate those who think books should be solidly constructed, unified, and with an intellectual space defined by clear and resolute boundaries. Perhaps *Glas* has all these qualities of real estate. But like art of a certain caliber, it begins by confusing and even estranging us, and the difficult question is how long this estrangement should last, how genuine it is. Not since *Finnegans Wake* has there been such a deliberate and curious work: less original (but what does "original" mean to Derrida?) and mosaic than the *Wake*, even flushed and overreaching, but as intriguingly, wearyingly allusive. It is hard, at the same time, to shake off a feeling that high seriousness is mixed here with high frivolity, and that we may wake up from the beautiful strangeness of *Glas* into a handful of provocative epigrams and strongly contextual ruminations. What form does this book have? Is it a book at all?

Derrida has said that traditionally the idea of a book sends us back to a totality that claims to be founded in nature ("totalité naturelle") and that this claim is a theological and bookish defense against the "aphoristic energy" of writing itself. It is precisely this energy which makes me want to call *Glas* an epigrammatology. "La dialectique de la langue est dialectophage." Or, "La glu de l'aléa fait sens"—a phrase in which we hear *g-l-a-s* persisting as alliterative undersong. And because of the way things are "glued" together by the "aleatory" method, we find ourselves in a maze of texts or fragments of texts that at once fascinate and bewilder. The disorderly philosophical conduct of this work is so magnificent that it defies linear exposition.

A contradiction remains, though, as to form, even if *Glas* is considered an aphoristic sparagmos of form. "Aphorism" comes from a Greek word meaning to mark off by boundaries, and so to mark off for oneself, or appropriate; whereas these aphorisms constitute a metaphoric movement that perpetually transgresses the limits of word and concept, signifier and signified, until they become, in their expropriating virtue, "aporisms" (I coin the word from the Greek *aporia*); places or topoi that belong to no one and everyone, or a wilderness of passages that seem at first to lead nowhere except further into the bush (*Buch*, book) of textuality.

At this point other images too, in addition to bush, suggest themselves: ambush, web, trap, labyrinth. Like all images or metaphors, they enter philosophical discourse casually: we come upon them ("tomber sur" is the idiomatic expression) in trying to illustrate an argument. They are free examples, instances, e.g.'s. But this instancing is less gratuitous than may appear, for often it compensates a felt abstractness or loss of immediacy in philosophical prose. It is a way of bringing presentness (the *hic* and *nunc*) back. Something in appearance marginal, supplementary, accidental (a "case" cited by chance, an illustrative metaphor) tells us that the essence or thing itself is missing. The thing instanced becomes, as it were, a disgruntled representative of the absent (perhaps always absent) thing, and paradoxically gains more authority than the argument it was intended to supplement. And here is where literary study sees *its* chance. (It is not its only chance, of course.) It seizes on the images and metaphors that slip, deliberately or not, into pure or scientific discourse, and reflects on whether this allowance of dream or icon may not be closer to the real subject. This "tomber sur," like the operation of chance, or the phrase "it fortuned" in Spenserian romance, becomes loaded: with each "case" we "fall" into the "Falle" of words (8i)*: into a necessary reflection on their status, on the word/thing relation.

In Derrida, then, as in Heidegger, we are often caught up in a paronomasia that reverses the "tomber sur" into an "Überfall." The latter is a Heideggerian word I would like to translate as "hyperbole" as well as "ambush," to indicate that words can only be words by not being things, by aiming referentially at things yet overshooting them—an error (almost a *hamartia*) that makes it appear as if things were lost to words.

Actually two types of loss may be felt: of things as such in their supposed presence, their Pongian or Stevensian cleanliness ("How clean the sun when seen in its idea / Washed in the remotest cleanliness of a heaven / That has expelled us and our images"), which also leads a poet like Rilke ("Wird euch langsam namenlos im Munde?") to ablute or anonymize the familiar object; and loss of the thing-as-such, the heaven-ground of essence. Perhaps the two are the same loss; but where the first implies a toleration of otherness in the

---

*Reference is made to Derrida's *Glas* by page number, followed by column indications: 8a would mean page 8 left column; 8b, page 8, right column; 8i, page 8, intercolumn. See figures 1 and 2. For full reference to works cited in the notes, see the Bibliography.

form of muteness or non-sense, the second expresses a wish to pierce through to a more substantial otherness, to a clarifying signature beneath the phenomena. Both movements in Derrida tend to eddy mothlike around the flame of the word *propre*, which can evoke an impossible appropriation as well as an unthinkable absence of properties or of desire for them.

Let me return, then, to Derrida's style. The French *moralistes* of the so-called Classical period reinvented the epigram: it helped their concise, unflattering attack on all the manifestations of "amour propre," which includes, for Derrida, an "amour" of the "propre"—the desire for the illusion of being in place, present to oneself. This kind of narcissism can be a cheap target; and the rapier thrust of the epigram may be too clean in its attack to make us feel properly "improper." There is a problem of style here, of how to be a thorough moralist, one who dirties conscience, without becoming a divagating pedant, an explicator or dribbler of words. What magic instrument can set words against words, cut through their waste, self-indulgence, the grease of rhetoric, the antiquarian detritus? A love-hate of words is clear in Derrida; and to say so is not to say much. When he writes, "Le texte est craché," he covers the sentiment by a complex metaphoric web that involves thirst, agglutination, insult, and the structure of textuality as an aggressive and sticky conduit. "O Lord!" Coleridge exclaims, after the ingenious deduction that stands as an epigraph to this essay, "What thousands of Threads in how large a Web may not a Metaphysical Spider spin out of the Dirt of his own Guts/but alas! it is a net for his own super-ingenious Spidership alone!"

Derrida's aphoristic energy disseminates given texts as epigrammatic fragments but also reconstitutes them into a seemingly interminable—insatiable—web of his own. What he calls writing ("écriture") is in opposition to the very thing he honors as a philosopher: totalization of knowledge as an encyclopedic system or Hegelian absolute knowledge ("savoir absolu," 7a). The problem of form connects with a remarkable method of analysis, applied in *Glas* to Hegel (left) and Genet (right), and previously tested on Rousseau but even more radically on Plato and Mallarmé in *La dissémination* (1972). The question of style is also a question of method when Derrida "decenters" all themes or metaphors in philosophy as in literature, to reveal that nothing can be "proper," "present," "in place." It is as if the unities were disappearing from the stage of philosophy as well. The "scene of writing" is a multi-ring but intersecting circus leading to one intense, ongoing act of reading. Nothing is here subjected in a simple way to a dominant subject, whether identified as author, cogito, archetype, or field of knowledge.

The new method has its connections with Heidegger's critique of thematization in *Being and Time*, as well as with Nietzsche's famous reduction of truth to an illusion established by a "mobile army of metaphors, metonymies, anthropomorphisms." It is also indebted to historical semantics and to more structural or semiotic models of the "chain" of signification. But the mobility itself is what is remarkable in Derrida, and the sense of a serious, unending game, both in the writer who plays language against itself and in the reader who must uncover, without losing track, the gamut of language: rules, conventions, sedimentations, intersecting themes, crossing texts. . . . The issue of intention or meaning ("vouloir dire"), as of authorial guarantees or "logocentric" unity, is exposed to its strongest challenge yet.

Glas therefore questions at the start Hegel's understanding of a "savoir absolu" in which substance and subjective thinker coincide. It does so by drawing even the name of the author into the game. Hegel, who he? ("qui, lui?"). The imperial, eaglelike hubris of Hegel's project is brought out, not to mock it but to show its hyperbolic character. Derrida's opening "Quoi" is not much better, after all: it too is rhetorical as well as philosophic, and points to an overriding "interjection." We can still suggest, like Heidegger, that in questioning moments like this not the philosopher himself but "Die Sprache spricht" ("Language itself is the speaking subject"). But even where, as in this axiom, the ego is dethroned as the magisterial or controlling center, a new illusion surfaces.

The personification of "Sprache" shows that those who put author or ego down are still potentially mastered by the idea of presence itself, which persists even without the concept of a sovereign subject, because of the privilege accorded to voice ("Die Sprach *spricht*") as the foundation of the written word. In his study of Husserl, therefore, Derrida makes us *hear* "phonème" in the word "phénomène" as he degrades voice from its "leading" position to be merely the "phénomène du labyrinthe."[2] Voice does not found but reveals in a blind, overidentifying movement (the hyperbole, also, in Icarus's flight, called "la voie d'Icare," that is, "la voix d'Icare") the archi-texture of significa- tion (the detours or postponements of the "absolute" in Daedalus's labyrinth). The flight of the eagle called Hegel reveals something similar. It involves relations of *voix* and *voie*, of father and son, of foundation and filiation. *Glas* can only be understood if we begin "with" and "beyond" the "savoir absolu" mentioned in its opening pages, so that what Derrida names untranslatably "pensées inouïes" can be reclaimed by working through that labyrinth of Daedalian-Hegelian signs already inscribed in language and language- memory.

THE SOUND-WORD *glas*, which provides the title of Derrida's book, refers to death knell or passing bell. It is endlessly "joyced" by the author, to suggest that voice has no monument except in the form of a rattle in the throat covered or sublimed by the passing bell. The sound reverberates in the labyrinth of writing and, in dying, lights it up. Even the labyrinth, of course, is not to be put on the side of permanence: it is simply "as darkness to a dying flame." Voice *passes*, like the immediacy of perception to which, from Husserl to Merleau-Ponty, it had been related. "Contrairement à ce que la phénoménologie—qui est toujours phénoménologie de la perception—a tenté de nous faire croire, . . . la chose même se dérobe toujours. Contrairement à l'assurance que nous en donne Husserl un peu plus loin, 'le regard' ne peut pas 'demeurer.' "[3]

That ends the book on Husserl. Yet if we elide both voice and look, or allow them to slip away as purely phenomenal, what is left? What "demeure," substance, rock, foundation, house, path? Even if we do not seek to monumentalize our nothingness in the form of some permanent double, that colossus of Memnon which clangs like "glas" (8a–9a), even if we understand the need for sacrifice and dissemination, must we spend our intellectual lives decomposing the vanity of the monumentalists: the writers, artists, philosophers, and theologians among us?

So, if prematurely, we say to ourselves: *Glas* is but another owl-howl, philosophy trying to do itself in. We know that Derrida is the leading philosopher in France; that his first important work was on Husserl; and that *Glas* is in part an ambitious "mise en scène" if not "mise à mort" of Hegel. As in Hegel too there is no branch of the "sciences humaines" that does not find its way into an omnivorous prose. And Derrida's embrace of all that knowledge is curiously *terminal*: the murder of texts becomes a fine art, and what Hegel aspired to, that "savoir absolu," is simply, now, the "ton de l'on," as befits the elegant demise of ego, voice, corpus, world-spirit, and other "monumental" desires.

Yet someone must be speaking here. Who is this "on," or "l'alibi du Il indifférent" (Maurice Blanchot)? It is precisely at this point that we understand Derrida's attack on what he calls the "logocentric" tradition. For this impersonification ("l'impersonnifié, le texte . . ."), which Mallarmé recovered for French thought, is all too easily explained or mollified by a reference to the logos: "In the Beginning was the Word." So, by a characteristic and false turn, after Mallarmé comes Claudel. "Nous savons que le monde est en effet un texte et qu'il nous parle, humblement et joyeusement, de sa propre absence, mais aussi de la présence éternelle de quelqu'un d'autre, à savoir son Créateur" (cited by Derrida in *La dissémination*, pp. 53–54). Claudel goes on to associate *Igitur* and its depersonalizing mirror with the dark glass of Paul's Letter to the Corinthians, and the enigmatic Book of the Creatures.

That wrong turn—at once rhetorical and conceptual, which can be felt in Claudel's Augustinian style, so vocative in the void—that wrong turn, Derrida claims, has been taken so often that it has left its mark, frayed its path, in language, and perhaps has become language itself. We cannot but follow it even when we realize its deception. It is indeed a lure; but unlike the lure, say, of fleshly love, its disabusement cannot lead to the idea of a more glorious body or a more perfect language. It leads to the method called by Derrida "deconstruction," which reveals that turn being taken, not only against the will of the author, since it is preinscribed in language, but also because any author who stands in that turn cannot express that experience, that impersonification, except by words that sound, willy-nilly, mystical, like a displaced or negative theology. It is impossible not to think of the logos when we read "Die Sprache spricht" or "le Texte y parlant de lui-même et sans voix d'auteur" (Mallarmé again). Voix d'auteur / voix d'hauteur: the logos, or *Ecriture* in contradistinction to *écriture*, is always hierarchical. Proudhon, earlier in the century, had already pointed to the problem, when, though arguing a materialist position, he found himself forced to "conclude in the language of a believer, because there exists no other; not knowing whether my formulas, theological despite myself, ought to be taken as literal or figurative. . . . We are full of the Divinity, Jovis omnia plena" (quoted by M. H. Abrams in *Natural Supernaturalism*).

The spell can only be broken by a development internal to language. For the illusion of mastering the hazards of language is itself suspect, full of the pathos to be voided. And to create a countermythology as Blake and other strong artists attempt (even when as sophisticated as Valéry in *Eupalinos*) is only partially effective because it is so hard to tell parody from pathos. The only way to exit from the labyrinth of language seems to be by way of the center. Or, as in Blanchot, the labyrinth is itself conceived to be a scattering of the center, "l'étrange roue ardente privée de centre," the labyrinth of *écriture*.

Glas: a labyrinth. The theme of form returns, and strangely so, because whatever "demeure" this book may be, it must be a house of words and not a temple. The structural or architectonic metaphor, encouraged by the two "columns" confronting us, as by the Hegel passage on Memnon's statue and symbolic art, is at once undermined by that oldest of themes, the Ruins of Time: "Quoi du reste aujourd'hui" (7a).

The pages of *Glas* ruin words, in fact. There is a sense of débris, which is the obverse of an awareness of the treacherous flow ("glissement") of language. Time, though, is not against language (or vice versa) but coterminous with it: to be in the one is to be in the other. If, then, the page fractures itself with blank spaces and inserts, it is because God created the world not by the logos but by a slip of the tongue. There is no single, unifying logos: there is, at most, a divine parapraxis imitated alike by medieval jongleur and modern grammatologist.[4]

To create the world it needed six slips of the tongue . . . . Or, to adapt a talmudic speculation on the burning sword that guards paradise—we don't know how many sides a slip of the tongue has (any more than how many sides a dream has, "For the phenomenon of dreaming is not of one solution, but many" as Christopher Smart declared). The illusion of the logos is that saying and meaning coincide, that the exact or just word can be found and need not, or need only, be repeated. But writing is serpentine, that is, temporal. The serpent is the first deconstructor of the logos. He proves that the Word may have more than one sense or a sense other than intended. "Let Ziba rejoice with Glottis, whose tongue is wreathed in his throat" (Smart).

The unity or autonomy of the text becomes uncertain, therefore, as texts interlace like that wreathed tongue. Using words that have been used already, we trace or cite or echo them in ways that change and perhaps distort. This serpentine slippage is not mysterious, and founds both Derrida's notion of *freeplay* and Owen Barfield's of *tarning*. It is seen in such doublings as "glas" and "glace"; in the "fall" (cas/case) of grammatical endings; in paragrammatic effects of alliteration; in ballad or other variants; in the variorum of interpretive readings; in the scrambling of Milton's "Amara" as Coleridge's "Abora"; and in the principle that differentiates, in time, "grammar" and "glamor."

Derrida's concept of ecriture (I shall naturalize the word in this form), his attack on those who privilege voice or oral perspectives, is not meant to argue that writing is primary in any literal or genetic sense. He knows perfectly well that what evidence we have indicates that writing is an after-birth: *nachträglich*, to use Freud's word. Its relation to speech, of which it seems to be a (phonetic) transcription, may be compared to Jacob and Esau, who struggle out of the womb together and continue to fight for the firstborn's privilege. The *Nachträglichkeit* of written language is an after-pregnancy comparable to that of interpretation: the transcription in other or apparently secondary terms of something already given. The structure of interpretable events, which includes writing in an essential rather than adventitious way, is that there are always two sets of terms, a dyad that may be a hendiadys. We are quite free, by a "self-determined indetermination," to put in question the privileged status of the prior or first term or else to construct a narrative that gives more weight to the second by a special theory of progress or meaning. We can also construe the relation between these terms as a chiasmus. Even a quarrel as important as that between Ancients and Moderns, which still partially determines our historical consciousness today, can be charted this way. It seems to be a "rhetorical" quarrel also in this larger sense.

The fact that writing is belated or *nachträglich* relates it to time, even if in the form of art it seeks to overcome time by a dream of monumentality. *Nachträglichkeit*, as a concept, founds interpretation and reveals the heterogeneous yet dyadic (two without one or one as two) structure of intentional events. The two columns of *Glas* to which we now turn also respect this structure: however peculiar it must be to see in Hegel and Genet struggling twins. And since Derrida, by his interpretive act or mise en scène is later than both, we are again introduced to a *Nachträglichkeit* that is not simple belatedness but a self-inscription ("insemination" "grafting") of the "present" in a text that has already begun and is almost all quotation. "Quoi du reste *aujourd'hui. . . .*"

ON FIRST looking into *Glas*, since both columns begin with quotations (though only one with quotation marks), and since Hegel's name surfaces immediately ("quoi . . . d'un Hegel"), the impression is that we have entered a play near the end: the end of the Hegelian drama of mind in the *Phenomenology.* Yet is what we are given to see, in these double-columned and elliptical pages, the bacchic yet sober tumult of thoughts in the last philosopher (that Hegelian master of the revels), or a mere graveyard, perhaps Golgotha, of dissociated names and notions?

> Nous autres, civilisations, nous savons maintenant que nous sommes mortelles. . . . *Elam, Ninive, Babylone* étaient de beaux noms vagues, et la ruine totale de ces mondes avait aussi peu de signification pour nous que leur existence même. Mais *France, Angleterre, Russie* . . . ce seraient aussi de beaux noms. . . . Maintenant, sur une immense terrasse d'Elsinore . . . l'Hamlet européen regarde des millions des spectres.

So Valéry after the First World War,[5] in an essay strictly contemporary with Eliot's *Waste Land:*

> Jerusalem Athens Alexandria
> Vienna London
> Unreal

A dangerous juncture for comparatists. Should we call *Glas* a Hegelian Rag? Or a fashionable meditation in the graveyard of Western culture? Let us agree that it is full of strange noises. The ruins echo as if not only the tombs but the inscriptions, the hieroglyphs or names themselves, were empty. We don't hear what we read or read what we hear. Is that name Hegel or *aigle* (7a)? Could this *imperator spiritus* be a figure out of some medieval bestiary? And what is that "IC" in the left-hand extra margin (7a), and that strangulated "je m'éc . . . " in the right (7b)?

Much is effaced, or self-effacing, yet too much remains. The less ego the more echo seems to be the rule. Echo has no purely phonetic transcription: it is here and there, a dim sound (½) or a redoubled one (2). *Ai/gle, glace, gel, si/gle* is only one scrambled series. The Mallarméan *aigu* rhymes (a "glacier de vols") provide another series: *qui, lui, emblémi* (7a). What of the contagious or ablauted *laissé, enseigner, signer, ensigner,* preceded by *Sa* (7a)?

quoi du reste aujourd'hui, pour nous, ici, maintenant, d'un Hegel?

Pour nous, ici, maintenant : voilà ce qu'on n'aura pu désormais penser sans lui.

Pour nous, ici, maintenant : ces mots sont des citations, déjà, toujours, nous l'aurons appris de lui.

Qui, lui?

Son nom est si étrange. De l'aigle il tient la puissance impériale ou historique. Ceux qui le prononcent encore à la française, il y en a, ne sont ridicules que jusqu'à un certain point : la restitution, sémantiquement infaillible, pour qui l'a un peu lu, un peu seulement, de la froideur magistrale et du sérieux imperturbable, l'aigle pris dans la glace et le gel.

Soit ainsi figé le philosophe emblémi.

Qui, lui? L'aigle de plomb ou d'or, blanc ou noir, n'a pas signé le texte du savoir absolu. Encore moins l'aigle rouge. D'ailleurs on ne sait pas encore si *Sa* est un texte, a donné lieu à un texte, s'il a été écrit ou s'il a écrit, fait écrire, laissé écrire.

On ne sait pas encore s'il s'est laissé enseigner, signer, ensigner. Peut-être y a-t-il une incompatibilité, plus qu'une contradiction dialectique, entre l'enseignement et la signature, un magister et un signataire. Se laisser penser et se laisser signer, peut-être ces deux opérations ne peuvent-elles en aucun cas se recouper.

Sa sera désormais le sigle du savoir absolu. Et l'IC, notons-le déjà puisque les deux portées se représentent l'une l'autre, de l'Immaculée Conception. Tachygraphie proprement singulière : elle ne va pas d'abord à disloquer, comme on pourrait croire, un code c'est-à-dire ce sur quoi l'on table trop. Mais peut-être, beaucoup plus tard et lentement cette fois, à en exhiber les bords

Sa signature, comme la pensée du reste, enveloppera ce corpus mais n'y sera sans doute pas comprise.

Ceci est — une légende.

Non pas une fable : une légende. Non pas un roman, un roman familial puisque s'y agit la famille de Hegel, mais une légende.

Elle ne prétend pas donner à lire le tout du corpus, textes et desseins de Hegel, seulement deux figures. Plus justement deux figures en train de s'effacer : deux passages.

reste à penser : ça ne s'accentue pas ici maintenant mais se sera déjà mis à l'épreuve de l'autre côté. Le sens doit répondre, plus ou moins, aux calculs de ce qu'en termes de gravure on appelle contre-épreuve

« *ce qui est resté d'un Rembrandt déchiré en petits carrés bien réguliers, et foutu aux chiottes* » se divise en deux.

Comme le reste.

Deux colonnes inégales, disent-ils, dont chaque — enveloppe ou gaine, incalculablement renverse, retourne, remplace, remarque, recoupe l'autre.

L'incalculable de *ce qui est resté* se calcule, élabore tous les coups, les tord ou les échafaude en silence, vous vous épuiseriez plus vite à les compter. Chaque petit carré se délimite, chaque colonne s'enlève avec une impassible suffisance et pourtant l'élément de la contagion, la circulation infinie de l'équivalence générale rapporte chaque phrase, chaque mot, chaque moignon d'écriture (par exemple « *je m'éc...* ») à chaque autre, dans chaque colonne et d'une colonne à l'autre de *ce qui est resté* infiniment calculable.

A peu près.

Il y a du reste, toujours, qui se recoupent, deux fonctions.

L'une assure, garde, assimile, intériorise, idéalise, relève la chute dans le monument. La chute s'y maintient, embaume et momifie, monu-mémorise, s'y nomme — tombe. Donc, mais comme chute, s'y érige.

Figure 1. Jacques Derrida, *Glas* (Paris: Editions Galilée, 1975), p. 7. Courtesy, Editions Galilée.

Deux passages très déterminés, partiels, particuliers, deux exemples. Mais de l'essence l'exemple se joue peut-être.

Premier passage : la religion des fleurs. Dans la *Phénoménologie de l'esprit*, le développement de la religion naturelle a comme toujours la forme d'un syllogisme : le moment médiat, « la plante et l'animal », comporte une religion des fleurs. Celle-ci n'est pas même un moment, une station. Elle s'épuise presque dans un passage *(Übergehen)*, un mouvement évanouissant, l'effluve flottant au-dessus d'une procession, la marche de l'innocence à la culpabilité. La religion des fleurs serait innocente, la religion des animaux coupable. La religion des fleurs (l'exemple factuel en viendrait d'Afrique, mais surtout de l'Inde) ne reste pas, ou à peine, elle procède à sa propre mise en culpabilité, à sa propre animalisation, au devenir coupable et donc sérieux de l'innocence. Et cela dans la mesure où le même, le soi-même *(Selbst)* n'y a pas encore lieu, ne se donne, encore, que (dans) sa représentation *(Vorstellung)*. « L'innocence de la *religion des fleurs*, qui est seulement représentation de soi-même sans le soi-même, passe dans le sérieux de la vie agonistique, dans la culpabilité de la *religion des animaux* ; la quiétude et l'impuissance de l'individualité contemplative passe dans l'être-pour-soi destructeur. »

« Die Unschuld der *Blumenreligion*, die nur selbstlose Vorstellung des Selbsts ist, geht in den Ernst des kämpfenden Lebens, in die Schuld der *Tierreligion*, die Ruhe und Ohnmacht der anschauenden Individualität in das zerstörende Fürsichsein über. »

Deuxième passage: la colonne phallique de l'Inde. L'*Esthétique* en décrit la forme au chapitre de l'*Architecture indépendante ou symbolique*. Elle se serait propagée vers la Phrygie, la Syrie, la Grèce où, au cours des fêtes dionysiaques, selon Hérodote cité par Hegel, les femmes tiraient le fil d'un phallus

toujours regarder de côté vers l'Inde pour suivre ce passage énigmatique, qui passe très mal, entre l'Extrême-Occident et l'Extrême-Orient. L'Inde, ni l'Europe ni la Chine. Sorte de goulot d'étranglement historique. Resserré comme Gibraltar, « roc stérile et dispendieux », colonnes d'Hercule dont l'histoire appartient à celle de la route des Indes. En ce détroit un peu louche, le panorama est-ouest-eurafrique se rétrécit infiniment. Point de devenir. La pointe rocheuse a souvent changé de nom, néanmoins. Le promontoire s'est appelé Mons Calpe, Notre-Dame-du-Roc, Djebel Tarik (Gibraltar)

qui se dressait alors en l'air, « presque aussi grand que le reste du corps ». A l'origine, donc, les colonnes phalliques de l'Inde, énormes formations, piliers, tours, plus larges

L'autre — laisse tomber le reste. Risquant de revenir au même. Tombe — deux fois les colonnes, les trombes — reste.

Peut-être le cas *(Fall)* du seing.

Si *Fall* marque le cas, la chute, la décadence, la faillite ou la fente, *Falle* égale piège, trappe, collet, la machine à vous prendre par le cou.

Le seing tombe.

Le reste est indicible, ou presque : non par approximation empirique mais à la rigueur indécidable.

« *Catachrèse*, s.f. 1. Trope par lequel un mot détourné de son sens propre est accepté dans le langage commun pour désigner une autre chose qui a quelque analogie avec l'objet qu'il exprimait d'abord; par exemple, une langue, parce que la langue est le principal organe de la parole articulée; une glace [...] une feuille de papier [...]. C'est aussi par catachrèse qu'on dit : ferré d'argent; aller à cheval sur un bâton. [...] 2. Terme de musique. Dissonance dure et inusitée. E. Κατάχρησις, abus, de κατὰ, contre, et χρῆσις, usage.

Catafalque, s.m. Estrade élevée, par honneur, au milieu d'une église, pour recevoir le cercueil ou la représentation d'un mort [...] E. Ital. *catafalco*; bas-lat. *catafaltus, cadafaldus, cadaffalle, cadapallus, cadaphallus, chafallus*. *Cata* est selon Du Cange le bas-latin *catus*, machine de guerre appelée *chat* d'après l'animal; et selon Diez *catare*, voir, regarder; du reste, finalement, ces deux étymologies se confondent, vu que *catus*, chat, et *catare*, regarder, ont le même radical. Reste *falco*, qui, vu les variantes du bas-latin où le *p* se montre, ne peut être que le mot germanique *balk* (voy. **balcon**). *Catafalque* est le même mot que *échafaud* (voy. ce mot).

Cataglottisme, s.m. Terme de littérature ancienne. Emploi de mots recherchés. E. Καταγλωττισμός, de κατὰ, indiquant recherche, et γλῶσσα, mot, langue (voy. **glose**). » Littré.
Les ALC sonnent, claquent, éclatent, se réfléchissent et se retournent dans tous les sens, comptent et se décomptent, ouvrant — ici — dans la pierre de chaque colonne des sortes de judas incrustés, créneaux, jalousies, meurtrières pour voir à ne pas se laisser emprisonner dans le colosse, tatouages dans la peau plissée d'un corps

Figure 2.   Jacques Derrida, *Glas*, p. 8. Courtesy, Editions Galilée.

The right-hand margin (7b) strives to make us believe that the two columns before us are emblematic. Perhaps, then, Hegel ("Soit ainsi figé le philosophe emblémi") is monumentalized—no, echo says "monumemorized" (7b)—by the left column as Genet is by the right. But how solid is this architecture made of skulls of words? Why does it echo so archly? Must spirit or corpus become unbound as mere name, mere signifier, to renounce itself? *Renoncer, résonner (raisonner), renommé:* does my verbal trick win against Death, or must I trump myself with the chance alliteration of "gloire" and "glas"? If there is a primal scene of writing it is having one's name inscribed on a monument or tomb. *Tombe, tome, le tombeau de.*

Whatever is being constructed is based on competing principles: the equivocal and equi-vocal character of words. The balance of the whole is therefore incalculable and a hazard; for while one system wishes to balance out, the other differentiates—organizes inequality, like Valéry's demiurge. Writing may be on the side of equi-vocality, when drawn toward an infinitely self-stabilizing exchange. Voicing the written word may be on the side of differentiation, for the gap between graphemic and phonic appears most acutely when an equivocal or homophonic word generates allophones. Yet these relations could be reversed. The dead (mute) letter may be more differential (because of its reserve) than the living (voiced) letter. The border between dead and living (including Hegel and Genet, or what is living and dead in Hegel's philosophy[6]) is indeterminate. Or if it has a more precise form, chiastic.

Nothing could be more mistaken than to think of Derrida as derogating what he calls the "cas de la phonè." The case of the *phonè* is never closed; its cadence cannot be encased in grammar or meaning. It falls through, into, both. Writing manifests it as ambiguity, irony, equivocation. Even unvoiced letters like the *s* in *glas* or the *H* in (French) *Hegel* pose a problem of retention or restitution that leads to the problematic of substance: *what remains?* Not forever, but in our case, here and now, already passing as the hand writes those words, like Hegel's or Valéry's "main-tenant": "Quoi du reste aujourd'hui, ici, maintenant, d'un Hegel?"

THE ANSWER to what remains is, deceptively, quotation. Words, however direct—and what could be more so than "ici, maintenant" in the inaugural sentence of this book—are already mediated, already quotation. For Derrida's "ici, maintenant" alludes not only to a problem in philosophy, Husserl's or Heidegger's discussion of the "now," but also, more precisely and textually, to the famous demonstration concerning "Das Dieses" that opens Hegel's *Phenomenology*. Hegel remarks that if in answer to the question "What is the

Now?" we write down "The Now is the Night" and look at this "written truth" the next day when we would have to write it as "The Now is the Noon," we realize how shallow this truth, this now, has become. A complex argument follows on how the abstract immediacy of the here and now is negated, or inserted into a dialectical movement that contains more truth than the moments subsumed by it. But if Hegel anticipates in this way the development of the *Phenomenology* as a whole, he seems unaware of the importance to it of writing; not only of a curious wordplay prospectively reminiscent of Heidegger. Though from his point of view those pieces of writing are incidental, a *Beispiel* (example or sideplay) that changes nothing, from another point of view the entire process seems based on those pieces of paper, which certainly lead into Derrida's emphasis on the "scene of writing."

The "ici, maintenant," then, is a complex quote; and these quotes and ibids remain. They remain not only in the sense that, as Hegel states, they preserve a certain moment for a later inspection that will betray them—by opening to our awareness the gap between *meinen* (to mean: *vouloir-dire*) and *sagen* (to say: *dire*)—but also in the sense that a later inspection (characterized by the equally vulnerable terms "aujourd'hui" and "pour nous") may find in Hegel's text a remainder ("du reste") that reveals a still more powerful and elided negativity, his nontreatment of the status of writing.

These quotes and ibids, then, "remain." We can also call them, more elegantly, overdetermined words or floating signifiers, at once the *symbols* and the *ruins* of other texts. They are terms which, though not proper nouns, at least not formally, have significance because like Saussure's hypograms (see the *Notebooks* published by Jean Starobinski)[7] they are potentially capable of "motivating" texts, even of evoking an intertextual situation. The wasting-power of language or time heaps the mind with these remnants, but mind cannot bear waste, and Derrida begins *Glas* with a punning meditation on the insidious conjunction "moreover," which in French contains the restless noun *reste*.

A symbol, then, might be redefined as a trace, remnant, or stubborn surplus capable of motivating a text or being remotivated by it. The mind is always being trashed: nothing is resolved enough to be dissolved. There is no *alchimie du verbe* or philosopher's stone that could turn the treasure of trash each thinker thinks into the gold of certain knowledge ("savoir absolu").

If there were just one act of mind that did not have to be repeated, one word that could disappear and lighten language: purged, sublimated, *aufgehoben*, annihilated! But all terms seem to be what Kenneth Burke has aptly named "god terms," and like Joyce's "etyms" can only be joyced, chewed, adulterated, contaminated, and so . . . reinscribed. The conception of form or symbol as the translucence of the universal in the concrete (to the point where the linguistic material is totally sublimated in the concept) is an illusion made, like an exotic toy, in Greece: in Hegel's and Germany's nostalgia, that is, for the chastened Asiatic style they describe as, somehow, both serene and sublime. But "gl reste gl" (137b).

Glas: a science of remnants. Perhaps philosophy has always been such because it finds remainders (mere sounds, waste-products, contradictions, excrement, death) intolerable. Or an antiscience, what Georges Bataille called *heterology,* which tries to undo Hegel's dialectic swathing of the Discourse of the Other. "The element of contagion, the infinite circulation of general equivalence" (7b), which in Roland Barthes's S/Z comes to subsume or expropriate even the "property" of sex, alludes in Derrida to Bataille's "Hegelianism without reserve," which implodes the principle of *Aufhebung* until all possibility of closure is denied and every attempt at a "limited economy" is transgressed. One column tolerates, while it questions, Hegel's "savoir absolu," but the other immediately evokes the drive toward a "nonsavoir."

Hence that sinister right-hand opening: *"'ce qui est resté d'un Rembrandt déchiré en petits carrés bien réguliers, et foutu aux chiottes' se divise en deux. Comme le reste."* In Bataille, heterology is also the science of the low-down, the *bas.* The quoted words, of course, are Genet's, and even the bipolarity of a page divided into columns was suggested by Genet.[8] But just as the Hegel opening on the left may recall Blanchot (is there a play on *emblémi, blêmi, Blanch-ot?*), so this passage in the context of what follows may recall Bataille, though his name is so inward to the text that its presence—Bataille: bastailler—would be an impossibly literal restitution. It is, at most, the ironic "motivation" of an "unmotivated" act by the interpretative mind.[9]

Yet the Genet column proceeds to treat just this question of a style so remarkable, so inwardly inscribed, that we say: this is a Rembrandt, this is by Genet. The concept of style, in brief, is based on a signature-feeling that saturates the text it authenticates yet is not actually there as a proper noun, as "Genet" or "Rembrandt." It is unquotable, expropriated ab initio, quartered—if only into four-sided column or page. Yet *Rembrandt* in the Genet text stands as a parallel to the "ici, maintenant" in the unmarked allusion to Hegel. The tearing of the name (or the manuscript bearing it as title?) into small pieces must be a deliberate canceling of yet another mode of presence: an iconoclastic (onomatoclastic) act, with sacrificial and purgative overtones, and all the more disturbing because a painter, and Rembrandt in particular, is involved.

But is painting too, as the act suggests, ecriture? What would correspond, in painting, to the aphoristic or transgressive energy of ecriture vis-à-vis Book or "savoir absolu"? Or does the domain of images insist on a presence that defeats the assertion I have already quoted from the end of Derrida's work on Husserl: "le 'regard' ne peut pas 'demeurer'"? But the *look* does abide in

Rembrandt and through him. Rembrandt is to modern art what the concept of Greek art, illusory or not, was to Hegel. The translucence of the spiritual in the *pays bas* of the carnal ("une infinie, une infernale transparence" are Genet's words) suggests an incomparable synthesis or embodiment, which Chardin later can only "cite" in his beautifully overdressed figures performing simple acts like reading. Rembrandt is monumental, the creation of a mirror of art that maintains the glance of subject or beholder, as subject becomes substance without (or even with, like Genet) passing through a Medusa or Narcissus complex.

Hebrew tradition holds that both the oral and the written law were given to Moses on Sinai. Writing, moreover, exempt from the prohibition against graven images, developed as more than a useful or necessary device to prevent a religious code from being lost to the pressure of time and the diaspora. The prohibition against images obliged a channeling into the written word of imaginal energies. Derrida in this is Hebrew rather than Hellene: aniconic yet intensely graphic. It may be more than the accident of entering the philosophical tradition at a certain point in its history that made him choose as his polemical instrument the notion of ecriture. The discussion of painting in this deflected form is peculiar for one so deeply engaged in the critique of presence as it bears on modes of representation. (His *Derrière le miroir* essay, [10] on the painter Adami, still evades the problem of the painterly moment in favor of the penetration of the graphic into picturemaking. So his use of "regard" is generally in the sense of "perspective" or "aspect": He swerves [clin / clinamen] from its meaning as *Augenblick*.)

What he takes up in the subsequent discussion of Genet is not the role of the canceled image so much as that of the canceled name. Where the right- and left-hand disposition of the text might remind us of the right and left hemispheres of the brain, distinguished by a discontinuity between verbalizing and visualizing functions, and where a similar discontinuity, though not physically localized, between horizontal and vertical impressions (the division into columns tending to increase, at times, the sense of verticality) might actually support Gaston Bachelard's understanding of the role of the intuition of the instant in literature (see his text of 1939, "Instant poétique et instant métaphysique," especially section 3; but also Genet's "instant" revelation in *Rembrandt déchiré*), Derrida tries to limit the visual effect to certain emblematic and tensile properties.

While it is perfectly consistent for Derrida to keep within the sphere of textuality and seek a theory that could deduce texts not simply from other texts but also from a "sacrifice" or "dissemination" of the identity-feeling encased in one's proper name, there are overtones in this curious quotation that disturb us precisely because they point to a "remainder" in it which even Derrida, who comes back to the quotation in an intricate discussion of Hebraism versus Hellenism in Hegel juxtaposed with Genet's discussion of the powerful, glancing effect of Rembrandt's pictures, cannot, admittedly, fathom. Though it might be argued that Rembrandt is the most graphic of artists, and that what we feel may be precisely a pictorial script, signature becoming image, or canceling—disseminating—itself as the presence of an image, Derrida glides away from such hints into a new theory of how literary works are generated by the dispersal of a name that seems to be and never is "proper"—that vacillates between being proper and common, so that the writings of Genet, perhaps we should say the works "au nom de Genet," are a perpetually displaced self-quotation, singular yet infinitely divided, *détaillé*.

Inevitably, then, the issue of castration, or of the "vide solide," as Genet calls it, describing his experience of alterity, is raised. On the second page of *Glas* as the phallic statue is being erected in one column (8a), the signature falls in the other column (8i), and changes are rung in the third (8b) on terms that begin with the Greek *cata* (down or against). A polyphonic style develops which insinuates an unreadable word that could be "castration" yet never is, that could be "catastrophe" yet never is, that is never more, in fact, than a technical term from rhetoric, and leaves us with "Klang und nicht Sprache," the Klang of Glas, a polyglot and mocking sound-trace of some primal cleavage: fall, division, babel, parricide, castration.

Castration as a theme surfaces pointedly in Derrida's attempt to find in Hegel's commentary on the story of Abraham the conceptual articulation between "*Aufhebung*, castration, truth, law, etc." (53a), at the same time that the columns running opposite on the page return to Genet's description of the *look*—the medusaing look—of Rembrandt's pictures. "X, chiasme presque parfait, plus que parfait, deux textes mis en regard l'un de l'autre" (53b). A "regard" that might castrate or turn into stone is put "en abîme": writing deflects, reflects, decenters it, it is figuralized, anagrammatized, apotropaically or symbolically cut as in circumcision or the endless découpage of name and text in Derrida, *déchiré (déchié)* until the logo-phallus or its absence, signification or its void, the whole, dizzying metaphysical desire for presence or absence is infinitely mediated not only in language but as language.

This *Aufhebung* of the theme of castration involves a polemic with Lacan on the central role of the phallus as signifier or "transcendental key" (38b) in the process of sexual differentiation. The undifferentiated life, to misquote Socrates, is not worth living. The acceptance of sexual differentiation is inherently tied to both the institution of the family (Derrida's major theme in the column on Hegel) and the institution of language (his major theme in the column on Genet). These themes, because they are each other's margin, are not confined by them but intersect chiastically, and one can only hint at the plenitude of *Glas* as (I must pun as I must sneeze) a *sematics*. Though it is an antiencyclopedia, a book that refuses to be a book—that does not wish to gather in but rather to express the disseminated or diasporic state of the logos as language—yet, as in some medieval Speculum or Book of Creatures, the strange, exotic, glyphic, incomprehensible word-world becomes a kind of household through Adam's power of naming and Abraham's gift of substitution. As we read *Glas* we feel the protest of the entire Linnaean realm: a protest of the living creatures, or natural language, against posttypological typing, as if each being were able, even when mute, to contribute its own mark or seal, if not signature. The passing bell of *Glas* becomes a wedding bell; and though Derrida's phrase "the economy of death" is one that should chill (and naming, no doubt, is an anticipation of death, a formal and often fixating recognition of self or other), there is here a barely refrained antimessianic exuberance that lifts the burden of circumcision even from the heart, because it is already, and endlessly, in language. The "scheiden" or "coup" or "ur-teil," the cutting edge of language on every page of this text, all the devices of découpage (Derrida's *coup de dés*) seem to undercut the worry about "Entscheidung" that Heidegger pursues so intently.

For "Entscheidung" has already fallen, or is always falling. No throw of language will "master" philosophy and, through philosophy, the human condition by dividing time into a B.C./A.D. pattern, or positing an absolute present. Caesuras are not caesareans. There is no more a fullness of time than there is a fullness of language. Derrida lets language be, not by nonchalance but by giving it its "to be," as he deconstructs a text or moves within, rather than simply against, equivocation and the multiple register of words. As in the Hebrew liturgy that quotes God against God to plead a covenant in danger, so here words are quoted against words to save the contract between word and thing: a contract always being foreclosed by this or that philosophical simplification or "Endzeit" ideology. Let no one mistake this nonbook: *Glas* is of the House of Galilee.

Who else but Reb Derissa could go from the dissemination/castration or flower/sword theme to the Wartburg dictionary (59 ff.), and by an error or *Bedeutungswandel* as bewildering as any semanticist has traced, show how sword and lily lie together (*lis/lit*) in "glaïeuil" (gladiolus: *Schwertlilie*) with its *Blütenstaub* of phonic or dialectal resonances: *glageuil* ("klage," "deuil"?); *glaudius, claudio, gaudio* ("joy"?); *glaviol* ("viol"?); *glaive, glai, englasi* ("terrify," "freeze," "glaze"?); *glai, glace, glisser*? These flowers of language, though not simples, have a medicine in their "phonème" as well as "phénomène." "Y a-t-il gl dans toute langue *naturelle*? gl. . . ph . . . Ça brille et se brise" (62b).

ÇA BRILLE *et se brise.* Hardly an aphorism, because thrown off so casually. Does the *ça* really refer to *gl* or *ph*? Its airy, gestural quality makes it a "surjet" rather than a "sujet." Is the suggested therapy again the deposing of the sovereign subject? Derrida in his pharmacy, his panglossalium, mixes phonemes like a medicine man, a shaman, or what he calls "sfeinctor" (280b). But if he has learned from Freud that there is a talking cure, he has also learned that there is no triumph of the therapeutic, only an endless analysis. Consider again this *ça* and how it puts the phrase it introduces "en abîme."

If we were to substitute the symbol X for *ça*, the phrase could easily evoke a kind of mirror: "X brille et se brise." Derrida has just shown how fragile—and fertile by that fact—are the proper names of flowers. A name is meant to hold an identity fast, to mirror or mime it as best it can, but analysis reveals at most a "miroitement," the shimmer-fragments of that insistence. This imago of the proper name, everywhere, not only in flowers, points to the "phantasme absolu comme s'avoir absolu."

Instinctively, of course, we take *ça* as "things in general," or things belonging to a large, undefined class. Yet the other side of this referential vagueness is a grammatical constriction: the grammar, almost defensively, makes *ça* the subject: it is "*ça*" that shines and breaks. The reflexive *se* ("se brise") intensifies this feeling that *ça* is a name or a noun. *Ça* moves back into a pronominal position and assumes more fully the force of "it." But what noun does "it" stand for?

The dead end of grammatical analysis is now aided by the "forgotten" phoneme. *Ça* is homophonic with *Sa*. On the first page Derrida condenses "savoir absolu" as "*Sa*." Then let us substitute *Sa* for *ça*. "*Sa* brille et se brise" means that Hegel's "savoir absolu" is a mirage (*Schein/glanz*/glance) that must break. Derrida says it with flowers, but he says it. His dictionary analysis of "glaïeul" has revealed the lawful instability of phoneme or signifier, one that leads to the creation not only of new verbal forms but also of new meanings by such "dissemination." The motto of a famous dictionary is "Je sème à tout vent." Derrida's "*Sa* brille et se brise" is an equivalent heraldry.

But *Sa* as tachygraph, as artificial abbreviation, was already there before Derrida. All he does is to reinscribe or superimpose through that phoneme another text. For *Sa* is homophonic with the abbreviation for "signifiant" when distinguished in Saussure from *Sé*, the "signifié." This doubled *Sa* not only suggests that so-called absolute knowledge is as unstable as the volatile phoneme or signifier but also makes the text of Saussure into an additional "signifié." Because of this double or false-bottomed *Sa*, we can hardly keep track. We have something like three signifiants (*ça*, *Sa*[1], *Sa*[2]) and I'm not sure how many signifiés (mirror, things in general, dissemination, *gl* or *ph*, "savoir absolu," Saussure). *Ça* is too sassy.[11]

To cap it all we must also reluctantly consider the possibility that *ça* is a *Sa* (signifiant) born directly of language, that is, without being authored by the verbal tricks of "un sujet nommé Derrida." When he says, "*Sa* sera désormais le sigle du savoir absolu" (7a), he is parodying the logocentric fiat. But the "other side" of this movement (which includes the discussion of Genet) is an immaculate *ça*, the always already canceled name of *la chose*. "Ça brille et se brise" refers then to the most haunting question of all in this work: what is the *Sa* (*signifiant*/signature/"savoir absolu") of the *ça*? A question that both Heidegger and Lacan raise in different ways, Lacan importing the *Sa* into the Freudian *ça* (S/Es/ID) and Heidegger straining to find the right language-turn back through the bush or *Holzweg* of language to the "nom de chose" (11b): Being as otherness, or es-sence. At this "semidiotic" point, however, philosophy begins to speak in tongues or to sound like a gag out of Ionesco; and we realize that discourse is in danger of moving toward silence. Or toward a stutter (*Sa, Sa, gl, gl*) signifying nothing ("les glas de la signification") though full of sound and analytic fury.

A question like "Que signifie le glas du nom propre? Plus tôt: est-ce que ça signifie?" (27b) only exacerbates the Mallarméan equivocations. Mallarmé, the "aïeul" of Derrida's "glaïeul." (See the "Prose pour des Esseintes." Mallarmé's method is the subject of "La Double Séance," in *La dissémination*.) "Savoir" includes ". . . voire" (52b), that is (voire!) an indeterminacy principle, "le vrai (*verus, voirement*), mais aussi le suspens indécidé de ce qui reste en marche ou en marge dans le vrai, n'étant néanmoins pas faux de ne plus se réduire au vrai" (52b). As when "Ça brille et se brise" suggests, in the context of the sword-flower and dissemination theme—what Derrida calls his "anthèmes" (anthos theme/anthem)—a link between decollation and castration, present not only in Jean Genet but also, undecidably, in Mallarmé's "Cantique de Saint Jean," with its symbol of an imperceptible climactic halt (the *nunc stans* of solstice), which is like the theoretic stability of identity or verbal meaning ("ça brille") before its fragmenting or dissemination ("et se brise"). Or when Mallarmé writes of a danseuse (as if every such were a potential Salomé) that she was not a woman "mais une métaphore résumant un des aspects élémentaires de notre forme, glaive, coupe, fleur, etc . . . " ("Crayonné au Théâtre"). Or when Derrida, in column 52a opposite "voire," speculates that Hegel may have taken the circumcision and the sacrifice of Isaac to be "simulacra of castration." "Si Hegel avait pensé ça, il aurait fait et dit comme ça." Ah, ça . . .

What does it come to, then? A monstrous head-birth? Or an acephalic theory of meaning, decapitated like the Mallarméan i-vers ("hiver"), which contains both "verre" and "air"? "Ça brille et se brise." Only one thing is certain. There is no putting the djinn back into the bottle.

DERRIDA'S style is not unique, though its extravagance (to use Thoreau's word) confronts the reader from an English text-milieu with as much of a problem as the heavier Heidegger. The problem does not lie primarily in the difficult mingling or montage of all kinds of subject matter, which a purer criticism might reject as aleatory and overburdening. Nor does it lie primarily in the habit of inner or esoteric, as distinct from exoteric quotation, which one expects in art but not to this degree in philosophical and critical writing. The problem, on the surface at least, is the persistence, the seriousness, with which an intelligence of this order employs devices that may seem to be at best witty and at worst trivial.

We have all been to school with Empson, yet to transfer to one's prose these puns, equivocations, catachreses, and abusive etymologies, these *double entendres* and double takes, these ellipses and purely speculative chains of words and associations, has a desacralizing and leveling effect that the generic neutrality of the word *ecriture* reenforces. Many readers are left fascinated yet cold, seduced and angry. All the more so as the tone is so even or absent that despite all its paronomasia *Glas* seems as elegantly humorless as Sade's *Philosophie dans le boudoir*. Herein, of course, one difference with Joyce, who shocks and delights, rather than teaches. Every pun, in Derrida, is philosophically accountable, every *sottie* or *sortie* must contribute further to the *déniaisement* of the European Mind, still so virginal after all the attempts on it: by Sade, Rousseau, Nietzsche, Marx, Freud, Sartre, Genet, Bataille.

Glas, with a style that the French Classical tradition has nurtured and made ductile, is philosophy's *Fleurs du mal* rather than its death knell. Yet, to insist, how do we take all those verbal tricks, so productive yet so easy to parody? So functional in foregrounding language, in making us aware of it as the only subject, compared to which ego and author are episodic notions discarded by an interminable demonstration?

Indeed, it is not the devices themselves but the interminable character of the analysis they impose that may tire us into antagonism. The dialectophage or boa-deconstructor aspects of Derrida's systematic play, his *serio ludere*, is the real issue. To call it "freeplay" seems understated even if we remember that the term is adapted from the world of machines. For a machine with this much play in it is either a surrealist, erotic, morphological fantasy, like Marcel Duchamp's *Grand verre*, or a language game with so many trick-possibilities that to say there are seven types of ambiguity is suddenly of the same order of truth as to say there are four humors or seven cardinal sins. The point is not that they are without number—there may be less than seven sorts of ambiguity, and Derrida relies heavily on one device of *coupure*, that of tmesis or variable juncture—but that the reentry into consciousness of contradiction or equivocation through such "freeplay" appears to be unbounded.

For there is endless material at hand, and the possibility of working it through in this interminable way cannot be foreclosed.

Yet has this not always been the case? If Derrida brings us to the brink of a new vertigo, it is the old one produced by looking at the whelming tide of interpretation. That consciousness makes cowards of us all. Or leads into anti-intellectualism. Science, however, has somehow not recoiled from discoveries of this kind, not in the long run. The concept of infinity in mathematics, or what each of us can see looking through a microscope (and which confirms another kind of infinity); the discoveries, similarly, of linguistics and semiotics, which have the same infinitizing taint about them—these have fascinated rather than repelled, and led to an openness of thought and inquiry even protected by a society which knows that ideological inferences from such openness could subvert it.

We may not be able to use the instrument properly, though its best use is as a critical rather than positive or ideological philosophy. Derrida deconstructs not only others but also himself: the activity, that is, of philosophizing in general. He shows how much metaphor remains and must remain, how much equivocation and palimpsest-residue. He does not advocate a more literary philosophy, but he doubts that philosophy can get beyond being a form of language. The very desire of philosophy to be itself only, in and for itself, absolute knowledge is the ultimate pathos. Literature too can suffer from this "metaphysical" pathos, when it seeks to be itself by paradoxically aspiring to be like something else: philosophy, for instance. The term *ecriture* is handy because it reminds us of the verbal condition that all these disciplines share and perpetuate.

Derrida tells literary people only what they have always known and repressed. Repressed too much, perhaps. The fullness of equivocation in literary structures should now be thought about to the point where Joyce's wordplay seems normal and Empson's *Seven Types* archaic. A thousand and one nights of literary analysis lie before, a Scheherazade to keep an emperor awake beyond his intentions. Until a new concept of *reserve*, not merely panic or defensive, is developed, one that could result in as fine a sense of decorum as literature itself often displays.

BLAKE in "Night the Ninth" of the *Zoas* goes on and on with his fireworks because there is so much "mystery" to fuel the flames. Potentially, all Western philosophy and literature lie before Derrida as before Hegel, and now they include Hegel. Yet nothing is really destroyed in the curiously memorial conflagration staged by Hegel or Derrida. The flames of intellect reveal a structure, that is all. It is like Blake ending his inferno with:

"How is it we have walk'd thro' fires & yet are not consum'd?
How is it that all things are chang'd, even as in ancient times?"

Or like Blanchot in *Le dernier homme* (1957), who modulates the apocalyptic
thought into something less assured, which anticipates the theory of Writing
in *Glas*:

> Le feu ne brûle que pour mettre au jour le plan vivant du grand édifice, il le
> détruit mais selon son unité, il le révèle en le consumant. Croyance que le grand
> édifice n'est plus maintenant capable d'alimenter un feu central assez fort pour
> tout illuminer en un flamboiement d'ensemble. Croyance qu'on en est arrivé à ce
> moment où tout brûle, tout s'éteint joyeusement au hasard, par myriades de
> foyers distincts qui travaillent où ils veulent, comme ils veulent, avec la froide
> passion des feux séparés. Croyance que nous serions les signes brillants de l'écri-
> ture de feu.

It may seem ingenious to characterize Derrida as a conservative thinker. Yet
the "Monuments of unageing intellect" are not pulled down. They are, in
any case, so strong, or our desire is so engaged with them, that the deconstructive activity becomes part of their structure. No cargo cult is in view. The
subversive devices used in *Glas* trap us into rethinking a great many texts. It is
true they are not there as direct objects of study, not presented as such—no
more than the Bible is in Blake. But one might say that Hegel, Genet, Freud,
and others are *elated* (a term I prefer to *sublated*), and if there is little humor
and mother wit in Derrida, there is nevertheless what the German Romantics,
who founded a certain notion of ironic transcendence, called *Heiterkeit:*
"hilarity," perhaps, or Nietzsche's "gaiety." Even though texts often become
pretexts here, even a kind of libretto, it is not always so. Hegel and Genet are
given the most sustained analysis and yet the effect remains musical. A deconstructive machine that sings: *Glas*.

It is easy to slip from metaphor to metaphor in describing this book. What
we are still puzzling about, though, is the high nonseriousness of it. The
gravamen of its renewed attempt to jest in earnest. One can sense a certain
fatigue: nothing of the freshness here of Homeric lying or Socratic irony. The
attempted elation is rather grim and involves demands on self and reader that
cannot be stated as an indefinitely ironized "Know thyself." There is, it
seems, no knowledge except in the form of a text—of ecriture—and that is
devious and dissolving, very unabsolute, as it leads always to other texts and
further writing. Both the "knowing" and the "thyself" are constantly deferred
by the very act of writing that might define them in black and white.

Indeed, even the black and white or typographic effect is in *Glas* a
haunting and essential aspect of this deferment, this *calcul* of ecriture. The
disjunct or aleatory form, which includes variable spacing of paragraphs
within columns as well as the insert of new columns or columnar boxes

(*Aushöhlungen*, 9a, 282a), is soon perceived to be less an experiment than a deliberate technique underwritten by concepts developed previously. It inscribes the theory of ecriture, differance, dissemination, deconstruction, freeplay. Intertextuality founds its space, as in Mallarmé. For the impression of equivalence is always broken, always reasserted. There is a paravisual effect, emblematic rather than pictorial, which plays on the idea of columns as (1) independent structures like the early phallic statues that could also be funerary monuments, and through *Aushöhlung*, sounding pits rather than pyramids; (2) dependent structures, like columns of a Greek temple, self-supporting as well as supportive, and associated with the achievement of equilibrium or an Apollonian "Gleichgewicht" (291a); (3) broken columns, or those whose monumental quality is put in question, because being variably elided by the spacing of the paragraph-blocks they are *decapitalized*, to suggest tensiles of cohesion that must now come from writing itself.

Writing, that is, is not a capitalization. It spaces out rather than dots the columnar *i*. Ecriture, in fact, might almost be defined as the deconstruction of those columns: of the Greek "support" of French culture (an aspect really of the tyranny of *Rome* over France, of a Latinity very different from Nietzsche's view of either Classic style or Greek joyousness), and of capital-istic thinking generally.

In *Glas*, then, and not for the first time, Derrida engages Marx. It is a mediated engagement that proceeds via Hegel, Feuerbach, and contemporary thinkers like Sartre and Bataille. That may be inevitable here, where texts are so consciously intertextual. The Marxist contribution is, like all others, "dépensé" according to a principle of freeplay that for the serious thinker may seem to be an aestheticizing maneuver. The decapitalized columns may allude to Marx's own struggle with Greco-Roman antiquity, as alienation becomes a form of alineation. Marx too is "emblémi." Was Marx meant to end as a visual joke, however sustained, in a fine book?

The ingenious engineering of *Glas* cannot but become an issue. What sustains these extraordinary three hundred pages, and what sustaining power do they exert in turn? A game that lasts so long must be more than a game. Even if *Glas* were a "self-consuming artifact," we would be left to admire its stylish sense of the vanity of all things. As in Nietzsche, the void itself would become a ground, the "womb of nature and perhaps her grave." Though the play of text and text could be mere "Schein," and the march of the columns more subversive than Valéry's

Un temple sur les yeux
Noirs pour l'éternité
Nous allons sans les dieux
A la divinité,

the void is made so solid that a material question must be faced: Can we
tolerate and live in this verbal revel, or do we seek to end it by passing to a
stage beyond, that metaphysical "beyond" or "real presence," which has gone
under so many names?

That we are left with something is something. To be made conscious to
what degree one lives in the void, in an "economy of death," is the oldest
imperative of both religion and philosophy. For Cicero, thinking of Socrates,
the philosopher is the virtuous man whose study is death. So for John Donne,
always already in his shroud:

> As virtuous men passe mildly away,
> And whisper to their soules, to goe,
> Whilst some of their sad friends doe say,
> The breath goes now, and some say, no. . . .

The mere breathing space between "now" and "no" is the economy of death
as a principle of phonemics, the subtlest "glas." Thanatopraxis, in a conscience like Donne's, is at one with interstitial thinking and has made the
boundary between what is living and what is dead so fine that Charon may be
cheated of his fare.

Was hat es da eigentlich geschlagen?
                                    Nietzsche

Sei ein klingendes Glas das sich im Klang schon erschlug.
                                                      Rilke

DERRIDA knows that this study of death, also named philosophy, took a
strange turn when Freud's metapsychology introduced the notion of a death
instinct indissociable from life and Eros. Jacques Lacan's revision of that
metapsychology reenforced and exacerbated the issue by postulating specific
"figures de la mort" said to determine, like the ancient Fates, the psyche. One
of these, perhaps the most potent because directed against the eristic and
erotic games ("jeux sériels") of verbal symbolism, is described by Lacan as the
source of monumental image-making: whether in the form of statues, spec-
ters, or automata. Lacan's famous idea of a "mirror stage" suggests that when
the infant discovers prematurely its full-formed image in the mirror, it is as a
double rather than a genuine other, and for the rest of its psychic life is
tempted to accede to that type of image-fixation because it allows a denial of
the insistence of words, their interminable, identity-deferring nature.[12] The
Identity (to adopt a Blakean term for Lacan's "je"), once it has appeared as this

mirror image, is pregnant with correspondences to the monumental themes being undone by the "jeux sériels" of Derrida's columniad.

The eternizing character of desire is therefore the obverse of an economy of death. Eros too can be a capitalist. This difficult conjunction of eternity-desire and death (Lacan: "When we wish to reach in the *sujet* what was there before the serial games of language, what is primordial for the birth of symbols, we find it in death, from which his existence takes all the meaning it has. It is as a desire for death that the *sujet* affirms himself vis-à-vis others; if he identifies with the other, it is by congealing the latter [by specular identification] into the metamorphosis of his own image-essence, and no being is ever evoked by him unless amid these shadows of death") not only constitutes the psyche but all our mythologies.

The importance of this point of view, however, is not exhausted by showing that the psyche emanates doubles like the funerary statues described in the opening pages of *Glas*. Thomas Mann in "Freud and the Future" (1936) had already glimpsed this truth and made it, as in Lacan, the basis of a theory of identity-building through ecstatic identification. A more insidious implication of this view includes the psychoanalytic concept of the psyche as a myth among these myths. A myth, moreover, which evolved into a full-fledged mythology only after Anna Freud had codified the mechanisms of defense (1936) and parlayed a metaphor ("defense") into a formidable model of the ego as adaptive machine: one as resourceful, if precarious, as the warrior-soul in psychomachias of old. It is no accident, then, that Lacan's theory of the mirror stage (1936 and 1949) was formulated as an at first cautious and then increasingly vigorous critique of the ensuing "ego psychology" that institutionalized itself most successfully in America.

Against this psychology Lacan asserts that the ego is not an adaptive or synthesizing power but something that rises up and smites language, that desires a fixed image, a nondifferential, glassy essence. Hence Derrida, going perhaps beyond Lacan, tries to smite the mirror-principle itself. The transgressive or liberating if always phantasmagoric crime is not, for Derrida, thing-murder by language, but mirror-murder or the end of mimetological versions of Identity. That means an elaboration of the notion of writing, and, coterminously, the movement in *Glas* from the heavy opening theme of the *colossus*, statue and funerary double, to the lyrical theme of a *calculus*, associated either with Nietzsche's shuttle-play between Dionysus and Apollo, or other kinds of music or writing machines. The "inexhaustible inventiveness, the dreamlike renewal of mechanical models" that Derrida so admires in Freud not only associates metaphoricity with scientific model-making, but once again projects the ideal of writing as a fantastic machine, an antimirror mirroring device that wards off the dark Lacanian trinity of statue, specter, automaton. Almost too smoothly, then, the freeplay in *Glas* oscillates between bel canto and bel cento.[13] It is not only the Freudian unconscious that is "Aufgehoben," as in Lacan: the psychoanalytic form of the Psyche myth is itself elated into a "question of style."

Hence the style of *Glas*. Its columns become shape-shifters that do not allow us to fix them by "glassification" as an eternity-structure of either a mythic or a psychic kind. They subsume the clanging colossus of Memnon (left), as well as the fixating glance of the Lacanian mirror (right), by a potentially chiastic positioning of "deux textes mis en regard l'un de l'autre." The perspective point of the columns recedes "en abîme" in two directions at once. One is the past, starting with Hegel who is still with us; the other is the future, starting with Nietzsche who is once again with us, having been rediscovered by recent French thought. There is an intersection of Hegel and Nietzsche, so that rays of inquiry that might regress indefinitely into a "precapitalistic" era are available for us here and now, through that double focus.

"WE DON'T know yet if *Sa* is a text, has given rise to a text, if it has been written, or has written, caused writing, let writing come about" (7a). Do we know by the end of *Glas*? In what sense is the text of *Glas* also the text of *Sa*?

We know at least "what remains today for us." It is quite a legacy, this too much and too little. There is Hegel, or the near-interminable shadow of historical knowledge extending itself through the "negative labor" of dialectic thinking. There is Nietzsche, or his attempt (after Schopenhauer) to clear that shadow away, to demystify the will to knowledge itself. But Nietzsche's labor resulted only in new kinds of interminable analysis. At first psychoanalysis, and now the clearing of the ground called deconstruction.

Deconstruction may lead to a new construction, of which we are here seeing a first installment or prelude. But the deconstructive, or let us simply call it "-analytic" work (the hyphen leaving the subject-phrase open, as if "analytic" would necessarily bestow anaclitic status on any such phrase), also magically conserves the texts it works through. It conserves them in a peculiar way, of course. Not as quasi-autonomous wholes but as fragments with the force often of aphorisms, and whose evocative power reminds us of extracts from works now lost and known only through being quoted by an ancient commentator. Even when we can go back to the "original," it seems either less original now or finds its wholeness, its aspiration to monumental status, made partial by intertextual fragmentation.

The deconstructive clearing of the ground is, then, quite different from Wittgenstein's. The *Philosophical Investigations* and *Zettel* have their own aphoristic energy: they are bulletins (little papal bulls) surviving the silent labor, silence itself. But the "text," for Wittgenstein, insofar as it exists, is the common word as concept, or the concept put to the test of idiom and common words. There is still a similarity in this between our two philosophers: both reflect on the status of conceptualization, on Hegel's question, absolutely basic, on what and where the "concept" is *today*. That Derrida worries the distinction between common and proper nouns is also a sign of affinity.

The conceptual given, for Wittgenstein, seems very different, however. There is no prerequisite for his intellectual labor except language and thought—thought that tries to free language to say what it means. The nature of the constriction or obstruction is not clear, though clearly there. The blockage or spell, "bewitchment," is simply something to be undone. But for Derrida, or as he would insist with Hegel, "for us," the conceptual given is always, already, a text. It is a text that is mediated by other texts, whether past or to come; and this is not an epistemological problem only but also a temporal and cultural one. Derrida's prerequisite for thinking is the very cumulus Wittgenstein would like to start without (he knows words have a "Dunst," or aura, but he remains unseduced): that heavy historical sedimentation which made Hegel aspire toward the elation of a "savoir absolu," toward a dance of thoughts characterized by the "interchangeable supremacy" of all stages in the odyssey—or calvary—of the human spirit. An intertextual dance if you will, as in some unimaginably assured act of reading. Or, in psychoanalytic terms, a working-through of the *coupure* (whether or not we thematize it as castration) until it no longer crucifies discourse.

On the final page of *Glas* (figure 16) philosophy takes back from literature its own, which includes a certain rhythm, a certain clang, "l'impair," perhaps, the off-rhyming of columns or even a harsher note ("les cordes graissées se tendent, on n'entend qu'elles"); and out of this, something other than tragedy is born. What is born, though? Clearly, if only in the form of an earnest jest, an *Aufhebung* (291b). This "elation" follows on the most lyrical moment in *Glas*, where we are given, in German, a passage from the section "Vor Sonnen-Aufgang" in Nietzsche's *Also sprach Zarathustra* (291b, "Vor der Sonne kamst du zu mir"). A musical and moving passage, which smooths "the raven down of darkness" and lets us glimpse what Nietzsche meant by elation, or Heiterkeit, or "fröhliche Wissenschaft."

An elation, then, that seems to be an elision of knowledge: "Da" (Dasein) and "Sa" ("savoir absolu") become a simple "Ja," an unspoken but also unbounded affirmation of all that has been, and will be again. "We share our knowledge by smiling at each other." It is, so to say, Nietzsche's version of Pater's Mona Lisa; a newborn virginity—reserve—with regard to the will to knowledge that becomes the main subject of Nietzsche's preface to the reedition (1887) of *Die fröhliche Wissenschaft:*

If we convalescents still need art, it is a *different* art—a mocking, light, fleeting, divinely ungraced, divinely artful art. . . . We do not believe any longer that truth will still be truth, its veil gone . . . we do not have to see everything naked . . . we do not have to be in the know about everything. . . . We should honor more the modesty [*Scham*] which aids a Nature that hides behind riddles and colorful uncertainties. Perhaps truth is a woman who has her reasons [*Gründe*] for not allowing us to see into her [*ihre Gründe*]. . . . O those Greeks! They understood how to live . . . to remain at the surface . . . praying to semblance [*Schein*], trusting in forms, tones, words, in the entire Olympus of Semblance! The Greeks were superficial—because of their depth.

Here *Glas* might have ended, in this Greek dawn more telling than Memnon's statue.

But an *Aufhebung* follows, which is not a recapitulation of the movement of *Glas* as a whole nor merely an affirmation of the art called for by Nietzsche. It is, indeed, more *Anhang* than *Aufhebung*, a disturbing supplement that turns the "end" into an "and." Even in style it is a strange rebus-form, almost a bricolage of words, mimic notation without a personal or lyric center. It describes an *Aufhebung*, to be sure, but as the precarious interplay of chance and calculation, and as (it is part of the grim joke) a laborious phallic erection, as just another—yet another—raising up (re-lève), equivalent to the retelling-republishing (ré-édite) alluded to in the next and last sentence of the book.

There is no finality, then; as one side (column) depicts a rising, the other may fall; the theme of balancing prevails as a countervailing movement begins again, perhaps the negative labor of the Hegelian dialectic (291a) that disturbs every Apollonian pose. The *Aufhebung* we witness is reenacted as a primal scene of clearing the ground, of path-finding, construction, and now, "ici, dès maintenant," writing. Nietzsche's morning knowledge (even earlier, "früh" as well as "froh," "Vor der Sonne kamst du zu mir," like the Shechinah or Sophia of Proverbs 8) turns to mourning ("glas") once more, reminds us of the interminable *work* of mourning ("lait de deuil" 290b), or of psychoanalysis working itself through to its own *Aufhebung*: a purging of the issue of the logo-phallus, of a castration that was "In the Beginning," "Vor der Sonne."

Why perplex the mind of the fair sex with metaphysics? as John Dryden might have said. Whether the rebarbative notion be castration or the logos or the Immaculate Conception. But the fair sex, by a deep joke, has become philosophy itself. The movement here, as in *Glas* generally, is not that of an *undressing*, subtle or rapacious, of a naked truth. It is, first, an assumption of historical knowledge in the form of all these texts, which stand interminably between us and absolute knowledge; and this between, this "inter" space of textuality may be the only knowledge. It is also, therefore, an alleviation of the quest for—will to—knowledge. By diffusing the theme of *coupure* or castration ("the stubborn center must / Be scattered," Shelley wrote), a powerfully reductive, quasi-theological assumption is disseminated, plowed back into the furrow of writing. "Ça brille et se brise."

Derrida carries Nietzsche's evangelic quip—that the idea became a woman in the transition from Plato to Christianity—into the transition of philosophy from Christianity to Hegel. "What if the *Aufhebung* were a Christian mother?" (225a) Philosophy, as a genealogy of morals, brought forth, according to Nietzsche, a relation to knowledge that represented our access to it as necessitating a shameful rape, the stealing, rending, forceful unveiling of hidden truth. In Hegel, however, this feminization, or feminine hypostasis—which Derrida finds even in Lacan's esoteric style and specifically in his understanding of what the possession of "secret" knowledge may do to the possessor who identifies with it (like the Minister in Poe's "Purloined Letter")—is transcended insofar as we find the model of an inevitable and near-endless *Aufheben* of whatever passes as truth, so that knowledge is neither capitalized nor an object of rape or theft. The thief Genet, in this light, is an exalted if daemonic version of the difficulty that inheres in making the "Christian" mother, Mary Immaculate, a form of *Aufhebung*. But the problem has been clarified: "Sa" ("savoir absolu") and "sa" (the feminine possessive pronoun) are once more, potentially, in a relation that does not reductively image otherness (*ça*) as a sexual and motivating split between feminine secret and masculine force. Perhaps *Sa* has found its text.

So at the end, which is not the end, the furrow of writing opens up again, and the night-knowledge plowed back into it, forgotten, silenced, comes to the ear as a dissonant music. It is the obverse as well as opposite of Théophile Gautier's velleities about the eternity of art. What we find in this furrow is not a sign of mastery, the "imperator spiritus" threatened always yet triumphant:

> Tout passe.—L'art robuste
> Seul a l'éternité.
>   Le buste
> Survit à la cité.
>
> Et la médaille austère
> Que trouve un laboureur
>   Sous terre
> Révèle un empereur.

Nor the "buckling" of a "heart in hiding" under the stress of a mastery greater than the cameo-mastery of art, as in Hopkins:

>   My heart in hiding
> Stirred for a bird,—the achieve of, the mastery of the thing!

Brute beauty and valour and act, oh, air, pride, plume, here
Buckle!

"Sheer plod," the poet continues, "makes plough down sillion / Shine," as if
this laborer too has found a medal in the earth, the metal of earth itself,
uncovered by the mettle—the buckling down—of spiritual labor on earth. But
his imagery remains within the sphere of mastery and being mastered, of the
"thing" being forced open, or released through a dying fall ("ah my dear").
How close all this remains to the era of Mallarmé, Nietzsche, Pater! A
hundred years is itself like the breathing space between "now" and "no." So
the "débris de" with which *Glas* trails off is the "quoi du reste" with which it
began, and scatters or tears to bits ("petits carrés bien réguliers") an elated
proper noun, a signature, le débris de . . . Derrida.

2 *Epiphony in Echoland*

"*Dingo*, adj. et n.m. (Dingot, fin XIXe; de *dingue*). Fam. fou,
V. *Cinglé, dingue...*" "*Dingue*, adj. et n. (1915; o. i.; p.-ê de
*dengue,** cf. arg. la dingue 'paludisme' (1890); ou de *dinguer*).
Pop. Fou, dingo. Il est un peu dingue. On devrait t'envoyer
chez les dingues." *Dinguer*, v. intr. (1833; d'un rad. onomat.
din-, ding-, exprimant le balancement [des cloches, etc.]).
Fam. (Après un verbe). Tomber [*Glas*, 110b].

Overture

FOR those who come in late, there should be an overture, even if no
curtain rises.

Derrida leaves his name suspended at the end of *Glas*. One of Adami's
pictures in *Derrière le miroir* (see figure 3) reproduces the signature "J. Derrida" with the "da" cut off. Not only is "da" the syllable Adami and Derrida
have in common, but *Glas* plays obsessively on *Da* as the tachygraph of
presence, "Dasein." In Adami's picture the *Da* is *Fort*. "Le da n'est pas là,
hic et *nunc*, mais il ne manque pas... il faudra voir plus tard: ce *qui* se fait
fort de la chute monumentale—tombe par dessus bord."

Derridadaism? The illustrious fish, suspended in page or picture, is surely
an exmonument or erection, a J(e)(u) "ang*l*ed with meditation," strang*l*ed by
the graphic energies that overflow the mirror surface of this doubled and
caesuraed page. With scales that seem to become Xs, and, near the base, a
chiastic *DA*, or the first letters of the painter's surname, it could be a modern
hieroglyph: a "picto-idéo-phonogram" as Derrida calls it, complicating the
older term of "speaking picture."

For if this picture speaks it is only to make the "ding" (the thingy,
representational content) a "dingue": a "glas" or "Je / tombe" (*Glas*, 197b).
Adami's design does not, according to Derrida, illustrate or energize language
as a *devise* might its *mot* but releases instead the graphic potential within art
itself. "Non pas l'éclat de voix dans la peinture, mais l'éclatement de la parole

33

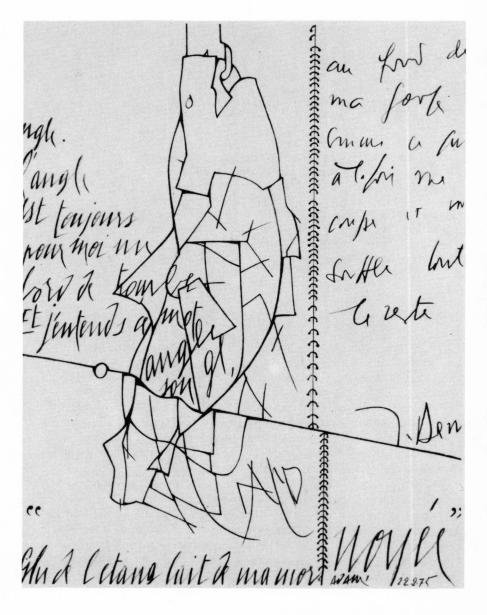

Figure 3. Valerio Adami, *Ich*, signature painting (1975). Reprinted from *Derrière le Miroir*, no. 214 (May 1975), by permission of Valerio Adami and Galerie Maeght.

dans le dessein." Pictorial art too is a form of writing (ecriture); and the false dichotomy of "painting" and "voice," similar to that of writing and voice, is modified by a differential but not absolute contrast between "design" and "words." Adami epigrammatizes art and shows there is as much "trait" as "portrait" in the strong yet graphic silence of his still life. To fully decipher, however, the relation between grapheme and phoneme, or eye and ear, in such a *Je d'esprit*, would need a science as baroquely transformative as Freud's dream theory or the wittiest devices of the Mannerist canon.

The Philosopher as Wit

Had Derrida begun his career with *Glas* or the essay on Adami, our perplexed judgment could hardly have avoided raising the issue of Mannerism, or of the resurgence of wit ("esprit") in philosophy. In modern art this resurgence has been an obvious feature for some time. Magritte (figures 4, 5, and 6) can create a new "domaine enchanté" by jokes that question the frame though not the force of art. Claes Oldenburg, Bill Lombardo, and others practice their equally good-humored deconstructions on American monumentalism (figures 7 and 8), but in the wake of a French tradition founded by Boullée, whose designs were too visionary to be realized (figures 9 and 10). Apollinaire's "idéogrammes lyriques," Duchamp's ready-mades, the beginnings of concrete poetry in Marinetti, Kurt Schwitters, Paul Klee and others, and even the "scenarios" of Robbe-Grillet are witty projects or *graffiti*. As in Adami's sketch or in the double-columned and variable paragraphing of *Glas*, it is the *cadre* (quatre, carré, carte) that is being changed into an *écart* by a "systematic and canny exploration."[1]

To some extent, then, *Glas* is an art form itself, related to these witty typographic and pictographic explorations. It questions philosophy's Hegelian ambition to be more than art or more than language—to subsume these on the way to certain knowledge. More positively stated, Derrida saves the face of language: the character of the written character. Yet if he does so, if he insists with so many contemporary artists that the materializing imprint of words is more than the deformation of some ideal thought-sound—if "l'errance joyeuse du *graphein*" reminds us strangely of another slogan, Marinetti's "les mots en liberté"—he is also the most radical critic of naïve, phonocentric materialism. It is not the sin against the phonè committed by writing (i.e., by the phonetic alphabet) that concerns him. The singular power of the phonè is not in question: indeed it is seen to be the real *mal*, as demonic in its historical and artistic sway as the mad, sad trajectory of Poe's poem "The Bells." Speech, in the form of an *imago vocis*, is forced to sin, explosively,

Figure 4. René Magritte, *L'île au trésor* (1942). Collection of Mme. René Magritte. Courtesy, Mme. René Magritte.

Figure 5. René Magritte, *La légende des siècles* (1958). Collection of Harry Torczyner. Courtesy, Harry Torczyner.

Figure 6. René Magritte, *Le domaine d'Arnheim* (1962). Collection of Mme. René Magritte. Courtesy, Mme. René Magritte.

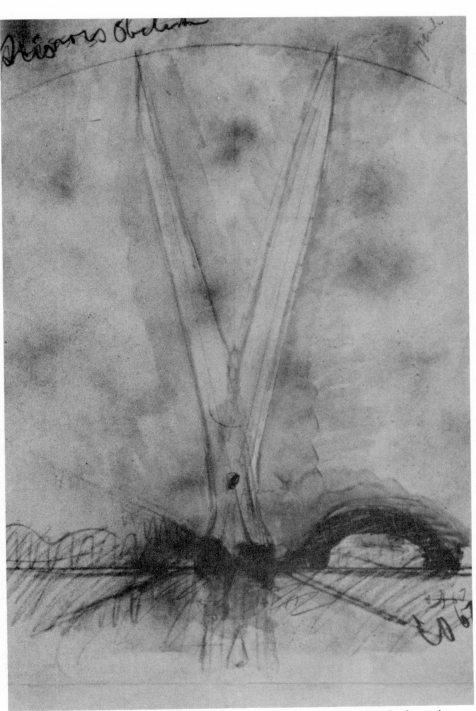

Figure 7. Claes Oldenburg, *Proposed Colossal Monument to Replace the Washington Monument: Scissors in Movement* (1967). Collection of David Whitney. Courtesy, David Whitney. Photo by Geoffrey Clements.

Figure 8. Bill Lombardo, *Monument Sculpture* (1975). Courtesy, Bill Lombardo.

Figure 9. Etienne-Louis Boullée, *Tour en cône tronqué* (18th century). Bibliothèque nationale, Paris.

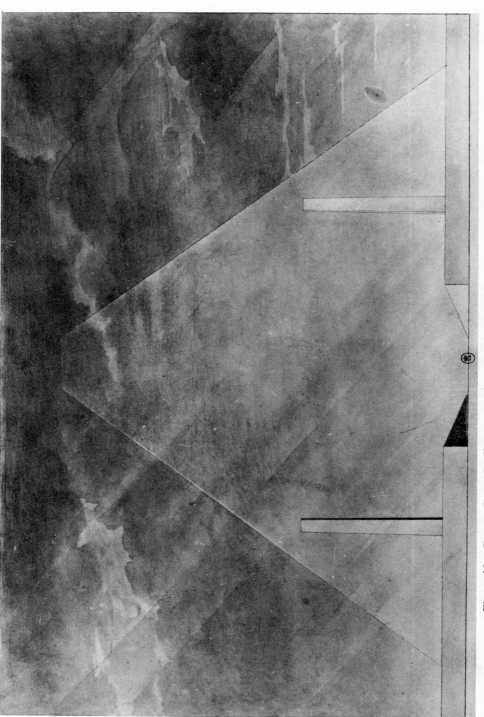

Figure 10. Etienne-Louis Boullée, *Pyramide sous ciel gris* (18th century). Bibliothèque nationale, Paris.

Figure 11. *Top,* Thomas Bewick, *Ass; bottom,* Thomas Bewick, *Thumbprint* (signature), from A *History of British Birds* (circa 1800).

against any language or philosophy of language, including Saussure's, that tries to contain acoustic conceptualization within a single, reduced writing system.

In the West, as the *Grammatology* already argued, writing is reductively conceived as stored speech. The idea arises, therefore, that the energy or sensuous presence of speech must be restored by some counterentropic, revolutionary science, reversing the loss incurred when written speech puts sounds on ice. This magical or restorative science is, for example, the new art Ezra Pound, Apollinaire, and others set against the dead letter. Derrida, however, does not credit this newest search for a "real character" except as it shows the "fragility now recognized of our notions of pictogram, ideogram, etc. . . . the uncertainty of the border separating such *écritures* as go by the name of pictographic, ideographic, phonetic."[2] For writing exceeds not just the specialized form of what we call writing—that is, the Western phonetic alphabet—but other special forms as well: the Chinese written character, cuneiform, hieroglyphs, the rebus, and so on.

Adami's picture-writing, therefore, simply expands the picture we have of writing. It is not touted as an ideal script. *Glas,* moreover, uses a deconstructed version of Hegel's analysis of signs in the *Encyclopedia of the Philosophical Sciences* (paragraphs 457–61) as well as of Saussure's semiotic theory, to distance itself from any naïve idea of the phonè as phoenix. Indeed, the phonè is more sphinx than phoenix, and at most a "foenix culprit," to echo Joyce. *Glas* approaches a theory of writing purged of all *phony* perspectives.

Wit and Wound

The importance attached to living speech, to *viva voce* discourse, is only one obstacle to such a theory. It can delude us with the hope that the phonè may be caught, a big fish, in the angle of words. Or that writing may become a "s'entendre parler," a conversation with oneself in which, as in Hegel's ultimate thought process, every tone is registered and organized by the sound-machine (see *Glas*, 251b, figure 12). A subtler obstacle still, which is the obverse of the hope we place in living speech, is our capacity for being wounded through the ear.

This is not immediately obvious, because our myths deal more with the power of the voice, with Orphic effects or Milton's "omnific Word," than with its power to hurt us, to echo internally, and wound and even madden. The eyes are vulnerable enough, yet ears are, if anything, chaster than eyes. Words penetrate deeper into the labyrinth of the ear. The very notion of depth is difficult to associate with the eyes, and writing is brought in contact with that depth only through the mysterious formula *l'oeil écoute*. What is the "eery" connection between "coup d'oeil" and castration in Genet's Rembrandt experience? Does his "je m'éc..." imply also a percé-phonic violence?[3]

The wounded ear is not as common a theme as the wounded eye, which proliferates in lovers' complaints and in religious confession. Genet's experience, close to Sartrean nausea, also seems to come via the eyes. Yet we know the role "You are a thief" played in his psychic history. The fixation of identity ("Thou art that") can also evoke the unsoundness of sound. It is precisely the imaginative relation of ear to eye, or of eye-writing to ear-writing, that is at issue.

A systematic analysis would probably start with Freud's understanding of the rebus in *The Interpretation of Dreams*. I prefer to remain unsystematic when there is so much exploration still to be done. The phrase "the wounded ear," for instance, contains a metonymic substitution: it is not the ear that is wounded but the wound comes via the ear as organ of hearing. Yet the metonymy cannot be resolved because we do not know what is wounded. To say the *psyche* is wounded merely leads to the further question, What is the psyche?, and so to more figures of speech. Similarly, if the question is—radically stated—How sound is sound?, the equivocation undermines the very idea of a cure, whether *of* speech or *through* speech. We then fall back on an easier or more traditional notion, which defines "cure" as "care," the care we should take of language.

Yet psychiatry—especially the Lacanian kind—moves within this eery domain of "tour d'écoute" or "tour d'écriture." It giddies us with its turnings, whether rising or falling; for *tour* itself is an equivocal word, and what we really feel, in listening or writing with sensitivity, is that the screw of language can always be turned further. Hence a nausea, or *écoeurement*, coming from language itself. We know meaning always gets screwed.

Derrida often creates a deceptive prose, modeled in part on Mallarmé, that evokes a radical equivocation. This ordinary yet artificial prose is described in *Positions* as an "écriture bifide" facing in at least two directions and presupposing more than one author's "signature" (as in *Derrière le miroir*'s interlacing of painter and writer). We seem to skirt Joyce's words within words, his "echoland"[4]; yet Derrida would probably object that Joyce achieves his polyglot or palimpsest effects by driving to the limit the privilege accorded to the oral within the written, and proceeding logocentrically, word for word. Yet Derrida cannot do more than to make the domino effect of equivocation appear strangely ordinary: not exotic as in Joyce, nor precarious as in Coleridge, but an impropriety proper to language.

No nausea or vertigo is therefore induced. Equivocation is illimitable, but only because it is imitable. The screw of language can always be turned further. The trick is in the open and suggests an indefinite series of variations. Consider in the sentence quoted from the essay on Adami the polyglot turn on *fort* ("gone" in German, "strong" in French) and *qui* ("chi" in Greek, that is X or the chiasmus), or the conjunction of the ideas of margin (of a page), frame (of a picture) and board (of a boat) in the phrase "par dessus bord." Add "tombe"—"tombe par dessus bord"—and construe it as a noun, and the syntax continues to dissolve into words beneath words that yield a rattle-repetition of the themes of "chute monumentale" and "glas."

Pinking Philosophy

By bringing word-*techne* so openly into philosophical discourse, Derrida moves away from a *pudeur* surrounding the relation of language to the machine, including the machine of the body. It is hard to define this *pudeur*, which has pervaded literary criticism since the attack on wit (false wit) in Neoclassical theories of decorum. Perhaps it was felt that wit in its extreme forms exhibited a wound, although no theory before Freud said more than that wit's abuse of language was also an abuse of nature. The ingenious gardener, wit, deals in forbidden mixtures, grafting, adulterating, producing puns or "Pinks" as double as man's mind (see Andrew Marvell's "The Mower against Gardens"). The difference between art and nature is in danger of being lost. The infectious or promiscuous variety that results threatens to bring a leprous insubstantiality into language and nature. But in Marvell, as in Derrida, we never lose sight of the reversibility of the theme: their witty, over-developed flowers of language suggest a *precious wound* associated with the language of flowers. The wound of wit, in brief, lies close to the wound of love.

Nature's shameless use of the machine of "antherection" (also, anti-erection) or "dissemination" should make art blush; and Derrida's methodical use of wit in philosophic discourse is this blush—or flush—methodized. The hurt to the ego that the indifference of lust inflicts stands in a complex relation to the reassertion of difference (e.g., "esteem" of the opposite sex) which that indifference can produce, but by mechanical or impersonal means that operate more reliably than the affected, vulnerable ego.

Now philosophy, strangely enough, has always tried to deflower language instead of appreciating it as a fertile machine for figures and metaphors. Yet how can you deflower a *machine à fleurs?* Derrida knows that philosophy is *in* language, and that its style is radically metaphoric. Then what can he do for philosophy, or for our word-consciousness? Is his punsterish, catachretic style good or bad?

There is no such thing as a good pun. Puns are the only thing beyond good and evil. Perhaps we could talk, like Horace, of curious felicities or splendid vices of style—I don't know. Philosophy is more shameless because of Derrida, but not therefore less veiled. Our consciousness of words is raised to the point where an embarrassment of riches returns us to a state of reserve and uncertainty: to an appreciation of the *mute* letter. Mute letters are the discreet jewels of meaning. Their potential, their reserve, is eloquent (*l'oeil écoute*) yet they suggest a *chose* (perhaps "la chose freudienne," perhaps "la chose heideggerienne") that cannot be named as such. They introduce, there-fore, an indeterminacy affecting both nomination and interpretation. A "Je ne sais quoi" or a "Quoi du reste" that is as coy as it is uncanny.

Of course, the distinction between the mute letter and the muteness of the written character generally is a relative one. Theory must respect both. Derrida suggests that to interpret this muteness as a positive negation is in-adequate, if not mistaken. Silence speaks, but as silence. He also suggests that there is no *relève*, no *Aufhebung* of that fact. We are free to understand it, that is all.

Shall we say that we need that reserve, as if nurturance were at stake? Or that it is the portion put aside, not for use, made sacred . . . a sacred no-thing? Making sense of it is not put in doubt, but rather theories that have tried to make sense of making sense, and made nonsense. Yet their nonsense is itself often valued by Derrida. He does not fear the seemingly absurd or anomalous idea a strong theory may bring to birth. That risk, in fact, is the very result of intellectual gestation, as if the chance of strange but also remarkable issue increased with the age of the parent. When Sarah overhears God promising Abraham a child, she laughs; and perhaps that is what philosophy is doing in Nietzsche and Derrida.

The Fortunes of Wit

Glas, therefore, puts "philosophèmes en liberté." As if to realize Jean Paul Richter's definition of wit, it reduces philosophic systems to clauses and mixes ideas like cards in an intellectual gaming, good only for those who know how to win because they understand play.[5] For the first time since Nietzsche and the German Romantics, the question of play and wit is renewed in so radical a fashion that intellectual and aesthetic history is unable to absorb it.

We know, of course, what happened to the German aestheticians, to Jean Paul and Friedrich Schlegel. (Others might be mentioned: Derrida quotes Novalis in *La dissémination*.) Their ideas on the "chemical" or combinatory force of wit in philosophy, or on Romantic irony as a quality of art subverting even while it embraced all genres and positions, were swallowed up by Hegel's vast dialectical enterprise. Hegel's dialectic is seemingly based on something more concrete than mere play of wit or an infinitizing irony. It embodies "the cunning of reason." Yet this cunning shows itself, *in Hegel*, as an endless kind of wit, or the interpreter's will to overcome *Willkür* (arbitrariness). Reason, through the dialectic, represents as something always already on the way to reason what remains subversive of it. Nietzsche, drawing his own conclusion from this "representation," extracted from Hegel the contrary principles of a will to power (or truth) and of artistic illusion (*Schein*). The wit of art, he implies, is a will to power over the will to power. Art represents as something on the way to art what is subversive of it. It makes the truth—that is, untruth, error, the endlessness of desire or will or wit itself—bearable.

Derrida, then, goes through Hegel to Nietzsche. One might have expected him to go through Hegel to the foundation of contemporary aesthetics ("Kunstkritik," says the young Walter Benjamin) in the fragmentary, counterencyclopedic work of the German Romantics—itself inspired by further sources, by Shakespeare, Cervantes, Sterne's *Tristram Shandy*. This he fails to do, except for remarks on Novalis. The problem of historical regress is the one infinity not faced by Derrida. Nor did he have to go to Germany: though Romantic irony set itself against the superficialities of Gallic wit, there is always the paradoxical and many-sided Diderot. Which is not to the point unless it affects Derrida's outwitting of the principle of closure in historicizing kinds of criticism, those that value the institutionalization of specific genres or orders of discourse. Juxtaposing Hegel and Genet is itself a subversion of historical or genre criticism.

"Dissemination"

That the labor of wit may abort we take for granted. Wit may even be a disease of language, but then only as lust is of sex. For the point of wit is that it has more language than language knows of. Freud showed clearly enough that wit is language-libido. These two infinities of wit and lust have always plagued the decorum of social existence. Pascal tried so hard to be an honest man! Yet the very ideal of "l'honnête homme," or that it had to be put forward as an explicit ethos, betrays the degree to which wit was feared.

What could Pascal's "honnête homme" say to Derrida's "sfeinctor"? The danger sensed by European Classicism was not simply false wit (a trivial and aesthetic fault) but the prospect of endless fakery. With the spread of technical skills, and a secularized principle of imitation, the sacred patterns were in danger not only of being profaned but also of being counterfeited.

There might be no way a father could easily recognize his child, or the true line, in this coming age of bastardy. "Let Rehob rejoice with Caucalis Bastard Parsley," Smart writes in his madness, or in the "errance joyeuse du *graphein*." That he pairs a biblical figure with a common plant, and a proper name with a multiplying mouthful, is a miraculous cast of the tongue. It is wit as Jean Paul, or Freud, understood it, "wild pairings without a priest." If there is a priest, it is the author—whose authority, however, is put in question by such promiscuous yokings. There is no way to reconcile Dr. Johnson's protest against "heterogeneous ideas linked by violence together" with Smart's practice, except through the Blakean proposition that contraries are not simply negations.

The rich darkness or "famillionaire" quality of Smart's verses expresses a strange economy. We may call it, after Derrida, and risking paradox, an economy of *dissemination*, one that reflects the unleashing of vernacular wit in Reformation and Renaissance, its attempted repression by the neoclassical reaction, and its renewed upsurge (sometimes as madness) leading to Derrida's appraisal of "dissemination" as "that which does not return to the father."

The word, that is, cannot be justified by a reference to the logos, or sacred origins, even when it still desires this. It is a word cast on the waters, a prodigal without hope of return. The "imitation of nature" now takes nature literally and substitutes the image of a creative self-scattering for the "collected" imitation of a divine pattern: the "legein" of the logos. The rock parsley in which Rehob rejoices is not the rock on which Peter built his church, yet "parsley," as a word, roots back to "petersilie" and "petroselinum." Smart's proliferating verses heed the first, imperative blessing uttered in the Bible: "Be fruitful and multiply" (Gen. 1:14).

The concept of mimesis changes, is changeable. Yet Derrida fails to provide a history that charts the path from "imitation" to "dissemination." Perhaps he thinks that such a history would show nothing but a self-deceived consciousness: deceived repeatedly, endlessly, by the logocentric fallacy.[6] As mystery stories start with death, so the joyful mystery he has learned from Nietzsche starts with the death of God: with the abandonment of all hope of returning to the father by imitating a Word that was "in the Beginning." But so global and undifferentiated a view leads to arbitrary soundings and selections. Why the importance accorded to Genet? Why the emphasis on Mallarmé (even if doubled by a discussion of Plato)? What of the great Romantics, other than Hegel, or the fertile writers of the Renaissance: Rabelais, Ronsard, Erasmus?

The joyful wandering of the written word begins, if anywhere, in Romance, although it is hard to say where Romance begins. Perhaps with Homer's *Odyssey*. But leaving aside that speculation (developed in Northrop Frye's emphasis on the design of Romance as a perpetual displacement of sacred patterns or archetypal myths), it is important to remark that nearer home—near enough for verifiability—the literary evolution of the vulgar or vernacular tongues is essential for an understanding of the concept of dissemination, which clearly belongs in a differentiated series with imitation, translation, contamination, secularization, and (sacred) parody. Otherwise the concept's probative value is lost in the abstract and monotonous vigor of its application to this or that slice of text.

To extend these remarks. The developing vernaculars had to sow their wild oats and did so by "imitation." But this "imitation" was a witty and varied bootlegging of older and sacred texts, the pater-patterns. The great vernacular authors betrayed as well as translated these patterns: they ransacked the paternal store and plowed what they found into their national poems. In short, they praised Rehob but cultivated bastard parsley. Vergil was helpful here, and especially the *Georgics*, for the Romans had faced a similar problem with the absorption of Greek and Italic riches ("munera"). That this activity of translation or contamination—Santayana somewhere gives its formula as Santa Maria sopra Minerva, which Kenneth Burke alters to ecclesia supra cloacam—was joyous as well as pious or anxious is suggested when Vergil asks the divinities of Greece and Italy to join the Roman tutelary gods in a dance at the opening of the *Georgics*: "ferte simul Faunique pedem."

This literary efflorescence, then, whether of Latin or Renaissance literature, should be considered a "first" stage of the dissemination Derrida talks of:

what is cultivated here only returns to the father nominally. Not everything, of course, goes in this direction. The Counter-Reformation, and Loyola's "exercises," restore the principle of imitation in a militant way, even if in a John Donne or Christopher Smart meditational verse becomes prodigal once again. Moreover, what could not return to the father tended to "adorn" or "illustrate" the mother: either a Mary substitute, or the mother tongue.

Each revival of wit is therefore already a "second" stage of this dissemination; and while the notion of stages can produce a naïve historicity, it is unconscionable not to consider the development of the national literatures in their specific and peculiar relations to the history of religion: one should at least raise the question of what translating the Bible meant to language (Luther's pithiness and even grossness still influences the "Mutterwitz" of Jean Paul), what theologies or theories of reading evolved, and what attempts were made to subordinate art to a regulated principle of imitation.

The place of the Romantic poets in this history of dissemination is among its most fascinating chapters. When, for example, in his earliest verses, Blake invites Autumn, "laden with fruit, and stained / With the blood of the grape" to stay with him, "and all the daughters of the year shall dance" (see "To Autumn" in *Poetical Sketches*, published 1783), he is still echoing the "ferte pedem" of *Georgics* I, as well as the "huc, pater o Lenaee, veni" of *Georgics* II. His imitation is, however, so removed from the "father-text" that the latter ceases to exist except in one respect: Blake has understood the "translation of empire" theme in Vergil, and substituted (according to the Vergilian model itself, at least in the *Georgics*) the arts of peace for those of war. Hence "blood of the grape" is more than an apt Hebraism. The poet is fashioning georgics in or against the reign of the Georges. In his later, more explicitly visionary poems, the "dissemination" here conveyed through intertwining themes of harvesting, rest, wine, song, and festivity becomes large-scale, ambivalent denial of the principle of imitation—or the "ragging" (in the form of a repetitive, quasi-dithyrambic dismembering) of biblical Creation and regeneration myths:

> Then fell the Legions of Mystery in madd'ning confusion,
> Down, down thro' the immense, with outcry, fury & despair,
> Into the wine presses of Luvah; howling fell the clusters
> Of human families thro' the deep; the wine presses were fill'd;
> The blood of life flow'd plentiful. Odors of life arose
> All round the heavenly arches, & the Odors rose singing this song:
>
> "O terrible wine presses of Luvah! O caverns of the Grave!
> How lovely the delights of those risen again from death!
> O trembling joy! excess of joy is like Excess of grief."

Urthona call'd his sons around him: Tharmas call'd his sons
Numerous; they took the wine, they separated the Lees,
And Luvah was put for dung on the ground by the Sons of Tharmas & Urthona.
They formed heavens of sweetest woods, of gold & silver & ivory,
Of glass & precious stones. They loaded all the waggons of heaven
And took away the wine of ages with solemn songs & joy.

The Four Zoas

With Derrida dissemination enters a new phase. It is now directed
analytically—prosaically, if you wish—against the mimetic principle (the
"collect" or "legein" of the logos) in major texts of the Western tradition.
They are so separated from a direct logo-imitative intention by his deconstructive readings that they cannot be returned to the father: their author, or their
author in heaven. Instead of converting the straying text to a central truth by a
mode of interpretation similar to allegoresis or sacred parody, Derrida ab-
solutizes the text's "error."

What emerges is an anti-allegoresis, and perhaps for the first time since
Philo of Alexandria. (Kenneth Burke stands nearest to Derrida in this.) Interpretation no longer aims at the reconciliation or unification of warring
truths. Literature is always "bifide," as in Mallarmé. More "bifide" than the
often happy and enriching conflict between Latin and the vernacular, or a
hieratic high style and the corruscating wit of a sprouting, idiomatic mother
tongue. For the movement away from the father does not lead to the redemptive
adornment of a complementary, maternal presence, except in certain Jungian
or mythological versions of the attack on the "masculine trinity" of the logos.
Instead the prestige of all origins, of all ultimate sources (spermatic word or
immaculate womb), is questioned.

A Two-handed Engine

What does it mean, though, for practical criticism? Derrida argues that it
is the mother who "speaks" through Jean Genet's style, despite its classical and
biblical resonance. The style is taken to be a dissemination, or ultimate denial
of patrology. From a historical perspective, however—the one we have
sketched—Genet's style is rather the revenge of the mother on a Neoclassical
tradition that almost strangled vernacular literature in its cradle. An impossible counterpurity is posited, an idealization of the (original and lost) mother
tongue.[7] The Anglo-American tradition, which did not experience so strongly
the neoclassical *episteme*—which did not, in other words, suffer academic or
social censorship from the seventeenth into the nineteenth centuries—is
much less productive of such gifted *aliénés* as Genet, of "martyrs" of language

like Roussel, Artaud, and Leiris, or of exemplary madmen like Brissot. It never totally repressed, in the name of purity of diction, the fertile, even promiscuous, mix of idioms in Shakespeare and Donne or in the visionary satire of Swift and Blake; and what it lost it recovered in Joyce and the philological exorbitance of Smart's *Jubilate Agno* (first published in 1939).

There is much less fuss over origins in our tradition, because, in literature at least, no doctrine of purity prevailed long enough to cause an overestimation of excluded, hence "lost," tendencies. Derrida's attack on originary thinking is, nevertheless, important for criticism. He shows that the more we penetrate a text the more its textual and intertextual weaving appears; and this is not a matter, simply, of coming to know through the chosen book more and more sources. That would be source study and *explication de texte* all over again. What one comes to know is the unintelligibility—the "abysmation" or "échappé de vue ins Unendliche" (F. Schlegel)—of the literary work. To approach, tendentially, absolute knowledge is also, as in science, to approach a form of understanding that faces toward scepticism or unknowingness. Derrida is thus closer to Jost Amman's remarkable Shandylike genealogy (figure 13) than to Hiltensperger's logocentric labyrinth (figure 14). Reading should be an *errance joyeuse* rather than the capitalization of great books by interpretive safeguards.

It is hard to see how dissemination could be formalized. It is a *travail de textes*, their working-through, in which the texts themselves undergo a renewed birth-labor. Being attentive to the multiplicity of themes or the polysemy of a work of art constitutes a progress over "linear" explication, but is not sufficient. The horizon of criticism, which is the assumption of unity of meaning, has itself to be breached. "La dissémination . . . pour produire un nombre non-fini d'effets sémantiques, ne se laisse reconduire ni à un présent d'origine simple . . . ni à une présence eschatologique. Elle marque une multiplicité irréductible et *générative*" (*Positions*, pp. 61–62).

Can this disseminative kind of reading still be called a reading? Can a new "horizon" or "foundation" be discovered, as was attempted for mathematics at the turn of the nineteenth century? Or are we already in the presence of an unknown "geometry," perhaps an old one, if we think of the exegetical "gematria" proposed by Derrida's essay on Sollers' *Nombres*? I suspect that the disseminating commentary of *Glas* resembles the "two-handed engine" Milton alludes to in *Lycidas* when denouncing the clergy, who, in modern dress, are the clerisy, the provosts and purveyors of literary study.

Derrida's engine does not, of course, have the strength to smite once and for all. Its two-handedness remains symbolic of its impotence: it reproduces itself merely, giving us doubles that make us see more doubles still. The result for our time may be a factional split between simplifying types of reading that de la vérité, la vérité de la vérité. Alors le phantasme (absolu) de l'IC comme phantasme (absolu) est la vérité (absolue). La vérité est le phantasme même. L'IC, la différence sexuelle comme opposition (thèse contre thèse), le cercle familial absolu serait l'équivalence générale de la vérité et du phantasme. Enantiose homosexuelle.

Cette différence déterminée en contradiction ou en opposition, n'est-ce pas justement la religion (la représentation) résolue dans le Sa? Est-ce que le Sa ne permet pas, précisément, de penser la limite de cette limite, de faire apparaître cette limite comme telle, de voir le phantasme en sa vérité? Est-ce que le Sa, résolution de l'opposition absolue, réconciliation de l'en-soi et du pour-soi, du père et de la mère, n'est-ce pas le Sa même du phantasme?

En tant qu'il opère le passage de la représentation à la présence et qu'il produit la vérité (présente à soi dans le savoir) du phantasme absolu, qu'il est la vérité du phantasme absolu, son essence dévoilée (*Wesen : Gewesenheit :* le phantasme ayant-été), le *Sa* est l'accomplissement final du phantasme, l'être-auprès-de-soi du *logos.* Le phantasme absolu : *Sa.* Mais ne pas en conclure : *Sa,* ce n'est que — le phantasme, la vérité de la vérité *n'est* encore *que* phantasmatique. Dès lors que *Sa* accède à lui-même, tout ce qui lui est équivalent est infini. On ne peut plus dire d'un phantasme infini qu'il *n'est-que.* Le discours du *Sa* disqualifie le *ne-que.*

la hauteur du son.

Et compte tenu du « récit », des « jalousies » de la « boîte expressive », du « plein-jeu » et du « grand plein-jeu », de la bi-claviculation et des orgues classiques, baroques ou romantiques, ne pourrait-on reconstituer un modèle organigraphique, une nouvelle *De organographia*

Ja diese vielstimmige liebliche Werck begriff alles das in sich, was etwa in der Music erdacht vnd componiret werden kan, vnd gibt so einem rechten natürlichen Klang, laut vnd thon von sich, nicht anders als ein ganzer Chor voller Musicanten, do mancherley Melodeyen von junger Knaben vnd grosser Männer Stimmen gehörtworden. In summa die Orgel hat vnd begreifft alle andere Instrumenta musica, groß vnd klein, wie die Nahmen haben mögen, allein in sich. Wenn ein Trummet/Trummet/Posaun/Zincken/Blockflöt/Querpfeiffen/Pommern/Schallmeyen/Dolcian/Racketten/Sordounen/Krumphörner/Geigen/Leyern/&c. hören, so anstu diese alles vnd noch viel ander wunderliche liebligkeiten mehr in diesem künstlichen Werck haben: Also daß, wenn du dieses Instrument hast vnd hörest/ du nicht anderst denckest/ als habest bei diesen Instrumenta alle mitteinander.

Michael Praetorius « De Organographia » Wolfenbüttel 1619,

qui serait comme le savoir absolu de glas?

Mais le savoir absolu n'est, telle la " jalousie ", qu'une pièce de la machinerie, un effet de marche

un autre substitut de cas-

Figure 12. Jacques Derrida, *Glas,* p. 251 (part). Courtesy, Editions Galilée.

Figure 13. Jost Ammann, *Aus dem Geschlechterbuch der Familie Tucker* (1589). Handschrift auf Pergament (Schreibmeister).

Figure 14. Johann Kaspar Hiltensperger. *Logocentric Labyrinth* (18th century).

call themselves humanistic and indefinitizing kinds that call themselves scientific. The fate of reading is in the balance. In a classroom darkly.

New Literary History?

In this twilight, theories of literary progress or decadence are bound to emerge. A further battle of Ancients and Moderns, though it may never reach the Armageddon stage, seems to be in the making. McLuhanism, for instance, suggests a progress beyond the bookish or written word. The dead letter will be sounded or electrified once more, revived by a providence working in the guise of technology. Northrop Frye, though less materialistic, also remains firm and hopeful in his belief that the logos will continue to propagate. Not because the Bible, that book of books, is a sacred or privileged text, but because like any other strong depository of myth it produces "displacements" of itself.

The uncheerful obverse of such speculations is Harold Bloom's understanding of literary continuity, his revision of Oscar Wilde's "The Decay of Lying" as "The Necessity of Misreading." Bloom charts a recessional rather than evangelical movement of the logos. The difference in scope or literary power of Old and New Testament is a significant example of this. The scandal of the New Testament lies in its diminishment of the Old. The course of English poetry after Milton is similarly that of a decline, a negative progress. Bloom has reintroduced the Kabbalistic concepts of "zimzum" (God's shrinking of Himself) and the "breaking of the vessels" to dramatize a falling-off, which is the prerequisite for a quasi-divine creation or dissemination: any strong artistic achievement depends on this sacrificial scattering of the burden of tradition or imagination. As if, in order to escape the Sphinx that blocks us, or the incumbent shadow of literary heredity, we had to cut off limb after limb. One can only hope that, synecdoche being a rich device, this *coupure* into parts that save the whole may continue indefinitely.

Bloom, like Derrida, takes seriously Nietzsche's view that Christian asceticism is not what it seems to be, but a form of nihilism: a will to live, even a will to power, drawn from the very awareness that God is dead and life unmediated. Or mediated only by illusions like the "ideal" of asceticism. Bloom's analysis of the deepening twilight of art yields a grammar of illusions: six "bifide" or cloven fictions by which the literary sons arrogate enough authority to pretend to their father's kingdom.[8] In its parodistic motion, therefore, Bloom's chariot of wrath remains one of Urthona's "waggons of heaven" loaded with the "wine of ages," with "solemn songs and joy."

Even the most radical literary movement in contemporary America, the "oral poetry" of the school of Charles Olson, stays within the patriarchal aegis. It seeks, as is already clear in Pound, more than charm of cadence or fidelity of speech: can these tones (bones, stones) live, and be new hieroglyphs to us? It is strange how close, on occasion, "oral poetry" comes to the "errance joyeuse du *graphein*." Yet its theory hovers unresolved between imitation and dissemination. "Melville was agonized over paternity. He suffered as a son. He had lost the source. He demanded to know the father." So Charles Olson in *Call Me Ishmael,* waking the pathos of a tradition (the redemptive search of the son for the father, of the father for the son) that goes back, with ease, to Stephen Daedalus.

Who knows Ishmael's "proper" name? The biblical Ishmael's father was Abram, or Abraham. Does Ahab contain Abraham? Ahab, Ahb, Abba. "*Ahab* sera désormais le sigle du père absolu." The father, in Melville, is not to be known—except as the "antemosaic unsourced existence of the unspeakable terrors of the whale" (*Moby-Dick*). As an "unfathered vapour," then, or the divine voice speaking out of the whirlwind in the Book of Job.

That voice is fathomless, however. It has no sons or daughters. It can hardly be described as delighting in dissemination. Yet while demanding that Job gird up his loins, it also utters the image of the sea bursting from the womb, the uncovenantable Leviathan, and the sons of God shouting for joy at the foundation of the earth. And it restores to Job fourteen thousand sheep, six thousand camels, a thousand yoke of oxen, and a thousand she-asses, as well as seven sons and three daughters.

Melville's negative way leads him, ultimately, to stones instead of seed, to a nonsource among stones that cannot live. His Gothic gropings ("by horrible gropings we come to the central room") arrive at a sterile Golgotha. "Stones of Judea. We read a good deal about stones in Scripture. Monuments and memorials are set up of stones; men are stoned to death; the figurative seed falls in stony places; and no wonder. . . . Judea is one accumulation of stones."

"The figurative seed falls in stony places." Not only the seed, then, but the figure, the parable itself. The sower throws the parable in vain. "Even to the loose stones that cover the highway / I gave a moral life," Wordsworth writes, seeking his parable among the pebbles. What we need is a new Deucalion. "He who has ears, let him hear," says Matthew 13. But stones have no ears. Is this dissemination?

Die Frage nach dem Ohr

In children's verse, of course, pebbles may speak. Mute or insensate things can be heard. This "groping" of the ear, however, becomes "horrible" in Gothic fiction or simply in certain imaginations. Though Melville asked, "who can get a Voice out of Silence?" what is gropingly heard may be more horrifying than silence itself. What did Acteon *hear*?

In trying to understand in what way the psyche is like a text, Derrida remembers a famous passage from Freud's *Moses and Monotheism* that makes the analyst an exegete of darkness: in search of the erased primal crime through a text of traces. So Genet's "Je m'éc . . . ," evoked at the beginning of *Glas*, together with the tearing up of "Rembrandt," could be the sign of an internal discourse that has become lacunary, because censored or mutilated or converted into nonverbal symptoms. A self-suppressed "Je m'écoeure," it also points toward a "Je m'écris" in which we hear the *cri* of the torn or missing portion. . . . The silence speaks as in pictures; even screams, as in conversion neuroses. We understand better why Genet's reflexively formulated ("je me") experience of alterity is associated with the mute interrogation of certain Rembrandt paintings.

The "Je m'éc . . . " prevents, in the very act of writing down, the flowing out it denotes. Something is blocked as well as elided. By stopping (punctuating) the phrase this way, Genet suspends its flow and throws the emphasis back on the closed circuit of self-constitution. Feared loss of self produces a new self-affirmation, yet reveals in passing an ambiguity in the psychic mechanism of identification. The "je me" is a mirror kind of doubling, and the "éc . . . " evokes a sound common to both *écoule* (écris, écrie, etc.) and *extase*. Identification, according to Lacan, is a mode not simply of stasis but of ecstasy: temporality, or language as the foundation process of differential meaning, is arrested by the premature assumption of a fixating ego image. "Je m'éc . . . " considered as a complex *psycheme* could therefore be translated: I reexalt my identity by regressing through this experience of otherness to the primal ecstasy that fixed my now newly threatened identity—fixed it once and for all in the foreclosure of permanent exile.

To add "je m'exile" only emphasizes how dependent interpretation is, in this case, on an indeterminable, if self-constituted, equivocation and on what we know, from Genet or his interpreters, about Genet's life. The indeterminate "Je m'éc . . . " puts almost too much pressure on the interpreter, who has to supply (out of himself, as it were) a series of possible closures, all of which are at risk. If we see the episode as a whole in a dark religious light, it becomes an "Ecce homo." If we emphasize the element of aural narcissism, then "Je m'éc . . . " moves closer to "I echo myself." If we emphasize the physical disgust or *écoeurement*, then "Je m'éc . . . " reverts to a self-strangulated sound, as if words were, at that moment, a kind of vomit to be swallowed down.

What remains a constant, however, is that the experience as described by Genet does not involve an actual exchange of words. It is completely silent. The only words are those he writes (although they include patches of inner colloquy). He sees a stranger, and he juxtaposes with that his experience of certain paintings. The "Thou art that" emanates in its allocutory strength from purely visual sources.

Because Genet's eyes, and finally his sex, seem to sustain the wound, the interpreter gropes toward understanding the predominance of sight in the economy of (this) human experience. Something is wrong when all is done or suffered in pseudosilence. Wrong, precisely, with that "economy" ("je m'économise"?). Genet's text is merely a legend or *legomenon* that circles the mute *dromenon,* as if psychic life were ritual at the core, a continuous rebus. Then what is the status of words in all this?

The "Je m'éc..." punctures a dual discourse that is too suave. It breaches the pseudosilence; makes us aware of the physicality of words. The loss portrayed comes close to being a word-loss. The words continue, of course; their mental or masturbatory charm is not broken despite the castrating glance evoked. But to unriddle the rebus means, here, not only to word *things* but to word *words:* to understand, through the *coupure* of "Je m'éc..." and the symbolic wounding of "Rembrandt" that words themselves have become the actors, the "comedians" and "martyrs" of what is enacted. To get a voice out of this silence means to rescue "Genet": the relation of proper name or signature to meaning—to the possibility of a *proper* meaning, of a "cleanly," "pure" identity, rather than the unclean, improper "vide solide" experienced. The *nom propre* is *non-propre.* [9]

It is, then, after all, the ear that is cut off, and that must grope to restore either itself or a wounded name. "The signature is a wound and there is no other origin of the work of art" (*Glas,* 207b). Yet this groping is done not so much by the ear as by language, or "une référence irréductible à l'intervention muette d'un signe écrit" (*Positions,* p. 16). This "mute intervention" or *mimique* we call writing is the problem, since we can never get it to speak itself out: to sound its object definitively rather than to "economize" it by a complex exchange of words or representations.

A curious affinity is suggested, therefore, between "Genet" and the "Pierrot" of Mallarmé's *Mimique.* Pierrot is as mute as writing; his sex is uncertain or ambivalent; his action also a passion; and his representation undecidably sacred or obscene. And, as in *Hamlet* (which stages the dumb show of a king poisoned through the ear), nothing survives at the end but "a wounded name."

Signature and Wound

> If there be rule in unity itself,
> This is not she.... This is, and is not *Cressid.*
> Shakespeare

What wounds signature or name (figures 11 [bottom], 20, 21, 22, 23)? The fact that they are purely visionary tokens, or that they cannot be "proper" in the sense of coinciding fully with the text or corpus to which they are affixed.

In his *Thieves of Fire*, a study of Promethean or charismatic artists, Denis Donoghue describes the "aura of presence" that emanates from their work, yet cannot coincide with it, as if something ("du reste") always remained, which becomes associated with their name:

> In reading Promethean writers we have the impression that they feel themselves participating in an ancestral drama not limited to their own: their works are at once immediate and distant, these battles are taking place now and always. . . . So it is common to say of each that his most achieved work is himself, his identity as victim-hero of the ancestral drama: the self in question determines whatever is visible and actual in the work, but it is not fulfilled by the work, there is a remainder, an incorrigible excess which is visible only in the name. (p. 24)

Yet when we come to common nouns, the situation changes. *Nomen* is, and is not, *numen*. The common noun may aspire to the condition of proper noun; but even the proper noun is only equivocally "proper." When, through the equivocal character of words, or the interpretive process that brings it out, we lose the certainty that there is a proper meaning—or, at least, a "rule in unity"—the hurt strikes as deep as slander. We may sense this hurt even more in the interpreter than in the writer who is his object. For the very fullness of an interpreter's style, if richly allusive, or speculative, or contaminated by the writer under discussion, leaves us with a hollow feeling. The interpreter's words are conscious of meaning more than they can say, of being caught up in the *task* of equivocation. The writer may be doing exactly the same, but by becoming the "object" of another's view, the writer for another writer, he seems more natural, unself-conscious: more *out there*.

The French critical tradition has taken this task of equivocation on, while Anglo-American criticism still seeks to limit it and remain "proper." American psychoanalysis, similarly, continues to localize trauma or wound in various types of primal scenes. The one wound is hypostatized as the eloquent, repeatable trauma that determines all. Derrida's "The signature is a wound and there is no other origin of the work of art" still links the wound to identity loss but through the complex relation of signature and text, of the knotting and unknotting of would-be "proper" or "definitive" words.

Derrida's Knot

That the word "knot" may echo in the mind as "not" is one of those small changes that analyst or exegete are trained to hear. "When thou hast done, thou hast not done." There are so many knots: Donnean, Penelopean, Lacanian, Borromean, Derridean. At the beginning of *Glas*, the similarity in sound of *Sa* (acronym for "savoir absolu") and *Sa* ("signifiant") is such a knot with a positive philosophic yield. Yet because of the equivocal, echo-nature of language, even identities or homophonies sound on: the sound of *Sa* is knotted with that of *ça*, as if the text were signaling its intention to bring Hegel, Saussure, and Freud together. *Ça* corresponds to the Freudian Id ("Es"); and it may be that our only "savoir absolu" is that of a *ça* structured like the *Sa*-signifiant: a bacchic or Lacanian "primal process" where only signifier-signifying-signifiers exist.

Moreover, in the same marginal comment where the *Sa* makes its appearance, Derrida "invents" another acronym, IC, for the Immaculate Conception. By the time we actually reach this theme in his discussion of Genet we are pages further on, and its introduction here through so peculiar a device seems quite arbitrary. But again, as with *Sa*, another near homophone is involved, so that language seems to motivate itself, as in the paragrams of Saussure. IC is close to the *ici* of "ici, maintenant" (*Glas*, 7a) gliding via its sound-shape into a concept and so echo-deconstructing it. The doctrine of the IC is simply an *ici* writ large, the exemplary instance for Western tradition of a metaphysics of presence.

The doubling of *ici* (itself double, that is, reversible), like that of *Sa*, is in itself a sign of the impossibility of presence and reenforces what is implied by the split page and the dual commentary. Does Derrida know he is quoting himself in this *icitation*? The echo-montage is willed, no doubt, but one cannot be sure the intended effect is not accompanied by an unintended one: by a daemonic rather than courteous echo. Derrida evokes a language system so equivocal that we cannot distinguish between original and citation, yet he is also so anxious to make his point that he riddles *Glas* with devices and interventions.

On the next page, of course, "le seing tombe"; but Derrida's (de)construction of the IC is already like the emptying of some large concept or weighty word—its fall into the débris of isolated letters. The fall foregrounds them, at the same time: erects the possibility of a more lapidary alphabet or post-phonetic writing. Could the "Je m'éc . . .," opposite, echo the IC and suggest an impossibly dense thought-sound EC/IC that can only be decondensed, like the metaphysical *ici*, by ecriture?[10]

Derrida returns to *ici* near the end of *Glas*, after having conjoined the phantoms of Immediacy (Presence) and of the Immaculate Conception. He can therefore write their epitaph: their "ici gît." He does so by an *icitation* from Genet that hollows language into equivocation even while hallowing the death of "Divine" (the "mother" in *Pompes funèbres*):

> Je me forçai à dire, à me redire, avec l'agaçante répétition des scies I-ci, I-ci, I-ci, I-ci. Mon esprit s'aiguisait sur l'endroit que désignait "Ici." Je n'assistais même plus à un drame. Aucun drame n'avait pu se passer dans un lieu si étroit, insuffisant à toute présence. "I-ci, I-ci, I-ci, I-ci. Qu'on l'a tué, qu'on l'a tué, qu'on l'a tué, con l'a tué, con l'a tué . . ." et je fis mentalement cette épitaphe: "Ici con l'a tué" (287b).

Enough, you say. But Derrida adds: "Reste ici ou glas qu'on ne peut arrêter." In his pamphlet on Adami, Derrida plays further on IC, which now reappears in the form of ICH ("I" or "Je"), the abbreviated ICH (TOS) symbol for Christ (see the fish of Adami's picture), and by chiastic reversal both the chiasmus itself (X) transliterated as CHI, and the querulous pronoun QUI. Freeplay reaches here a methodical craziness that parallels Christopher Smart's. But taken altogether a series of slippery signifiers has now established itself on the basis of the problematics of the subject, its construction and subversion. Though this verbal gematria is no more, no less, persuasive than Lacan's diagrammatia, it has the same treacherously memorable effect, as if Lacan's imaginary and symbolic realms had finally come together in a sort of *specular script.*

Let me try to formulate this basic mirror-writing as

IC(ICH / CHI)INRI

I have added the last term, the acronym of Christ on the Cross, to that crossing or chiasmic middle term, which stands for the problematics of subject or ego, and to the first term, which evokes, together with fhe initials of Christ and the first syllable of ICarus (as in "la voie/voix d'Icare"), the Immaculate Conception.

The three terms in series repeat a scene of nomination. It focuses on ICH, the narcissistic shifter, a mere text-figure when CHI. It focuses equally on the "Name of the Game," whether "Je," "Jeu," or "Je est un autre." But if to enter language is not the same as to enter the law, it is also not merely to learn the rules of a game. As in Kafka's parable, we remain "before" the law, a situation that keeps us "profane" yet engages us in a hermeneutics based on hope even when we resist that hope. It is, in short, the relation of language and law that is always being worked out in "symbolic" situations.

To enter language means to risk being named, or recognized by name, to struggle against false names or identities, to live in the knowledge that *reconnaissance* and *mépris(e)* are intertwined, and that self and other are terms that glide eccentrically about an always im-proper ("metaphoric") naming of things or persons. There is no ultimate recognition scene. *Glas* keeps us looking in a glass, darkly. It disenchants the hope it expresses by playing language against itself, by dividing, spacing, splitting, joycing, tachygraphing, equivocating, reversing its charged words. This then is Derrida's crucifixion of the Word, that is, cruci-fiction: his crosswordings rag the story of Christ, tear a seamless garment into semes. For many this will cheapen or overintellectualize a sacred text. Yet Derrida's negative labor can also be understood as an anamnesis of the journey of the self from IC to INRI, from a scene of ideal or spectral naming to the slander of identity.

Quoi . . . d'un Derrida?

What reenactment of the past is needful today? *Anamnesis* implies that something is recalled that was forgotten, *remembrance* that something is recalled that is dead. *Repetition*, when conjoined with *tradition*, conjures up a chain of authoritative writings, as in the *Pirke Avot* (Sayings of the Fathers), where the law is said to pass directly from God to Moses to the Elders. All three terms value the past as having a survival, or a right to survival, in us.

Dissemination is an unlikely word to add. It acknowledges that we no longer live in a world defined by certain writings having testamentary force and bending us authoritatively to their yoke. Today Old and New Testaments are simply two "texts" in a series that is profane and endless (an "entretien infini," Blanchot suggests), and to which, say, *Krapp's Last Tape* is just another addition. There is no way to canonize or close a series whose very character is centrifugal, disseminative—like time in Kafka, which averts the decree or delays it long enough to allow a perplexed, erring, but very human action to take place, despite K's hope for justification.

In combating the violence of that "eschatological" hope, inscribed in the texture of both ordinary language and organized metaphysical thought, Derrida continues the work of Camus and Blanchot. Camus could not decide what was spiritual and what intellectual in this combat; while Blanchot reduces hope to its sparsest, most denuded verbal contact. Derrida seems to transfer the combat entirely to the rhetorical and intellectual side, even to the point of denying himself what Hannah Arendt names a "modern equivalent of ritual invocations": quotes that recall or re-present voices from the past.

Though Derrida quotes liberally, and understands the relation between quotation and fragment (both are homeless, or so aphoristic that they cannot be fully assimilated to any context), he does not try to explode the past out of its pastness, to give it a new and factitious presence. Quotations still imply a hope, that of being attributed as well as integrated, and so an ultimate recognition scene. "Je comprends enfin qu'au jour du jugement, c'est avec ma propre voix que Dieu m'appelera: 'Jean, Jean'" (*Glas*, 220b). Derrida prefers to intermingle signatures, and he creates in *Glas* a scandalous literary pudding or French trifle.

It is, in a sense, a heroic trifle, a farce or satura mimetic of history's own disdain for the Classicist separation of genres. A parallel could be made between *Glas* and Norman O. Brown's *Closing Time* (1973) that extends beyond their titles. Section 3 of Brown's book is called an "Interlude of Farce," and it mixes, as Brown does throughout, Vico, the Joyce of *Finnegans Wake*, and various other authors. As if Marx's famous statement in *The Eighteenth Brumaire* were being generalized: "Hegel says somewhere that, upon the stage of universal history, all great events and personalities reappear in one fashion or another. He forgot to add that, on the first occasion, they appear as tragedy; on the second as farce."

But Derrida's "inkenstink" seems to allow of no first or second. His interminable prose is the exfoliation or etiolation of all metaphors of innocence that view history as a succession of renaissances, of reenactments of the past, whether failed or triumphant. What is history, then, and what can motivate us to face it, as Hegel did—a history that now includes Hegel, and may one day include Derrida?

A Question of Ground

—Où se situe le livre?
—Dans le livre.
    E. Jabès, *Le livre des questions*

The foregrounding of IC and similar "émajusculations" only raises, in its strange and graphic vividness, a MENE TEKEL aspect, or the question of the ground against which words are readable. No question the ground is slippery, when words are grounded on words. The slippage is all around us, and the principle of stabilization not very conspicuous. We seem to be stepping on soap. In the macabre comedy called *Glas*, the philosopher-artist is like a clown always about to fall who recovers his balance by an outrageous mimicry of the machination involved in balancing. Walking measures the ground; talking measures language; thinking is peripatetic. But the thinker also finds that thinking is beyond *mésure*, or that man is not the measure, not even of his language. He discovers that where he thought he was on solid ground—whether terra firma or presuppositions or whatever you name the substratum—he is (also) on language; then, that language is not a ground but a groundless veiling of the hypothesis (itself a grounding term) of the ground.

The dilemma is historicized by Heidegger, who sees a shift from substantial- to word-thinking occurring in the "translation" of culture from Greece to Rome. Translator, traitor: but this Heideggerian version of history—whose sources go back to Hölderlin's attempt to "translate" the Greeks, and is paralleled in our time by Buber and Rosenzweig's effort to recapture biblical Hebrew in German—is something that occurs all the time in writing or art, as it discovers itself to be a palimpsest, at once full of layered inscriptions and riddled by lacunae or cruxes. Joyce's art, especially in *Finnegans Wake*, is symptomatic: the "nom propre," as Derrida might say, becomes unsound by releasing an improper sound, so that the book reads like a palimpsest in which the salacious echoes at once hinder and enrich readability. Ecclesia supra cloacam. . . .

The cloaca is still a bottom of a sort. *Finnegans Wake* remains curiously pastoral in its labor: the words sweat a sexual balm. Lust sings. It is hard to be frightened, as one can be when Blake, in his visionary machines, keeps taking the ground from under our feet, or castrates the whole body. But the void, in art, is always being exposed and limited at the same time. The opening of Genesis is exemplary in this respect. "In the beginning God created the heavens and the earth. Now the earth was unformed and void, and darkness was upon the face of the deep. . . ." The word for the deep, *t'hom*, is suspected to be the Canaanite primal Goddess Tiamat. It seems as if her proper name were taken away or never existed: she is voided into a mere noun that means "the deep." Canceled, sublated perhaps, it (she) enters a new discourse.

Yet we do not know with certainty what the signifier *t'hom* signified. We see it as part of the series "unformed and void, and darkness upon . . . the deep." Our own fiat, and numerous traditional guesses called translations, give the word a sort of constancy, and match—or stalemate—the signifier. When through historical research the suppressed Tiamat emerges again, we are both delighted and perplexed. What is more substantive here, the recovery of the original name, which must remain a hypothesis, and which may itself have an original, or the way the Hebrew Creation story glides over the abyss of contamination—the obscene or obscure word *Tiamat*—by a divine epigram that establishes its own word directly, as it were, on the abyss? Here too, then, is a translation that, in its exemplary "toils of grace," becomes accepted ground.

The specter of bricolage, sometimes dignified as syncretism, now arises. We know, with Valéry, that civilizations are mortal, that even biblical codes may fall apart, that the translation cannot hold. Everything is stolen from "the deep," which is really a bottomless trash heap of absolute, now obsolete, ideas, of pathetic rather than motivating words. A "fumier philosophique," Balzac called it, in describing an antiquarian store. Culture seems pieced together from bits and pieces salvaged by some conservative instinct. The doctrine of purity of diction, so dominant in France from Malherbe to almost the present, was but our latest attempt to insist on a grace beyond bricolage, a purifying labor that always admitted it contained an obscure magic, a *je ne sais quoi*. What remains of that today? Of that coy *quoi*? Or of other movements of sublation and translation, like the dialectophage (Derrida's word) dialectic of Hegel? "Quoi du reste aujourd'hui, pour nous, ici, maintenant, d'un Hegel?"

Strange, to think of Hegel as stylist, as discovering a new grace of style: that is, of cultural translation. This hobbling sentence of Derrida's already deconstructs Hegel's slippage over the abyss of words he helped us to think about: the "pour nous," "ici," "maintenant." It is the question of the subject as well, or of presence and place in relation to self-presence. The question of history too, and, more insidiously, of the "quoi du reste": the fact that there is a remainder which motivates thought or is remotivated by it.

We glue bitty words like *ici* and *pour nous* together, into some desired unity. That unity mocks us already in the form of the word *aujourd'hui*, a sticky compound that raises the question of word boundary or juncture. Suppose we alter one boundary slightly, using a glue like that of the liaison (the d'). Suppose we lift typographically the negative liaison of the comma, thereby transforming it into an apostrophe to create a new spacing of the sounds: "quoi du res t'aujourd'hui, pour nous. . . ." By so doing we release the elided name of Heidegger into a sentence that seems to deal only with Hegel, for now "quoi du res," that is, "Die Frage nach dem Ding," emerges (like Tiamat) from the word "reste," as if this question, today, were what remained for us, as the only possibility for grounding thought, though a question that keeps echoing and cannot be answered once for all ("Qu'est-ce qu'une chose? Qu'est-ce que le nom de chose" [*Glas*, 11b]).

"On a touché au vers," Mallarmé said; now, on touche à la prose. Boundaries are what one thinks. Fickle, punctuated sounds, wavering between prose and poetry, yet solid too, because of habit and of linguistic rules like the liaison, or the binary opposition of marked and unmarked. This interstitial kind of thinking, this margin-haunted and liminal discourse, prevents language from being reified into, on the one hand, poetry and literature, and on the other, prose and philosophy.

If thinking is for us, today, textual, then we should understand that grounding. To some extent it can and must be argued that we have fallen into the condition of viewing all things as texts, and even the "thing" itself is textual. Structured "like" language, Lacan says ambiguously of "la chose freudienne." Heidegger describes our condition, whether or not he is right in historicizing it on the theological or Platonic model of a fall.

Texts are a false bottom, no doubt; a ground as treacherously sustaining as Nature was for Blake. Nature, says Blake, is there because of God's mercy, for otherwise we would still be falling. God, says the Book of Genesis, has built the world on the deep, or on the monster Tiamat. Hell, in Milton's cosmogony, is likewise a false bottom, though unmerciful. To be in Hell is better than not to be, is Belial's argument; a sophism for theology but a truth for those who can bear it. Hence the metaphor of the fall that obtrudes toward the end of the opening page of *Glas*. Today, not to fall, means to accept the grounding of textual thought as well as to keep falling *through* the text, as Blake said we see *through* the eye. There is no "cure of the ground": there is only the "here hear!" of the text, or else what Belial feared: "And that must end us, that must be our cure, / To be no more."

3 How to Reap a Page

It is by naming that we think.
Hegel

In each age, the number of the dead, that dark society, acts on
the living with the force of an increasing majority working out
its affirmations, asserting its preferences ever more and more
distinctly, and with more completely universal assent.
Walter Pater

A PURELY artistic, and anti-Christian, countervaluation of life is how
Nietzsche describes in *Ecce Homo* (1886) his "questionable" book, *The
Birth of Tragedy out of the Spirit of Music* (1871). And he raises the problem
of *naming* his new perspective. "How to name it? As philologist and man of
words I baptized it, not without some license—for who can know the real
name of Anti-Christ—with the name of a Greek god: I called it dionysian."
    What sort of countervaluation is *Glas*? Does this equally questionable
book contain a new perspective on life like Nietzsche's, related to an artistic
and anti-Christian, that is, Dionysian philosophy?
    The disposition of Derrida's commentary into two columns, one on the
arch-Christian Hegel and the other on the Antichrist Genet, cannot be irrele-
vant. Nor that the issue of the relation of philosophy to art is immediately
raised, not only by the book's eccentric layout but also by initial excerpts from
Hegel, one from the *Phenomenology* (689)[1] dealing with "Natural Religion,"
the other from the *Aesthetics*. On the last pages of *Glas*, excerpts enter from
the section in the *Phenomenology* entitled "The Religion of Art" (especially
"The Living Work of Art," 720 ff.); these, together with a short treatment of
"Revealed Religion," are the approaches to "savoir absolu," or absolute
knowledge, the last station in the "calvary" of spirit, whose scripture the
Phenomenology seeks to be, and to which Derrida alludes on the first page of
Glas when he wonders whether *Sa* has found its text, and whether it could be
signed (see figures 1, 15 and 16).

67

circulation du jouir dans le culte. *Telos* du culte, spéculer la jouissance de Dieu et se la faire.

en suivant la galerie phénoménologique (« Ce devenir présente (stellt... dar) un mouvement lent et une conséquence d'esprits, une galerie d'images (eine Galerie von Bildern)... »), de station en station, on revient vers l'*IC* et le *Sa*, passé le « calvaire de l'esprit absolu ». On y retrouve, tout près du « calvaire », — à inspecter des deux côtés — la « certitude de son trône » (Gewissheit seines Throns).
Il suffit en somme, à peine, d'attendre.
Tout cela aura été projeté, mis en pièces, clos, cloué, tombé, relevé, répété, aux alentours de Pâques.
Le cercle de la galerie phénoménologique se reproduit et s'encercle dans la grande *Logique* et dans l'*Encyclopédie*. Quelle est la différence entre deux éditions du même cercle? Hegel qui vient d'apprendre « la vente rapide de la deuxième édition » de l'*Encyclopédie*, confie à Winter, en 1827, ses inquiétudes. Il lui demande de se porter « garant du paiement ponctuel des honoraires ». « Pour le nombre de feuilles primitif (18) dans la première édition, nous avons fixé les deux tiers de l'honoraire, se montant à 25 florins; pour le nombre de feuilles postérieur, nous sommes revenus à cet honoraire, et pour les 18 autres feuilles de la deuxième édition, nous nous sommes contentés de 22 florins par feuille; en concluant cet accord, je me suis réservé le droit de réclamer des honoraires pour ce qui serait ajouté dans une nouvelle édition. [...] Ce nombre de feuilles s'accroîtra-t-il dans la nouvelle édition, et de combien? Je ne puis encore en avoir aucune idée, étant donné que ce travail m'a surpris à l'improviste et que je n'ai encore pu parcourir l'ouvrage de ce point de vue; mais d'une façon générale, je prévois que je n'apporterai pas de modification ou d'addition importante. — Le tirage reste fixé comme auparavant à 1 000 exemplaires, avec 18 exemplaires d'auteur, 12 sur vélin et 6 sur papier à écrire.
« Du fait que j'ai reçu si tard l'annonce du besoin d'une nouvelle édition (la lettre de M. Oswald est datée du 13 juillet), il résulte que l'envoi du manuscrit ne pourra avoir lieu que tard — plus tard sans doute que vous ne le souhaitez; avec mes travaux, qui depuis se sont accumulés, je ne puis encore rien dire de précis sur la date; mais je ferai mon possible pour que l'édition puisse paraître à Pâques. »

gymnastique.

Nous sommes dans le cercle dionysiaque. Le troisième moment de l'art abstrait, la religion qui s'y inscrit, c'est déjà la phase la plus abstraite du moment ultérieur, l'œuvre d'art vivante. A travers son syllogisme, un procès de langage s'affaire encore à la relève du reste.

Le premier moment unilatéral, c'est le délire bachique, le *Taumel*, l'ivresse débordante au cours de laquelle le dieu se rend présent. L'essence lumineuse ascendante se dévoile comme ce qu'elle est. La jouissance est le mystère de cette révélation. Car le mystique ne réside pas dans la dissimulation d'un secret (*Geheimnis*) ou d'un insu. Mais ce qui se dénude ici appartient encore à l'esprit immédiat, à l'esprit-nature. Le mystère du pain et du vin *n'est pas encore ce* qu'il est, *déjà*, celui de la chair et du sang. Dionysos doit donc passer dans son contraire, s'apaiser pour exister, ne pas se laisser boire et consommer par la « horde des femmes exaltées ».

Il fait alors de la

Il est prêt. Comment fait-il? si démuni, tout nu. Tant de lettres manquent. Pas un A qui sonne dans son nom. Aucun R surtout, pas même un. Pas de G non plus qu'une consonne, un A ou un U viennent durcir ou raidir, arrêter, anguler. Graver. Empêcher de gémir, de geindre, de vagir. Il est tout seul, sans aucune des bonnes lettres, elle les a toutes gardées pour elle, pour son prénom. I lui fait aussi défaut. L, il ne l'a même pas.

L'a laissé tomber, sans faire cas, sans un, tout nu, juste de quoi spéculer, sans image, sans le savoir, sur son nom. Sans quoi.

Lait de deuil cacheté (coacté, pressé, serré, caché, coagulé, caillé).

Je commence à être jaloux de sa mère qui a pu, à l'infini, changer de phallus sans se détailler. Hypothèse dieuvenue père en soi de n'être pas là.

Figure 15.   Jacques Derrida, *Glas*, p. 290. Courtesy, Editions Galilée.

Apollon n'est pas nommé, certes ; mais l'opposé, la partie adverse, la stance contraire dans laquelle le dionysiaque doit passer pour « s'apaiser en se faisant objet *(sich zum Gegenstande beruhigen)* », se dresse comme le corps érigé dans la gymnastique grecque, la belle « *Körperlichkeit* ». La figure de l'homme se cultive à la place de la colonne sculpturale de la divinité. Le divin se laisse réapproprier dans l'humain : échange encore des deux érections, des deux institutions, mise en mouvement et regain de vie. Plus-value de la contradiction qui (se) contracte avec elle même, se fait du reste cadeau.

Mais une fois de plus, mouvement de balance, tout se fixe dans l'objectivité extérieure qu'on a opposée à l'embrasement dionysiaque. On a donc deux morceaux opposés qui se contredisent dans leur unilatéralité respective. L'équilibre *(Gleichgewicht)* est sans cesse rompu. Dans le délire, le soi-même *(Selbst)* perd connaissance ; sur le stade, c'est l'esprit qui est hors de lui-même.

A travers l'œuvre d'art spirituelle — langage de part en part — la réconciliation s'annonce : synthèse de la religion esthétique (abstraction, vie, esprit). Le syllogisme de l'art spirituel *(epos,* tragédie, comédie) conduit la religion esthétique à la religion révélée. A travers, donc, la comédie.

Un temps pour parfaire la ressemblance entre Dionysos et le Christ.
Entre les deux (déjà) s'élabore en somme l'origine de la littérature.
Mais elle court à sa perte, pour avoir compté sans

Lui reste léger, ne cesse de s'alléger. Comment vivre ainsi. Tout est bloqué au compte maternel. Echéance. Il eût fallu si peu, un A, un R, un G, pour que ça prenne autrement, que ça s'arrête ailleurs, pour que ça s'ancre dans un autre fond, griffe ou gratte une autre surface, la même pourtant. Pour que ça ne glisse plus. Avec soi, avec sa pompe funèbre, un autre contrat. Un autre legs. Pour solder, soudoyer le déjà de l'aïeul absolu.

« *Vor der Sonne kamst du zur mir, dem Einsamsten.*

Wir sind Freunde von Anbeginn : uns ist Gram und Grauen und Grund gemeinsam : noch die Sonne ist uns gemeinsam.

Wir reden nicht zueinander, weil wir zu vieles wissen -: wir schweigen uns an, wir lächeln uns unser Wissen zu.

[...] was uns gemein ist,- das ungeheure unbegrenzte Ja -... »

C'est très aride, sur l'esplanade immense, mais ça ne fait que commencer, le travail, ici, dès maintenant. Dès que ça commence à écrire. Ça commence à peine. Ne manque plus qu'une pièce.

Ça grince. Roule sur les troncs d'arbre couchés. Poulies. Les cordes graissées se tendent, on n'entend qu'elles, et le souffle des esclaves pliés en deux. Bons à tirer. Fouet cinglant du contremaître. Regain de force liée. La chose est oblique. Elle fait angle, déjà, avec le sol. Remord lentement son ombre, sûre de soi. Il eût fallu si peu, la moindre erreur de calcul, disent-ils si ça tombe, si ça se penche et cline vers le lit de l'autre, la machine est encore trop simple, le mode d'écriture précapitaliste.

Ce que j'avais redouté, naturellement, déjà, se réédite. Aujourd'hui, ici, maintenant, le débris de

Figure 16.   Jacques Derrida, *Glas*, p. 291. Courtesy, Editions Galilée.

So much, however, is already going on when we read those initial reflections, the new and startling form of *Glas* presupposes so much internalized and recoverable knowledge, that we are trapped from the outset in a final passageway, spellbound by crisscrossing phrases and resonances. The religion of art, a phrase we would ordinarily associate with the Romantics, then with Ruskin, Pater, and Proust, and which has its clear beginnings in Winckelmann, is about to turn into a philosophy of art extending indefinitely the border leading to Hegel's "savoir absolu."

This foregrounding of the artistic as the philosophical, or the birth of philosophy out of the spirit of art—and perhaps its return there—is what I would like to trace in Derrida. It is an open question whether we should call the spirit of his work Dionysian or Apollonian. Both enter, in a gymnastic kind of dialectic. The one certain thing about *Glas* is its cold, dispassionate ecstasy. There is an Apollonian elation, a spectatorial and sportive attitude that is difficult to characterize simply as knowledge. Like everything "aesthetic," it seems to stand beyond or below that designation. Derrida's gaiety, however, is both contrary and complementary to a second kind of impersonality: his disregard for the reader, the methodical madness with which he improvises relentlessly on heterogeneous texts, cut up or agglutinated ("les morceaux que je coupe et couds," 190b) against all decorum. This disregard for the reader is Dionysian in spirit, if we recall a remark of Nietzsche's: "It is of the very essence of dionysian art that it does not have any regard for its audience. . . If we try to think of a listener present when the endemic excitement of dionysian revelry breaks forth, then we must prophesy for him a fate like that of Pentheus, the discovered eavesdropper, torn up by the Maenads."[2]

For many readers *Glas* does emanate an incomprehensible or intolerable music. "Klang und nicht Sprache" is the sound attributed by Hegel to Memnon's colossus. Yet, to begin with, let Apollo be our golden theme. It is he who initiates the last page of Derrida's book (291a). Derrida has returned to the *Phenomenology* and the section on "The Religion of Art" previously mentioned. In Hegel every passage seems to describe a passing over. The text, Derrida's and Hegel's, is a passageway made of passages. These are disposed into columns separated horizontally and vertically by typography and rhetorical cuts—an unstable architecture of words, a mutely speaking colonnade, living pillars that emit confused words, as in Baudelaire's famous sonnet "Correspondances." But in this obscure wood or temple, we come across distinct symbols, objectifications comparable to pictures in a gallery. The final pages of *Glas*, verging always on the final paragraphs of the *Phenomenology*, evoke Hegel's "solemn procession of Spirits, a gallery of pictures" (290a, insert). At this juncture Apollo enters Derrida's text as the picturing or externalizing principle: resting point both for Dionysus and the overexercised reader. We seem to have reached at one and the same time

Easter and the most Westerly station of the spirit. Despite the crosswording, an epiphany or clarified symbol is anticipated.

Yet Apollo enters in a curiously muted manner. "Apollon n'est pas nommé, certes." Moreover, though he is the contrary state into which the Dionysian must pass to "sedate itself by becoming an object (*sich zum Gegenstande beruhigen*)," in the adjacent column (291b), also concerned with naming, a subversive prose continues to play off heterogenous themes of lightness, emergence, fall, foundation.

Zarathustra, the dancer, the light one, who winks with his wings

> Nietzsche, *Thus Spoke Zarathustra*

WHAT DOES the withholding of Apollo's name imply? Is it part of his "resting" or "remaining" in a light—sublated—form? "Lui reste léger, ne cesse de s'alléger." One cannot be sure what the "lui" refers to. It may be Apollo, it may be Genet, it may be the "father in himself" by virtue of "not being there" (last line, 290b). The sentence falls apart, like the unnamed name that might have contained an A, an R, a G, yet without them slips, floats, lacking a secure base ("pour que ça s'ancre dans un autre fond," which also is not unambiguous, since "ça" may stand for the Freudian *id*, and "s'ancre" puns on "s'encre"). The absence of a definite name extends into this general uncertainty of reference.

A name or noun stands for a person or thing, but a pronoun like *lui* stands for a noun. *Lui*, moreover, unless we agree to synthesize parts of speech in an *a priori* manner, sounds like a derivative of *luire*, to shine (like Apollo). "Lui reste léger" becomes the lateral montage of three isolated words: shine, rest ("Quoi du reste . . ."), lightly. A near-lapidary, epitaphic style seems to lead into "Comment vivre ainsi" and to suggest what Derrida elsewhere calls the "obsequent logic" of language. Let the shining one, now the indeterminate subject, rest lightly. Let a trace remain, as phenomenology (Hegel's "field of light") sets into a philosophy of names, of language.

A remarkable feature of Hegel's *Phenomenology* is that it is almost void of names. The periphrastic prose battens on their absence. The perspective, while not lapidary, is monu-memorizing (*Glas*, 7b). That which appears in the "phenomenological gallery" (top left, 290b) is already internalized; we are in the sphere of *Er-innerung*. Every concrete name or picture is subject to this posthumous development, this movement inward. But the function of language, rememorative, obsequent, is double. It makes things fall inward, but also outward, externalizing them as common if not proper nouns, as phonemes and syllables that inscribe even Apollo or draw a speech of sorts

from his name / tomb ("s'y nomme—tombe," 7b). That the god is not named
does not imply he cannot be named; for we are not in that early era in which
the spirit does not know itself, and so is dazzled or stupefied by its own
productions, its unconsciously alienated sublimity. In Hegel, as in Derrida,
the nonnaming or abluting of the name is a deliberate act, as in the playful
flourishes of Wallace Steven's "Notes toward a Supreme Fiction."

> Phoebus is dead, ephebe. But Phoebus was
> A name for something that never could be named.
> There was a project for the sun and is.
>
> There is a project for the sun. The sun
> Must bear no name, gold flourisher, but be
> In the difficulty of what it is to be.

Can there be a pure act of presence, then, Apollo not called Apollo? For
the name is still a shadow, a residue not entirely absorbed; a consciousness not
quite objectified or an object not wholly inward. Questions are raised that lead
to a convergence of metaphysics, linguistic philosophy, and aesthetics. The
placing of names in relation to things; reality-reference; the notion of
exemplification; the function of periphrasis, metaphor, and frame. Such
questions seem heavy for so casual, so "light" a mention of the fact that
Apollo is not named. Yet is it not his attribute that "lui reste léger, ne cesse de
s'alléger"? The gymnastics of the text make the heavier element (Dionysus)
appear light, or evoke a nuder (*gymnos*) mode of divine presence (290a),
characterized by a remission of the name and everything that is mysterious
rather than translucent. Dionysus seeks to come to rest in Apollo, and Apollo
to appear naked: that is, without the clothes or graveclothes of a proper name,
free and unfearful as to the question of identity, not needing that prop, casting
off even the residual concretion or sound-shape of a *proper* name.[3]

We new, nameless, and unfathomable beings

Nietzsche, *Ecce Homo*

LET US look closely at the last pages of *Glas* (figures 15 and 16). The "laisser
tomber" of the name in 290b and 291b repeats the action of the middle
column of page 8 (figure 2). The name is allowed to fall "sans faire cas," without making something of it, a thing or cause (*cas*); "sans un," without the comfort of presupposing a formalized identity; "tout nu," like Apollo or quasi-erotic
sport: "juste de quoi spéculer sans image," even giving up the specular image,
foundation according to Lacan of a first, false, narcissistic self-prehension,
and so speculating only with words (*nu*: specular obverse of *un*); "de quoi
spéculer . . . sans le savoir, sur son nom," the dissemination, elation, or quiet

entombing of the name ("laisser tomber . . . sur son nom," cf. "Je / tombe," *Glas*, 197b); "sans quoi," at rest, without a rest or residue, without the question ("quoi") that opens this very book: "Quoi du reste . . ."

Yet this "laisser tomber" of the name leaves out not only the name but also the pronoun, "L'a laissé tomber." Who has let "it" fall? The subject remains unclear, and the object of the verb, "L", is either the subject or undecidable. Yet coming at the base of this column as its subject-substratum, and toward the end of all the columns on Genet—drawing in, moreover, the punning relation of cas/Fall/phallus that involves the mother in the next lines—we can guess at the economy that founds the omission and the indeterminacy.

The economy is that of ellipsis (leaving out and eccentric doubling) and allows us to name the missing *it*. It, she, is the mother, who as "L" (*elle*) is both subject and object, who elides her son's life by stealing back her name perpetually through his conception of her. Within Genet's work, it is her name that is being redeemed, bought and brought back, or endlessly sold, exorcised, profaned (*A, R, G*, in 290b and 291b, seem to form a false prefix, ARGEN(E)T, but also coincide as ARG(O) with a more heroic theme). "She" (L) is the "purloined letter," one that returns inevitably in the "L'a" that follows, as well as the "Lait" of the next paragraph, and other versions of a pseudodeclensional chain ("Il fait alors de la" . . . "de n'être pas là"). The mother is the ultimate vamp of self-identity, the indeterminate subject of Genet's "grand discours sur le vol."

Looking once more at the right-hand column, we glimpse through that "sans image"—that hole or empty frame in the phenomenological gallery—the distinct if ghostly shape of the originary *elle* ("L"). See figure 17.

Derrida has constructed a symbolic equivalent to Hegel's "*Er*-innerung": an *L*-innerung, a textual internalization that evokes Genet's monumental labor of the negative, his erection or elevation of the fallen, phallic mother. "I begin to be jealous of his mother," writes Derrida, "one who could change phallus without going into details [dismembering the body or consciousness or language itself by a Dionysian sparagmos]."

The author's—Derrida's—jealousy is significant. For, once back with the mother, are we not also with Dionysus and in a drama that again plays itself out for Christ (291a)? There may not be a great distance, after all, between Christ and Antichrist or between Christ and Dionysus. Derrida is not only jealous of the absent, phantasmic mother, but also of the one who can "author" her son (by mutely possessing him, speaking through him this way) without having to articulate or disarticulate words. Derrida's hypothesis—which recovers from Genet this hypostasis of the mother, her action at a distance—stands to Derrida curiously as Genet or Christ stand to the immacu-

Il est prêt. Com-
ment fait-il? si dé-
muni, tout nu. Tant
de lettres manquent.
Pas un A qui sonne
dans son nom. Au-
cun R surtout, pas
même un. Pas de G
non   plus   qu'une
consonne, un A ou
un U viennent dur-
cir ou raidir, arrêter,
anguler.   Graver.
Empêcher de gémir,
de geindre, de vagir.
Il est tout seul, sans
aucune   des   bonnes
lettres, elle les   a
toutes gardées pour
elle, pour son pré-
nom. I lui fait aussi
défaut. L, il ne l'a
même pas.

L'a laissé tomber, sans faire cas, sans un, tout
nu, juste de quoi spéculer, sans image, sans le
savoir, sur son nom. Sans quoi.

Figure 17.   Jacques Derrida, *Glas*, p. 290 (part). Courtesy, Editions Galilée.

late mother who is so internalized that she is not there, or is (in) the son. The
interpreter's hypothesis manifests the absent father, not only the absent
mother: the father (Derrida as author-interpreter) whose impersonality
breached by this "Je"—"I begin to be jealous"—fills Genet's work with the
"name of the mother." This is the meaning of the untranslatable "Hypothèse
dieuvenue père en soi de n'être pas là."[4]

The bells, I say, the bells break down their tower
Hart Crane, "The Broken Tower"

NEAR THE beginning of *Glas* Derrida asks: "What does the death knell of the proper name signify?" (27b) We can now answer: it signifies the birth of the literary text. The fading of the name leaves no legacy ("legs," homonym of "*lait*" and near-anagram of "glas," as in 291b) except for the paranomasia of a text. "Reste ici ou glas qu'on ne peut arrêter" (287b). Yet this movement without term incorporates "terms" that displace the proper name. These terms are fixed or frozen particles (*glas* into *glace* and *classe*), coagulations in the stream of discourse, milk-stones (*galalithes*) or even body-stones ("le calcul de la mère" refers also to the organic, pathological kidney stone, *caillou*). They grow in language as in a culture; they are formed by a process analogous to introjection or incorporation; and there is a radical ambivalence about their value, whether they are blockage and detritus, or seminal and pregnant tissue. The letter *L*, signifying the pronoun "Elle," is a mock-up of such a term; so is the reduction of "savoir absolu" to *Sa*, which could be confused with another pronoun in the possessive case, also pointing to the feminine gender. "L'a," similarly, combines in Lacan's algebraic manner this capital *L* with what seems to be the *petit objet a* (standing for "autre" instead of "Autre," here within the feminine sphere).

Literary language, then, reflects an ultimate internalization. Yet something *remains*, like these overdetermined terms, and resists inwardness. An *X* or *L* factor extrudes at the deepest point: Hegel on *his* last page calls it "the lifting up of [the spirit's] depth" (*das Aufheben seiner Tiefe*). Though *Aufheben* here retains its technical sense, and evokes another quasi-final step in a dialectic that seems to stretch out infinitely, it recovers something of its physical connotation. "Monstrance of the deep" might be a good translation. The myth of depth is not deliberately effaced as in Robbe-Grillet, for we see that depth; but it is released from the brooding that held it in and made it invisible. The spirit gives itself away once more ("se fait du reste cadeau," 291a) or gives itself to be seen.

The fading of the proper name, then, is like the fading of the self in or into the literary work: its setting. "Impersonnifié, le volume . . ." (Mallarmé). Derrida's thought touches here, as it does often, that of Lacan, particularly what the latter calls the aphanisis or fading of the self (*sujet*) when inscribed in language.[5] But the common, if not absolute, ancestor of both Derrida and Lacan (as well as Mallarmé) is Hegel. What remains of Hegel, here and now, has taken the shape of Lacan; and it is with Lacan's version of Hegel that Derrida wrestles, as the following quotations from the *Phenomenology* can suggest:

[In language the] "I" is this particular "I"—but its manifesting is also at once the externalization and vanishing of *this* particular "I.". . . The "I" that utters itself is *heard* or *perceived*. . . . That it is *perceived* or *heard* means that its *real existence* dies away . . . its real existence is just this: that as a self-conscious Now, as a real existence, it is *not* a real existence, and through this vanishing it *is* a real existence [508].

The artist, then, learns in his work that he did not produce a being *like himself*. . . . The work of art therefore demands another element of its existence, the god another mode of coming forth than this, in which, out of the depth of his creative night, he descends into the opposite, into externality, into the determination of the Thing which lacks self-consciousness. This higher element is Language—an outer reality that is immediately self-conscious existence. . . . The god, therefore, who has language for the element of his shape is the work of art that is in its own self inspired [709 and 710].

The true self-conscious existence which Spirit receives in speech . . . is the work of art. . . . It stands in contrast to the Thing-like character of the statue. Whereas this exists at rest, speech is a vanishing existence; and whereas in the statue the liberated objectivity lacks an immediate self of its own, in speech, on the other hand, objectivity remains too much shut up within the self, falls short of attaining a lasting shape and is, like Time, no longer immediately present in the very moment of its being present [713].

There is always, then, one more kenosis, or surrender by the self of its achieved and destined position. Hegel's final paragraphs in the *Phenomenology* try to name the spirit's ultimate self-emptying as Nature and History, but this is merely a formal, if appropriate, ending to an act of naming that is itself part of the kenosis and must continue. What the *Phenomenology* has established is the relation of language to kenosis (or the "labor of the negative"): why "the many-named divine light of the risen Sun" (723) is named, and then is not named, or was never properly named. "There was a project for the sun and is." Apollo, golden theme of language, reveals the abyss opened by language: a dissemination through which "spirit" must pass before it can rise or rise again, in order to raise up its depth. That yeasty depth, however, from another perspective—Lacan's—is also its lack. Can we say Apollo reveals Dionysus?

I saw the birds being hatched, that later gave the key for new melodies. I saw how Hegel with his solemn almost comic face sat on the fatal eggs, and heard him cackling.

Heine

THIS CHAPTER, I fear, is becoming a detour to Dionysus. It began with Nietzsche's formal hesitation when he named his "purely artistic" and "anti-

Christian" world view after Dionysus. In Derrida that hesitation is everywhere—it is almost the formal principle of literature itself—and there is an obverse relation between his column on Hegel and that on Genet in respect to the proper name. Genet proliferates names; Hegel, at least in the *Phenomenology*, tends to withhold them: yet the opening and closing pages of *Glas* contrast Genet's tearing up of a proper name ("Rembrandt" or whatever it stands for) with Hegel's legerdemain. Hegel is named, and names himself, without hesitation; but Genet, and, on the last page, Derrida, cannot find their proper names. "Derrida n'est pas nommé, certes": the last column fades into what might have been his signature, "le débris de." Perhaps Derrida is merely the debris of Hegel (his second coming or reedition); while the name "Hegel" is turned, by joycing, into a questionable shape at the very beginning of *Glas*. "Hegel," detached from fading into a text to which it owes its resonance, is made to appear an unmotivated nonsense word.

If not unmotivated, then as *hors de texte* as Genet's title, which is like the extension of a name: "*ce qui est resté d'un Rembrandt déchiré*" (7b). Dangling and disjunct, linked to the essay it heads only through a concern for the body-feeling Genet experienced looking at Rembrandt, the nominal title cannot stop falling: it does not "stand" for anything, it is always in a state of sparagmos. There is a project for the name, but whose name, Apollo's or Dionysus's?

A time to perfect the resemblance of Dionysus and Christ.
Between the two (already) is elaborated summarily the origin of literature.
But it runs to its destruction for having counted without [291a]

Literature may have counted without Derrida, or the non-sense (*sans/ sens*) of his quasi-book. The paragraph immediately preceding raises the question of the genre of *Glas* by commenting on the transition from "Religion of Art" to "Revealed Religion" by way of comedy, the highest literary genre according to Hegel. What genre, or even gender, is *Glas*? Can we account for it?

There is a real danger of literature getting lost, running amok or running scared after Joyce's *Wake* and Derrida's *Glas*. Everything is infected by equivocation and the repetition of part-objects of language. Where the word was, the pun shall be. The reality-reference of literature is subdued to inter-textual allusions, omnivorous flowers of speech, metaphors, devices.

The rain has dispersed the spectators who run in all directions [*dans tous les sens*]. What is the matter that can be assured [*en somme*]? to cite, to recite the *genêt* through tediously long pages? To interpret it, to perform it like a piece of music? You're putting us on. What is being proposed. Flowery cadenzas [*fioritures*]? An anthology, that is, a lection of flower-words? by what legal right. And the complete text, it is kept from us? [135b]

There is a rain or ruin of unsummable meanings that seems to scatter us. A "hoard of destructions," to pun with Stevens; and how can we tell whether this fragmentation and expropriation of texts, this metacomic dissemination of the energies of language through an equivalent of seme-smashing, can be controlled? What if it is as nihilistic as Joyce's "abnihilization of the etym" suggests? Are we sliding toward a Dionysian revel which no longer knows its name, which cannot, that is, connect those energies with the legacy of a book that is contractual and covenanting: one which haunts us like an "absolute ancestor" (*aïeul absolu,* 291b) and therefore founds or funds the debt of commentary? Is *Glas* the last text that knows the deathduty it must pay? In the realm of commentary—commentary being that deathduty—*Glas* is its own wake.

Struggling for its name, for recognition, within a Hegelian context, *Glas* remains bound by the law it helps to reveal: the fading of the genre name it has never enjoyed. Commentary, when it becomes a philosophical work of art, a de facto genre by whatever name we call it, supersedes nothing, but signals or announces (*glas*) the relation of language to an "economy of death" that defines temporal existence and the works of men. It displays an "obsequent" logic because it is always both opening and closing the crypt of the dead—exhibiting their textual "remains." "Quoi du reste . . . d'un Hegel?"

In Derrida's own prose, therefore, as in hermeneutic reflection generally, words of the dead are entombed by inner quotation, allusion, or the verbatim presence of a piece of precursor. A passage from Hegel appears in an elaborate frame, like the portrait of an ancestor, or rather a relic; an extract from Nietzsche's *Zarathustra* startles us on the last page with its disjunctive lyricism; a "slowly-moving procession of Spirits" in the form of cryptic or encrypted fragments is presented. These Notes to a Supreme Commentary break through the Hegelian barrier that denominates comedy as the highest, most reconciled form of art, beyond which there is only revealed religion and absolute knowledge. *Glas* appears as a metacomic celebration of literature's power to externalize, to draw into the realm of appearance, the most deeply encrypted words, the extremest modes of internalization.

This may clarify several concerns of *Glas.* First the name breaking, which is really like removing the seal from a will or a crypt, violating that which guarantees it closure. The signature "Hegel," even if found on the title page, certifies and seals the work. Derrida therefore uses it against what it encloses as a false key or etymon. By the end of *Glas* such keys have faded back into the work.

Another concern is Apollo, the name of the father, or of the sun. This golden theme is so complex that I should summarize it once more. Derrida's first quotations from Hegel allude to a pre-Olympian age characterized by the religion of flowers and a "symbolic" architecture of colossal statues, funerary and heliotropic. They wait for the sun like Memnon's colossus, animated by the dawn's "rosy" fingers into a sound that is not yet speech ("Klang und nicht Sprache"). The sound is a boundary tone, less Greek-auroral than a hymn to the night, a shaping of darkness into stony echoes. We remain far from Keats's "tender eye-dawn of aurorean love" ("Ode to Psyche"). We remain far from that entire sphere of feeling, the "I-dawn" associated with psychology. And, strangely enough, we never reach it except as it fades or has always already faded. Love's first minute after noon is night, says Donne in his "Lecture upon a Shadow." At the close of *Glas*, with the interpolation of Nietzsche's "Vor der Sonne kamst du zu mir," we are still in a sound-sphere that is not Apollo's, though it is clearly, this time, *Sprache* as well as *Klang*. We hear through language either Nietzsche's Dionysus, his music, or Heidegger's silence. Even Apollo, then, or the name for the sun, is placed in the abyss of words. As language writes itself out, name after name, words under words, in an endless, disseminating movement of antonomasia (anthonomasia: *Glas*, 204b), it approaches the realm of the mothers, closer to Dionysus than to Apollo, and characterized by Nietzsche as Will, Delusion, Grief.[6] The Apollonian stance is ceaselessly broken, unbalanced, by the naming-and-questioning energy of writing, by a dissemination beyond that of the sun, yet as simple as "I should rather have said . . ."

> The Sun, its hand open: lavish forefather, magnificent Sower.
> Sower? I should rather have said . . .[7]

There is also, then, a Dionysian concern: the mother. "Reste—la mère" (132b). Her name, however, seems to have totally fallen out of the realm of appearance, even out of the text of *Glas*. It, rather than the name of the father, is "foreclosed" (Lacan). Yet it shows itself marginally in the playful stenography of *IC* and *Sa*, the gradual introduction of Hegel's thinking about family, his relation to his sister (with an implicit glance at Nietzsche's sister), and the importance of the *Antigone*; also in the homophony of *sein* (breast) and *seing* (signature or seal) and the graphic pun of both with "*Sein*" (German "being"); in the theme of the religion of flowers, of the genêt and the rose; and, most philosophically, in the post-Heideggerian question of what a *thing* is, and how it might be named. Compare the convergence of *la chose* and *la mère* in the following passages:

> The thing: magnificent and classified, at once raised beyond all taxonomy, all nomenclature, and already identifiable in a system [13b].

> The mother would not present for analysis the end term of a regression, a signified of last resort, unless you knew what the mother names or means, what she is heavy with. Now you could not know this without having exhausted all residues [*le reste*], all objects, all the names the text puts in her place [133b].

For ל is upon every hair both of man and beast

Christopher Smart, *Jubilate Agno*

... the first thing the voice of the first speaker uttered was the equivalent of God, namely *El*, whether in the way of a question or in the way of an answer.

Dante, *De Vulgari Eloquentia*

IT WOULD be a vulgar though affective simplification to say that Derrida is exhibiting in *Glas* the difficulty of bringing a truly womanly speech to light. But he may be going back, through the travesty of Genet's oeuvre, to the pathos that attends the question of how to redeem or illustrate the mother tongue. There is little that is vernacular in *Glas*: despite its abundant flow of words, we are never far from speaking statue or lapidary style. The L (*Elle*) is illuminated only like a letter in a breviary. Derrida's words are marbled, either because their matrix is the dictionary, or because the writer's imagination is fixed on the passage moment when the sculptured form begins to breathe and speak, or, undecidably, when the living body is arrested—turned into stone—by death.

Is there a truly native, original language that can be restored? How are we to find it here and now? The question makes sense only in its pathos: it is like Kleist saying that to lose self-consciousness we must eat a second time of the Tree of Knowledge. For we cannot leave exile, and the dictionary, behind. The double columns of *Glas* are a formal reminder of dictionary typography, of that kind of external and unreadable ordering.

Derrida is a great amateur of Littré and Wartburg.[8] The dictionary of the French Academy, which intended to fix and purify the language—an ideal that cooperated deeply with neoclassic restraints on the mutability and fertility of the mother tongue—suffered important changes at the hands of these makers. Although Littré was a Classicist in believing that certain words had undergone a "pathological" development, he boasted correctly that he was "the first to try and submit the dictionary completely to history." Each word or meaning was given historical exemplification (as in the OED, also conceived in the 1850s); and Littré did this by an enormous collection of instances drawn from significant writers. "Chaque écrivain formait un paquet de ces petits carrés déjà rangés alphabétiquement." The age of the slip has begun. It is as if Genet, or Derrida seeing through Genet, radicalized that procedure by tearing words into pieces to find their matrix. "Ce qui est resté d'un Rembrandt déchiré en petits carrés bien réguliers. . . ." What remains is either a matrix (*la mère*) or nothing, or both, undecidably, in the form of the slip.

With Wartburg's etymological dictionary the mother tongue, or rather the mother tongues, enter more substantially; and it is impossible not to realize how rich and promiscuous the *Bedeutungswandel* of words has been. This errancy of meaning cannot be gathered back: there is no one certain matrix. Language is error and cannot be purified. Wartburg can order the historical mass only by choosing a Latin word as *point de repère*.

But in the period between Littré and Wartburg, Ferdinand de Saussure raises the question of meaning itself. His notebooks experiment with the idea that words motivate words. The semblance of a rune-word—an undecidable matrix—is formed by certain Saturnalian and Vergilian verses. Saussure believes that the procedure is deliberate and calls these generative words, which tend to be proper names, anagrams or hypograms; but he is not sure that these "mannikins" are more than semblances. It is possible they are chance formations.[9]

The theory is important for Derrida; whether or not the motivating word was "In the Beginning," it seems to be there as a shadowy or disseminated trace. The relation of reference includes this detour whereby words refer to a word categorized as "divine" or "proper" yet always already dispersed. The "quoi du reste" (of this divine or charged name) is an echo-aspect of the "quoi de res"—the question of what happened to the notion of *thing* in the West, after the pre-Socratics. In Genet, the mute presence of the mother ("Reste—la mère") is like that hidden and motivating name-thing, always torn, always intact. Derrida calls this "name of the mother" not a mannikin but rather a *figurant*, because it is productive of the figures of the text, but also because the theater term points to the status of the spectral name as an *extra*. The *figurant* is marginal, or acts without significant speech, filling as if mutely a certain space. Yet this *extra* is, of course, the veritable *intra*.

Angulus ridet
        Horace

THE CONJUNCTION of mother and language in the infinite rebus of the text, a text that writes itself out by disabling or cas-trating ("la cicatrice visible d'une émajusculation," 13b) all visible names (those that have entered Apollo's realm or represent the father)—this fatal and subversive conjunction can be understood as a reaction to Apollonianism after the Neoclassical period and especially after Winckelmann. The notion of equilibrium on the final page of *Glas*, which had been disturbingly introduced on the first— disturbingly, because the *"je m'éc..."* suggests a nauseous ecstasy rather than an Attic shape and fair attitude—this notion of equilibrium, of a reconciliation of body and spirit in the verbal "symbol," comes in the form of a Greek statue interpreted and animated by a scholar.

The scholar was Winckelmann, who put into circulation the ideal of a work of art without any excess from the side of spirit or slag from the side of matter, without a residue (*du reste*) from whatever source. Or as Pater says in the preface to his book on *The Renaissance* (1873), which appends an essay on Winckelmann: "casting off all débris, and leaving us only what the heat of . . . imagination has wholly fused and transformed." (How different this from a work that ends, as if in contradiction, with the unfinished phrase "le débris de.") Winckelmann developed his ideal in powerful, ecphrastic descriptions of particular statues, especially of the Belvedere Apollo. What Hegel calls the "Religion of Art" is this Pygmalionic recovery of Greek statuary; and even the Apollo of Nietzsche remains Winckelmann's, or rather Winckelmann's subtly altered and historicized by Hegel. One of the most beautiful summaries of Hegel's understanding of Hellenism is found in Pater's chapter on Winckelmann:

> Take a work of Greek art,—the Venus of Melos. That is in no sense a symbol, a suggestion, of anything beyond its own victorious fairness. The mind begins and ends with the finite image, yet loses no part of the spiritual motive. That motive is not lightly and loosely attached to the sensuous form, as its meaning to an allegory, but saturates and is identical with it. The Greek mind had advanced to a particular stage of self-reflexion, but was careful not to pass beyond it. In oriental thought there is a vague conception of life everywhere, but no true appreciation of itself by the mind, no knowledge of the distinction of man's nature: in its consciousness of itself, humanity is still confused with the fantastic, indeterminate life of the animal and vegetable world. In Greek thought, on the other hand, the "lordship of the soul" is recognized; that lordship gives authority and divinity to human eyes and hands and feet; inanimate nature is thrown into the background. But just there Greek thought finds its happy limit; it has not yet become too inward; the mind has not yet learned to boast its independence of the flesh; the spirit has not yet absorbed everything with its emotions, nor reflected its own colour everywhere. It has indeed committed itself to a train of reflexion which must end in defiance of form, of all that is outward, in an exaggerated idealism. But that end is still distant.

Derrida's reading of Hegel catches the eternal return of that ideal of perfect balance associated with Hellenism. Hegel's dialectic never purges itself of its desire for a work of art that would realize the beautiful equilibrium. The spirit continually comes to rest, or arrests itself, in an object. "Chaque colonne," Derrida writes, "s'enlève avec une impassible suffisance." Yet something goes wrong, for which he uses a translation of the Hegelian word "Ansteckung" (French: *contagion*): "et pourtant l'élément de la contagion, la circulation infinie de l'équivalence générale rapporte chaque phrase, chaque

mot, chaque moignon d'écriture (par exemple '*je m'éc...*') à chaque autre"
(7b).

A strange economy this, and far from beautiful: the column becomes a
stump (*moignon*), and we approach once more a sense of unrest, unrestrained
exchange, even orgiastic dismemberment. The broken phrase "je m'éc..."
implies that the wish to find a classic point of repose must fall into an infinite
if calculable disorder. For the meanings of "je m'éc..." (see also chap.
2) cannot be computed. I equalize or equilibrate myself, even I square
myself (EC: *Ecke*, the German word for *carré*). *Ecke* also means corner, or
(French) *coin*, and may introduce a bilingual pun via the English *coin*, which
is what circulates in an economy. But *Ecke* is also the word for angle, or
(German) *Winkel*. All these meanings (except English "coin"), and some
others (e.g., the German word *Stück*, in French *pièce* or *morsure*, *pièce*
reintroducing the idea of coin or money) are joined in the Wartburg dictionary to the matricial word *Canthus*, from which also the German word for
board or edge, *Kante*, and, by antonomasia, *Kant*, the philosopher, who now
emerges as Winckel-mann (Angle-man).

Consider the notion of *Kante* as edge. In *Glas*, words are always falling
off the page or cut off, limited, by a frame. That frame is a *carré* angled
typographically to produce the "petits carrés" of paragraphs, words, of lineation. What the edge means is impossible to define in terms of inside and
outside or balance and imbalance. The equilibrium of page or book is like the
illusory concept of Greek repose; that balance, as in Hegel's dialectic, is
continually thrown off balance, the limit-boundary is crossed or sublated.
Title and signature, to use examples from the very first page of *Glas*, are in
principle *débordant*—outside the text, beyond its frame—yet are textualized
nevertheless. Obversely, anything can become a *parergon* or *rejet*, because of
this edge. Derrida carves out rectangles within rectangles, like the marginal
sections that first mention the *IC* and *Sa*. "Pour avoir compté sans" displays
the cutting edge of the *carré* in stylized fashion; "le débris de" more so by elid-
ing a name *diagonally* across from the specified nonnaming of Apollo. You
can't "count sense" ("compter sans" puns on that). The very frame of writing
is deconstructed. The form of the book is a Kantian limit that both justifies and
disables metaphysical (ontotheological) questions concerning the relation of
knowledge to truth, names to things, and writing to reality.

The plane geometry of reading is threatened by this. How many dimen-
sions does reading have? Must we understand this commentary on Hegel and
Genet as also a commentary on Kant? Was it not enough to bring in
Nietzsche and Winckelmann? But what matters is the antithetical *éc* in *écriture*, which writes something in (or out) without naming it. Once Kant has
been named it is hard not to see in the penultimate paragraph on 291b ("Ça

grince . . .") the depiction of a "chantier" (*Kantier*) with an ironclad wheel (see Wartburg s.v. *Canthus*) emitting the harsh music of the Kantian style and erecting a type of writing from the ground up ("De quoi s'agit-il au fond? Du fond").[10] Perhaps an image of ecriture is being raised here as a "chant du chantier."

To look at the penultimate paragraph as a "mode d'écriture" beyond genre or book is to notice its uncertain subject. It is a piece of nonrepresentational art, with glimpses of historical or natural reference. In "Elle fait angle, déjà, avec le sol," the pronoun refers back to "la chose," which is "oblique," but otherwise remains undetermined by a barely readable prose, a developed rebus apparently, with the *res* an ablative absolute (forever oblique) rather than a "savoir absolu." The thing, whatever it is, is caught in its rising or falling state, always on edge, leaning obliquely, and described by winks, "*signes clignants*," syntactical *membra disjecta*: a series of *morsures* or *clins d'oeil* (*Stücke, Augenwinkel*). As a mode of ecriture the paragraph "collideorscopes" picture-thinking (cf. *Phenomenology*, para. 764 ff), technical jargon, action language, the supposedly purer, "economical" diction of philosophy, and print technology (the edging-wedging of words on the angled page).

If Derrida is not directly interested in Nature and History, which participate in Hegel's absolute knowledge but are here present only in a schematic way, it is because the movement of writing is both more internal and external than these, both more immediate and mediated, limited and illimitable. How internalized the L is has been shown. Yet it remains external, a mere letter, unable to stand by itself, depending like writing on writing. Who really knows what the L stands for, falls toward: is it *Elle*, the mother? Is it an abbreviation for logos or language? L is also the second consonant of "glas" ("las!" says echo) and the last of "angle." "Elle fait angle, déjà, avec le sol." ("It [the unnamed object or subject] makes an angle, already, with the ground.") A question of ground? "Avec le soleil," too, for Derrida continues, "Remord lentement son ombre, sûr de soi." ("Slowly chews up its shadow, sure of itself.")[11] The angle that L (*Elle*)—and perhaps all writing—makes, is with Apollo (291a, top) as he emerges into himself ("sûr de soi") by substituting gymnastics (290a, bottom) for the orgy or *Taumel* of Dionysian revelry. Through this angular art, which writing already is, the L is elevated; it stands out as well as stands in for; we can spot it now, in fact, as an angle, L, *Winckel, Ecke*.

"Elle fait angle. . . ." The L appears, from this angle, as part of no name at all but as pure cadre or *carré*. It limits, even prescribes, all names, being the frame (*parergon*) that is not strictly part of the work (*ergon*) although the work is composed of nothing but such frames. The L is "l'être [*lettre*] à la limite" (cf. *Marges de la philosophie*, p. i).

Have you not heard, have you not seen that corps
Of shadows in the tower
Hart Crane, "The Broken Tower"

I HAVE argued myself into a corner; I wish I could rest there. Yet something prevents a writer from settling down even in a space so ingeniously arranged. To linger with Kant this way would be to thematize and overformalize *Glas*; it would contradict even the explicit use made of Kant within the book, the comparison of his view of the role of woman in the economy (*oikos*) of things with that of Hegel (*Glas*, 143 ff).[12] The question is made to center by Derrida on how to economize woman, libido, language-libido (*bavardage* or *écriture*). Like Mallarmé's faun, both Hegel and Kant seek "le *la*" (also, as shepherds of Being, in this strange philosophic pastoral, "le là" or *Dasein*), which like its rhymes *sa* and *da* keeps sounding in *glas*. *Glas*, a pastoral elegy? The L/*Elle*, then, is radically volatile; though hymeneal, like Goethe's "das ewig Weibliche," it cannot be stabilized any more than can the winged stamen or plumy pen: *elle* as *aile* (*d'étamine*). Flower, flight, and tissue metaphors converge as Derrida manifests his (or Genet's or Hegel's, any intense thinker's) compulsion to write for the dead, that is, to achieve a grand, detached, preposthumous style, whatever the apparent subject (see figure 18).[13]

What a magnificent dirge, death rattle, for a Classicism that cannot die, because it is always already in the shadow of the dead. Rousseau to the reader:

> Lecteur, si vous recevez ce dernier ouvrage avec indulgence, vous accueillerez mon ombre: car pour moi, je ne suis plus.

Mallarmé's faun to his, not unclassicist, illusions:

> . . . adieu! Je vais voir l'ombre que tu devins.

Yet this fugacity, this interlunation, the glimpsed embrace of love and death in seeking "le *la*" through a writing that is always working—and mourning—the fact that *la* or *elle* cannot take shape, rest, in a proper name—it had been foreshadowed by Mallarmé, master of the grand style in the modern period. Not in his poetry alone but also in his prose, especially his treatise *Les mots anglais*; and is not *Elle* a *mot anglé*?

Mallarmé plays, in the Cratylean manner, on many letters, including *L*. "Cette lettre semblerait parfois impuissante à exprimer par elle-même autre chose qu'une appétition point suivie de résultat" (cited, *Glas*, 180b). More significantly, both in a long "Introduction" and a summary conclusion to his book on the English language, having characterized the special richness of English but also its representative status ("Langue Contemporaine peut-être par excellence, elle qui accuse le double caractère de l'époque, rétrospectif et avancé")[14] and having specified certain "primordial laws" of language,

Car si les surnoms propres reviennent à (Notre-Dame) des fleurs, celles-ci sont coupées de la mère.

Détachées plutôt.

Détacher.

Peut-on ici se passer du mot? Détaché : comme le plus grand style.

La coupure, la déliaison, certes, mais aussi la délégation représentative, l'envoi d'un détachement, en mission auprès de l'autre, auprès de soi : « Elle [aile d'étamine, la Mort] avait détaché, pour La représenter, une cravate... »

Et comme tous les tissus, quand ou veut restaurer le texte de l'Immaculée Conception, la cravate se détache.

Avec ce détachement-là, réélaborer, comme problème du seing, de la signature et du nom de la mère, l'alternative du formalisme ou du biographisme, l'inénarrable et si classique question du sujet en littérature. « Ainsi, aux yeux de Notre-Dame ébahi, les petites tantes de Blanche à Pigalle perdaient leur plus belle parure : leurs noms

Figure 18.   Jacques Derrida, *Glas*, p. 113b. Courtesy, Editions Galilée.

such as agglutination, Mallarmé suggests that French too cannot escape a fundamental duplicity or impurity even when classically pure: "Everything, to the very disappearance of meaning, is but an alloy [*alliage*] of life and death and a medium, factitious and natural both." Given this fact, this law, Mallarmé foresees a third type of language formation, partially inspired by the "double treasure" or composite nature of English. What would happen if a "quasi-complete" language should mingle with an "almost complete" language, "perfect mixture resulting from the interaction between the two"? What if these two languages were French and English?

> Only grafting [*la greffe*] could offer an image to represent the new phenomenon; yes, of French which has been grafted onto [*s'est enté sur*] English: and the two plants have, all hesitation past, produced on the same stem a fraternal and splendiferous vegetation.

This "greffe" is the *Begriff* (concept) operative in Derrida's alloy of Hegel and Genet, their different languages and styles, but askew and aslant, detached from the residual pastoral vision that still motivates, with a discernible if purified pathos, Mallarmé's botanic metaphor. One text, in Derrida, haunts the other: the "s'est enté sur" becomes a "s'est hanté sur" ("sûr"?) by a development that seems as spontaneous as it is deliberate. All words live each other's life, die each other's death.

So the "Discours d'Elle" toward which the language of *Glas* aspires not only cannot rest, it cannot be identified with a class (mothers, women) or even, totally, with a particular historical language. In Hegel, and by slant appropriation in Derrida, this "Discours d'Elle" begins with Antigone, whose relation to her dead brother becomes a paradigm for the highest, most stabilizing point within the family and between the sexes. This stabilizing point is tantamount, however, to the erection of a sepulcher. A virgin sister accepts the tomb as her groom, and encrypts herself.

> Like Hegel, we have been fascinated by Antigone, by her incredible *rapport*, that powerful bond void of desire, that immense, impossible desire which was not viable, but could only reverse, paralyze or transgress a system and a story, interrupt the life of the concept, cut off its breath or, what amounts to the same thing, support it once it is the outside or underside of a crypt.

By the end of this passage in *Glas* (187a–88a) *Antigone* has become synonymous with *Aufhebung*, as if they were substitutable names. "L'a de gl agglutine les différents détachés" (188b).

Yet in Hegel "Antigone n'est pas proprement nommée" (*Glas*, 169a), because she is a limit, or to-be-excluded by the life of the concept, or because the work of mourning, as it coincides with dialectic sublation (*Aufhebung:* erection of crypt or monument), ablutes the personal name. This limit, which must be transgressed, remains in the system only as a name or monument that blocks it, either sublimely or pathologically. Name, tomb, milk-stone, fetish—monumentalized image or letter—there is always a cryptic point or period, an X or L factor that marks at one and the same time difference and identity. In the Identity-Philosophy preceding Hegel, it was called the "Indifferenz Punkt"; today it corresponds, perhaps, to Blanchot's "Le Neutre," or the idea of a "degré zéro," or the "freeplay" in language itself. The *a* in *Aufhebung* and Antigone, the "L'a de gl" and the "L'a laissé tomber," the *a* in Derrida's coinage "différance," perhaps even the *a* in "arrêt (de mort)" and "arête" (*quoin*)—as well as the "la" and the "là"—these show that the "appropriation absolue" that naming and especially the proper name try to achieve becomes by a fate of language "expropriation absolue" (*Glas*, 188a).

> . . . le fait même de l'expression est un vol de pensée
>
> Sartre
>
> . . . but as for their fingers, they were enveloped in some myth
>
> Melville, *The Confidence-Man*

I HAVE looked at *Glas* as a work of art and bracketed specific philosophical concepts developed by Derrida, especially in the *Grammatology*. The place of this book in the history of art, or its connection to the concept of art itself after Hegel—and, as it turned out, after Winckelmann—is the focus I found most fruitful. One problem is that every time I use an expression taken from *Glas*, or line it up with a colloquialism—say, "L'a laissé tomber" and "Let it be"—connotations press in from the language of philosophy as well. One begins to understand better, given this pressure of texts, this evocative stenography, what Derrida meant when he concluded the first chapter of the *Grammatology* with a suggestion that Hegel was "the last philosopher of the book and the first thinker about writing."

The heterogeneity of orders of discourse—of which Hegel and Genet, philosophy and art, classical diction and slang, are representative dichotomies, or necessary doublings, so that any text becomes intertextual, and "L'a laissé tomber," for instance, flirts, in its very difference, with Heideggerian concepts of art as disclosing the "Gelassenheit" or "Insich-ruhenlassen" of the "thing"—this heterogeneity can only be honored by writing itself as something worked through, *mise-en-oeuvre*. I say "something" because the status of this "thing" remains indeterminate; an energy, certainly; a *pulsion*, perhaps; also a machine. Language constructs a simulacrum that instead of disclosing thing or subject (even itself) is but a further baffle, screen, or veil; like Mallarmé, then, if less methodically, we are always weaving a shutter-style marked by a vacillation between parts of speech, a withholding of nouns as if they were all pronouns, a foregrounding, therefore, even a hyperbolic launching of divested noun elements, particles that seem to stand for or disseminate the "proper" term.

Can we talk, then, of an "economy" of language, at least of literature? Is there some kind of home rule, not auto-nomy so much as oiko-nomy? Like the second plot in Shakespeare's plays, the issue of the achievement of *Sittlichkeit*, of social morality or civility, takes up that question centering specifically on the role and regulation of women. But it is equally present in Derrida's curious appropriation (Heidegger: *Ereignis*) of phrases already charged, branded almost, by previous writers. The theme, curious in its psychological persistence, "How does language come to the column or statue?" (cf. *Glas*, 283a), is augmented by the theme of another coming-to, event or advent, best illustrated by Genet's reaction before Rembrandt's paintings or Giacometti's statues. The latter episode is comparable to Rousseau's Pygmalion animating his Galathea-Galalithe. What is revealed by these appropriations is the *hand of a thief*, a particular, peculiar *main-tenant*, writing considered as a Discourse of Theft going back to Prometheus and Jason. "My fingers do, then, what those of Giacometti have done, but while his sought a support in the wet plaster of the earth, mine put with sureness their steps in his steps. And—at last!—my hand lives, my hand sees" (Genet, *L'atelier d'Alberto Giacometti*). (See figure 19.)

From the perspective of writing, as from that of a jealous divinity, every-

Figure 19.   Alberto Giacometti, *La main* (1947). Courtesy, The Alberto Giacometti Foundation, on loan at the Kunsthaus, Zürich.

thing appears to be stolen: even the body of words. The stealing makes the hand alive. The writer is an Argonaut; and style is but *argot*, thieves' slang, however sublime. Every *Aufhebung* perpetrated by this "light" hand, every elevation or sublimation, betrays the desire for a "s'avoir absolu" that would demonstrate—monstrously if need be—one's hand, style, presence.

Property is theft.
      Proudhon

Psittacus, ecce, cano.
      John Skelton

AN ELOQUENT passage in the *Grammatology* argues that the "originary violence of language" is that of inscribing in a classifying and differentiating system—and so "suspending"—the "absolute vocative" (see below). The word *suspends* gives much away: it evokes the movement that connects *différence* with *différance* and institutes the economizing of an urge that is recognizably theurgic. For what can this absolute vocative be, if not, within all apostrophes, or all proper names by which we call men or gods, the fiat itself: the power of the logos to produce, out of itself as it were, a present and immediate response? "Let there be. . . . And there was. . . ." Can the work of art let the let-there-be be, suspend the absolute vocative *in* the system of language? Reverse that purloined or deferred L, and it looks like an instrument of suspense (gibbet or *potence*, see *Glas*, 223).

If this remains somewhat abstract, consider an instance of violent inscription whereby a word is stolen—appropriated and expropriated at the same time, becoming thieves' slang of an original kind. Genet's *"je m'éc . . ."* is indeed a vocative that seems curiously absolute. It cannot be reduced to one signification. The suspension points cut or strangle whatever might have made it into a recognizable phrase. This choking off is not, however, a device to achieve plurality of meaning, even if the latter is a by-product. In context, since Genet's experience is that of compulsive identification with a disgusting old man seen in a railway compartment, the *"je m'éc . . ."* combines the slang term *mec* (male) with *je m'équivale* or *je m'equus* (i.e., I return from the floral aura of my name to its more carnal sense: "genet" as a small Spanish horse), and also with *je m'écoeure* (I vomit), for Genet is primarily expressing the nausea that makes him try to throw up the *je* itself.[15] That this "cry" can be inscribed, that its very violence defers its meaning and produces plurisignification, exhibits the economy of writing as a whole. *"Je m'éc . . ."* is *je m'écris* (I write myself); its meaning is differentiated by a deferral (*différance*) equivalent to the written space of *Glas*.

In that space all properties are questioned until the *propre* itself—including the proper name—comes into question. Writing is always a *Journal du voleur.* "Lui reste léger, ne cesse de s'alléger." The writer, Genet or Derrida, cannot be taken seriously. He is the lightest of beings. Light-handed, certainly; if not Apollo then Hermes. So Derrida steals Genet's word, and makes it even more volatile. He first transposes it to his own page; it assumes, moreover, on the very first page of *Glas*, as we glance from one column to the other, the meaning of *je m'aigle* (making light of Hegel and introducing the Promethean theme). "Flighty theft [*vol*] without reference, textualized fiction, pure letters in the ear or throat, Eagle. . . . Stolen empire, empire in flight [*le vol de son empire*]—polysemy" (*Glas*, 68b, insert). By the last pages, that light-handed process—too heavy still—has passed through such meanings as *je m'équilibre* (the desire for coming to rest without a rest, as in Hellenic or statuesque repose) and *je m'ecke* (also intimating a kind of closure; I corner myself, psychologically, or by letting writing, in the form of a book, wedge me in. I *coince* myself). Writing *Glas* suspends the suspension marks, yet by this lightening or sublation reveals what is left out or left hanging—the L, for example, deferred over the space of the book, and which emerges near its close as a Kantian limit. *Je m'ecke* then becomes *je m'eckel*, a punning translation of *je m'écoeure*. Derrida has inscribed an *Ereignis* that is indeed a *perte du propre*: I disgust (German *Ekel*) myself, or "I" disgusts me. "Is it not always an element excluded from the system which assures the system possibility of space? The transcendental has always been, strictly, transcategorical, that which could not be received, formed, enclosed in any of the categories internal to the system. The vomit of the system" (*Glas*, 183a).

Yet what is *je m'eckel* but *interpreter's slang*, my own appropriation of Derrida's use of Genet? It is nothing but a kind of jargon. Argo(t) sum.

To name, to give names that it will on occasion be forbidden to pronounce, such is the originary violence of language which consists in inscribing within a difference, in classifying, in suspending the vocative absolute. To think the unique *within* the system, to inscribe it there, such is the gesture of the arche-writing: arche-violence, loss of the proper, of absolute proximity, of self-presence.[16]

Derrida

YET THERE is one dramatic moment in *Glas* when something like the forbidden name is named, or the absolute vocative is written out. It leads us into the underworld we began with, that of Dionysus. On p. 124 of *Glas* within a development too complex to summarize but which makes me think that *"je m'éc . . ."* means *je m'écoeure* in the literal sense of desiring so much to get at the heart of things, *au coeur du coeur*—to be so present to another or oneself, that one is ready, at least imaginatively, to kill and dismember as in Dionysian orgies—Derrida puts "Georg Wilhelm Friedrich Hegel" in the shade by a four-part name of his own:

> Dionysos Erigone Eriopétale Réséda.

This plush vocative with its internal doublings seems to restitute what was torn into little pieces at the beginning. Someone is named, certainly. But is it Dionysus alone? There is a word under the words, a disseminated sound. If we look at the cryptic fourfold as a Saussurean hypogram, then that other name is Derrida.

So that the one time Derrida names himself is within a feminine constellation and in conjunction with Dionysus. At the same time, what stands behind the naming is not a "sujet créateur" but rather a "mot inducteur."[17] In whose name does Derrida write this name, or his discourse as an extended name?

The parts of the agglutinated vocative seem to add up as a sum or matrix of sense. "La glu de l'aléa fait sens." Yet how to account for the effect of what appears to be a sequence of resonant syllables, a pure poetry? A word under the words is not sufficient to motivate them: it hollows as well as saturates. Can anything motivate or appropriate this name?

Erigone names a daughter of Icarus (Ic) who killed herself after her father's death, and is made into the constellation Virgo (IC). She was also a woman loved by Bacchus-Dionysus (cf. *Glas*, 83b–85b).

Eriopétale is a term from botany and belongs to the floral chain of metaphors: it describes petals that are fuzzy. The Greek *erion* means fleece; and Derrida connects text and pubis—theft of words and theft of love—through this term. "Le texte est la toison d'or" (79b). The "vol antique" or Argo motif is woven in.

Réséda, from the Latin *re-sedare*, to soothe or put an end to (cf. sedate), aptly ends the series. A plant, originally from Africa, Derrida's birthplace, it was used for the healing of tumors while a magic formula, "reseda morbos" etc., was intoned.

The fourfold name is thus expropriated from the language of the gods and the language of flowers, two staples of literary diction. The definition in the *Dictionnaire de l'Académie Française* (1694 edition) for the language of flowers may hold also for Derrida's stealing back of the language of the gods: "Langage symbolique dans lequel les fleurs, soit isolées, soit assemblées, suivant un certain choix, servent à exprimer une pensée, un sentiment secret."

It also happens that the reseda is a gaud, celebrated for its yellow dye, like the "genêt d'espagne." Associated, therefore, with the color of the sun, with golden Apollo, or golden Aphrodite, or the Argonaut's desire. Associated via "Genet" with the Dionysian passion to empathize, penetrate, ejaculate, and so vomit forth one's self. How can such different things enter a single mark of identity, a proper name? Has bricolage succeeded in drawing the sun into the abyss? Is meaning made present by surcharging these words, or by disclosing an unsettling difference: their beauty that lies precisely in having no proper meaning?

How ironic that *réséda* should settle nothing. For it comes at the end to mock the end. No wound is healed by it, or by this act of naming as a whole. "The signature is the wound, and there is no other origin of the work of art" (*Glas*, 207b). As a word, *réséda* seals this signature with a bad trilingual pun. *Res est da*. The thing is there. But it is not there.

The rest is silence. As in Nietzsche (291a): "Uns ist Gram und Grauen und Grund gemeinsam: noch die Sonne ist uns gemeinsam. Wir reden nicht zueinander, weil wir zu vieles wissen" (We have grieving, shudders, and ground in common: even the sun in common. We do not talk to each other, because we know too much). Part of this knowing silence is the link of reseda, not with a name but with a mark of identity. We learn about it from the Wartburg dictionary, which quotes a source of 1716. Reseda was called "Jew grass" (*herbe des juifs*) because "it furnishes the yellow color Jews were formerly obliged to wear in this region."

4 *Psychoanalysis: The French Connection*

To be stripped of every fiction save one
The fiction of an absolute
                    Wallace Stevens

THE LANGUAGE of Lacan and Derrida is shaped by a Heideggerian detour. Both writers see Western philosophy as reflecting through its grammar, its categories, and its now inbuilt manner of discourse a desire for reality-
mastery as aggressive and fatal as Freud's death instinct. Their critique of
metaphysics seems to blend with the findings of Freudian metapsychology.
The Western thinker gloats over reality like Shakespeare's Achilles over the
living body of Hector. Achilles, in a jocose and terrible taunt, inspects Hector
as if he were infinitely vulnerable:

> Tell me you heav'ns, in which part of his body
> Shall I destroy him? whether there, or there, or there,
> That I may give the local wound a name;
> And make distinct the very breach, whereout
> *Hector's* great spirit flew.
>
>   (*Troilus and Cressida* IV.ix.)

This fearful power of pointing out, or pointing at, expresses what Lacan
describes as the phantasm of morcellation, or of the "corps morcelé"—a
phantasm that the psyche is always seeking to allay. If we remember that
Achilles is almost immortal, that in theory he can only be wounded through a
heel left untouched by his immersion in the Styx, then we see the connection
between this taunt and a deeply human anxiety. In ordinary mortals the
Achilles heel is everywhere; psychic development is therefore a balance between the hope of immortality and the continuous fear of mortal exposure.

Directness—the "fingering" or "prenominating" mode of Achilles—has
its shadow side, which is part of the very subject of French investigations
linking language and the psyche. Yet to say we are crucified, or morcellated,
by language is as pathetic and exaggerated as to claim we are potentially

redeemed by it. The fundamental concern of Lacan and Derrida is with directness, or *intellectual* passion: that rigorous striving for truth, exposure, mastery, self-identification—in short, science and metaphysics—which at once defines and ravages the human actor.

Against this rigor, and often from within it, various doctors, including those of the Church, have sought to defend us; poetry, too, has been considered a *remedium intellectus* and the poet-humanist a "physician to all men." It is not surprising, then, that Derrida should open his tortuous and capital work, *Glas*, with reflections on Hegel's "absolute knowledge"—that immediacy of person to truth which is the exact obverse of the naïve immediacy Hegel calls "abstract" and which the absolute thinker sees filled or made concrete by historical experience in its very negativity, its morcellating if also self-healing movement.

Speaking of passion we evoke necessarily a family of words: *patience, patient, passio gloriosa,* even *crime passionel.* In the column opposite the one that opens with an allusion to Hegel's absolute thinker, Derrida quotes from Genet what seems to be a fit of passion or else a gratuitous act: the tearing to pieces of an essay manuscript on Rembrandt, rendered as if a picture itself, or the very name Rembrandt, had been defaced. "Ce qui est resté d'un Rembrandt déchiré en petits carrés réguliers et foutu aux chiottes" (*Glas*, 7b). This strange, onomatoclastic act is directed against what I will call "l'imago du nom propre" (the imago of the proper name) and it again evokes the fantasy of the "corps morcelé." We are made to realize how easily the psyche is punctured by image, photo, phantasm, or phrase. The terrible rigor of psychic, like logicistic, process sets this human vulnerability in a perversely radiant frame, one that may extend toward infinity like the Chinese torture of "a hundred pieces." Psychoanalysis, in this light, reveals once more the unresolvable ambivalence of passion as both suffering and ecstasy: as a *geometry* of beatitude achieved by submitting again and again to the wounding power of some ultimate penetration, or the illusion of coming "face to face" with life or death or truth or reality.

"I am half sick of shadows," says Tennyson's Lady of Shalott, before she turns to what she thinks is reality and dies. The wish to put ourselves in an unmediated relation to whatever "really" is, to know something absolutely, means a desire to be defined totally: marked or named once and for all, fixed in or by a word, and so—paradoxically—made indifferent. "He (She) desired to be without desire" is the underlying clue in the psychodrama of many Lacanian patients. The story of I (for identity) begins to cheapen into the Story of O, and can be more dehumanizing even in the noble form of Descartes's "cogito ergo sum" than the dangers of the Id. Pornosophy, so at home in France, so alien to English and American literature, depicts prophylactically the Ego's demanding a "divine" violation into thinghood or invulnerability.

The indeterminacy principle, however, that Lacan and Derrida develop from dream logic and literary language begins with the Id rather than with the Ego: or minimally with the *id est*, which, like the *à savoir* ("namely"), defers absolute knowledge and definitive naming in the very act of exemplary instancing. "Id est, ergo id non est." Exemplification is always serial, subversive, plural.

We return by this route to the subtle links between psyche and language. For one wonders, in reading Lacan, whether philosophical discussions concerning the *stigme*, or "here and now," are so removed, after all, from psychoanalytic speculations on the divine or hysterical stigmata, and the whole issue of ecstasy, identification, incorporation, conversion. Did Freud really succeed in ushering in an era of "deconversion" or of purely "psychological man"? With Lacan in particular, the project of psychoanalysis is not only involved in what the relation of analyst and analysand may mean for the "order of discourse" each embodies—just as Derrida, in *Glas*, explores simultaneously the question of a relation between the paternal discourse of a magister ludi called Hegel and the thievish, maternal "calculus" revealed by Genet. Lacan's project is not only this sensitive exploration of the power relations between codes or idioms within language; it is also an attempt to restructure them, in order to build a new communitarian model on the basis of psychiatric experience, Though we have entered the age of Freud we remain in the age of Saint-Simon.[1]

Lacan exposes the self-protective devices and rules so important to Freudian psychiatry, and demands of the clinician that he listen to the "Other" who is as much in himself as in the patient. This Other solicits the labor of recognition that must keep analyst and analysand apart despite transference and countertransference. The "pathos" of the analytic situation is linked to its representational character: something is acted out here-and-now to cure the here-and-now by a respect for there-and-then; for difference, otherness, change, mortality. The patient is to become patient rather than fitful-passionate, and the analyst must be patient too in order to *hear* what is going on, to decipher or even redeem from the *res* the *rebus* presented to him.

> Hieroglyphics of hysteria, blazons of phobia, labyrinths of the *Zwangsneurose*— charms of impotence, enigmas of inhibition, oracles of anxiety, talking arms of character, seals of self-punishment, disguises of perversion—these are the hermetic elements that our exegesis resolves, the equivocations that our invocation dissolves, the artifices that our dialectic absolves.[2]

Yet the analyst is attracted to and therefore protects himself from the ecstatic message, the heart of darkness in the patient, that is, in himself. He hunts that wounded hart as in some spiritual chase, but only to build on it (strange rock that weeps) an acknowledgment of a purely human crucifixion, of a secular, self-inflicted stigmatics.

Freud, according to Lacan, founded psychoanalysis on this attraction to the hysterical patient, usually a woman; and inattention to that origin means that theory must "cherchez la femme" once again, or take "le discours de la femme" (the woman's word) again into the method. A quasi-sacred detective story unfolds as Lacan follows the traces, semiobliterated, of Freud. He begins his own career with a thesis of 1932 that reflects on what is practically a literary theme: the self-inflicted wound of a woman he calls Aimée. The question elaborated since 1932 is that of the *Eigentlichkeit*, or "propriety," of this wound, one that is contagious in the sense that it cannot be localized, much less contained. Lacan's thesis is that the erotomanic woman who knifed an actress was really attacking her own person: the mystery is that the wound had to go through that detour.

In much of his work Lacan interprets a *blessure* (wound) that is so ambivalently a "blessing" as the *symptom* that acts out whatever is human in us. He names the wound, or makes "distinct the very breach" that renders the psyche visible. It is a movement of desire that cannot define itself except as a desire of, and belonging to, an other: a desire that may not be appropriated by the self, and so cannot build up (as ego psychology would have it) a stable self. In terms of sexual differentiation the breach is related to the (absent) phallus and in terms of noncarnal conversation it is related to a language where the signifier cannot be completed by the signified. The phallus as signifier is not circumscribed by its function of procreation but serves to open the wound, and womb, of signification. If the psyche is said to be structured like language it is because the symptom is always like a displaced or forgotten word, a repressed signifier that pretends to be *the* signified and a terminus to desire. The analyst recovers the signifier and with that not only the meaning of symptoms but a blocked mode or force of speech. Hence, all psychoanalysis draws others into its contagious orbit and stimulates an epidemic of soul-(un)making. The history of religion is full of such epidemics, of course; and Lacan's project, however self-aware, remains under that shadow.

I am consciously reading Lacan (and also Derrida) in the light of what Sartre called "la grande affaire"—the scandal of theological survivals in even the most secular thinkers. This survival may simply mean that the concept of secularization as presently understood is premature or crude. It is clear, however, that French thought in the area of psychoanalysis has removed language from the hope of being purified through a curative metalanguage. A language that is authentic, that lies beyond the eloquence of wounds or religious pathos or the desire for reality-mastery, is not to be found. Lacan, in this, must sometimes be distinguished from his followers, whose belief in the truth of words is more directly thaumaturgic and whose case histories can be more transparent and frightening in their reductionist clarity than those of the early Freud. At best both Lacan and Derrida remind us that language, like sexual difference or passion in general, is that in which we live and breathe and have our being. It cannot be subdued but remains part of the subtle knot that perplexes even as it binds together man and woman in the "scène familiale."

Que tu brilles enfin, terme pur de ma course.
                              Valéry, "Fragments du Narcisse"

IN A GLASS darkly. Lacan discovers a "stade du miroir" (mirror phase) in the early development of what is to be the child's ego. By the complaisance of the mirror the child sees itself for the first time as a coordinated being and, triumphantly, jubilantly, assumes that image. But what is found by means of this play ("je-jeu") with the mirror is really a double rather than a differentiated other. The myth of Narcissus is given clinical verisimilitude. The other (Rimbaud: "Je est un autre") is necessary for self-definition, but in the mirror is simply an illusory unification. The "corps morcelé," moreover, the fragmented or uncoordinated body image prior to the mirror phase, is only suspended. It remains active in the domain that Lacan names the verbal or symbolic in contrast to the nonverbal or imaginary.

    Beyond these observations lies a difficult psychopathology that we need not oversimplify except to say that the concept of a "corps morcelé" (cf. Glas, "un Rembrandt déchiré") is connected with Lacan's understanding of the castration complex, or how the phallus or the body part that "represents" the sexual foundation of otherness is enmeshed in an extraordinary developmental series of differential yet substitutive (compensatory) mechanisms. Acceptance of the (absent) phallus, or of the (absent) father, or, basically, of the mediacy of words, allows a genuine recognition of difference.

    Since the mirror phase, although using gestaltist and biological evidence, is not securely based on experimental data (especially when compared to the painstaking work of Piaget) it might be better to call it the Marienbad complex. Not only is Marienbad where the hypothesis was first made public, but also Resnais's film Last Year at Marienbad expresses Lacan's mirror domain as a fact of the imagination: the image or heroine in that film's mobile mirror seems to quest for a specular yet totally elusive identity, for some unique reduction to one place, one time, one bed, one fixative spectral event.

    The mirror phase, then, deals with images, with thing rather than word representation. (In Last Year at Marienbad, the sound track is dissociated from the life of the images, running nonparallel with it, an arbitrary or contrapuntal yet related experience. It is exactly like the somewhat mysterious juxtaposition, in Lacan, of symbolic and imaginary spheres.) The notion of a "corps morcelé" does, however, connect with the differential system of a psycholinguistics. The question therefore arises: Is there anything comparable to the mirror stage on the level of language?

Lacan's emphasis on the birth of language out of a "symbolic" rather than "imaginary" sphere seems to moot this line of inquiry. He suggests that the specular image, as the base of other imagery that serves an integrative or unifying function, is an illusory modification of a deeper or prior system, inherently differential. Thus, the question of what corresponds to the mirror phase on the level of language (to its unifying if illusory effect) may seem unanswerable in terms of Lacanian psychiatry.

Yet there is the well-known magical or religious ambition to possess *the* word. Does not the concept of Word or Logos in religion, or in such artists as Hölderlin, provide a clue? And is not the Lacanian psychopompos, who recovers an interior signifier, of that tradition? We are looking for a correlative in language to the specular image. The logos understood as that in whose "image" whatever it is signifying seems to motivate a logocentric phase of development—the very thing Derrida is seeking to expose.

Or consider the importance of the proper name in Shakespeare. "Had I it written, I would tear the word," Romeo says to Juliet, referring to his family name. The wounding of a name is too much like the wounding of the body not to be significant. We don't know why Genet tore "Rembrandt," but the effacing or defacing of the proper name suggests that there may be such a thing as a specular name or "imago du nom propre" in the fantasy development of the individual, a name more genuinely one's own than a signature or proper name. Signatures can always be faked. Is there something that cannot be faked? "The signature is a wound, and there is no other origin to the work of art" (*Glas*, 207b).[3] Is it possible to discern a specular word, logos phase, or imago of the proper name in the development of the individual?

Derrida's reflections on Hegel, in *Glas*, open with a play on the idea of "naming" or "nomination," a theme fully elaborated in his juxtaposed column on Genet. He implies, without calling it so, an imago of the proper name on the basis of what we know of the haunting, fixative, unifying effect of "being named." Just as the specular image produces a jubilant awareness tested and affirmed by the child's mirror mimicry, so the specular name can produce a hallelujah and magnifying language that mimics a sublimity associated with the divine logos. This is so even if the identifying name, the *nom unique* or *nom propre*, is accusatory. Indeed the *scene of nomination* (my own phrase) is bound to be accusative as well as nominative, or to include within it a reflexive, intense response to the act of vocative designation. "You are a thief," that commonplace accusation, that merest insult addressed to Genet as a child, strikes inward as a divine apostrophe and perhaps founds the perverse high ritualism of his style.

In such a scene of nomination, then, the mirror speaks. We suspect, of course, that our primary narcissism has already spoken to it, like the queen in *Snow White*. But whatever question has been put remains obscure: only the mirror's response is clear, indeed so clear that it obliges us to assume its answer as an identity, to construct or reconstruct some feature in us clarified by this defining response. At the same time, the specular name or identity phrase—our true rather than merely proper name—is reaffirmed *in time* by a textual mimicry, joyful, parodistic, or derisory, of the original "magnification." The repetition of the specular name gives rise to texts that seem to be anagrammatic or to conceal an unknown-unknowable key, a "pure" signifier. These texts are called literature.

Can we assert that the specular name "exists"? Derrida knows that such words as *exist* and *is* point to a static order of things, and he tries to avoid the trap of this inbuilt language-metaphysic. He suggests, instead, that if there is a Hegelian *Sa* ("*savoir absolu*") it may be incompatible with the *Sa* (*signifiant*) we call a signature: the proper name (Hegel) affixed to a text as its authenticating seal.

A similar counterpointing of proper and specular name is suggested in Genet's case. The "antherection" of his name in a given passage (that is, the flowery style that alludes to his flower name, "genêt") makes a tomb of it: as in Saussure's anagrams, the text generated by the name is bound to enlace and so to bury it. Like a child who will not believe his parents are his real parents but engages imaginatively in a "family romance," so the proper name, or signature, is always being "torn up" in favor of a specular name, whether or not it can be found:

> The grand stakes of discourse (I mean *discourse*) that is literary: the patient, tricky, quasi animalistic or vegetative transformation, unwearying, monumental, derisive also, but turning derision rather against itself—the transformation of the proper name, *rebus*, into things, into the name of things [*Glas*, 11b].

More radically still: writing is coterminous with that canceling movement, "la nécessité du passage par la détermination biffée, la nécessité de *ce tour d'écriture*." Every return, then, as in Genet, to a scene of nomination, must be unmasked as a figure. It introduces a factitious present or fictitious point of origin that may not be taken literally ("livré à la police") unless we are in search of an "ordinateur secret" leading back to baptism or birth.

> A text only exists, resists, consists, represses, lets itself be read or written if it is elaborated [*travaillé*] by the unreadability [*illisibilité*] of a proper name. I have not said—not yet—that such a proper name exists and that it becomes unreadable when it falls [or is entombed, *tombe*] into the signature. The proper name does

not ring forth [*résonne*], lost at once, save at the instant of its *débris*, when it breaks—embroils—checks itself on touching the signature [*seing*] (*Glas*, 41b).

Glas ends, therefore, with the words "le débris de" [Derrida]—that is, it touches, without actually stating, the "seing." The proper name seems to have been "disseminated": *Glas* has told (tolled) its demise. This concept of dissemination moves to the fore in Derrida's writings after the *Grammatology*. It is essential for his critique of Lacan or Sartre or any hermeneutic that relapses into a thematics (even a polythematics) by its insistence on an explanatory "key." In his grimly funny way, Derrida compares this procedure of "slipping the universal passkey into all lacunae of signification" to a police action. "It would mean arresting once again, in the name of the law, of veracity, of the symbolic order, the free movement [*marche*] of an unknown person" (*Glas*, 36b).

The signature, which denotes propriety through the proper name, is the *cas limite* of this arrest. Only courts of justice should insist on it, with their cumbersome machinery of registration, verification, ceremonial gravity, etc. Dissemination is, strangely enough, a pastoral though totally uninnocent protest against such restrictive or paralegal types of hermeneutic. It is the obverse, in fact, of classification. "What makes us write is also what scatters the semes, disperses *signacoupure* and *signacouture*" (*Glas*, 192b).

The passage from cl (for *class*, *clé*, *clue*) to gl (for *glas* or *glu*) analogizes these contraries: classification and dissemination. "At the very moment," Derrida continues,

> we try to seize, in a particular text, the workings of an idiom, linked to a chain of proper nouns and actual denotative configurations, *glas* also names *classification*, that is, their inscription in networks of generalities infinitely articulated, or in the genealogies of a structure whose crossweaving, coupling, switching, detouring, branching can never be derived merely from a semantic or a formal rule. There is no absolute idiom or signature. . . . The bell tolls always for the idiom or the signature. For the absolute precursor [*aïeul absolu*: perhaps "primal father"] (*Glas*, 169b).

Thus, we enter a chain of secondary elaborations stretching to infinity. There is no way of tracing them to an origin, to a logos that may have been "In the Beginning." When, in a quasi-heraldic moment—talking arms of character, Lacan might say—Nerval's *Desdichado* recites, "Je suis le ténébreux, le veuf, l'inconsolé," we know that the family name "Labrunie" has been cast out in favor of a specular identity that is the widowed logos itself: the babel of "à la tour abolie." The appropriate hermeneutic, therefore, is like the interminable work of mourning, like an endless affectional detachment from the identity theme as such, whether that is linked to the (absent) logos or to a maternal and sexual presence distanced by the logos into the idea of an Immaculate Conception.

Perhaps the most persistent—obsessive—theme in *Glas* is the Immaculate Conception. It surges into the opening page before its time. No sooner has the author said, in the margin, "*Sa* will henceforth be the mark [*sigle*] of absolute knowledge," than he adds, "And IC, let us note it already, because the two portals [i.e., columns on the page] represent each other mutually, the mark of the Immaculate Conception." The notion of *sigle* (of words represented by their first letter) enters a series including "signature" and "seing" (seal or mark at the end of a text, representing the signatory, with a possible interlingual pun on *seing/sein/Sein*: seal/breast/Being). This tripling could be explained by the special function assigned each term, but Derrida is more concerned with how language moves by marginal differentiation through a signifying series that can never quite circumscribe, or comprise, a body (corpus).

This term *Sa*, therefore, which he institutes but which is homophonic with Saussure's abbreviation for signifier (*signifiant*), although made of first and last (of *initial* letters that denote an *end* state) is neither a first or last term, for it enters an indefinite sequence that includes other words already mentioned, as well as *signe, ensigner, enseigner*. Writing *Glas* in two columns, or beginning with two Hegel passages, reinforces our awareness that the "scene of writing" never takes place in one place: its locus (corpus) is always also "ein anderer Schauplatz," as Freud put it: displaced from right to left, to a supplementary comment or even into a physical symptom, which Lacan rightly analogizes to a "truth" already written down elsewhere and therefore in part missing from present discourse. There is, in short, no absolute or transcendental *Sa* (signifier) any more than an absolute or certain *Sa* (knowledge of what is signified). We cannot say, like Christ, "This is my body" without being already dead: premonumentalized.

From the start of *Glas*, then, we are presented with two illusory moments of ecstatic identification some eighteen hundred years apart: absolute knowledge, or Hegel's vision of an end to dialectic and alienation in the thought process of the philosopher who has internalized history; and the phantasm of the Immaculate Conception. Why the latter? What bearing has it, as developed in the column on Genet, on the Hegelian "legend" unfolded opposite? And why emphasize, of all literary writers, Genet? Among Anglo-American readers the juxtaposition will cause a resistance that even the brilliance of the result may not remove.

These questions I will now try to explore a bit further. One must acknowledge, however, the problem of cultural difference that stands in the way. The pressure Derrida exerts on texts is admirable: through him we realize once more how consistently the human condition is a verbal condition. But there is little in English letters to compare with the *involution* of French or German commentary once it has singled out its exempla. A modern medievalism then takes over. So that, while the intertextual method opens its chosen books to endless interpretation, it also, paradoxically, affects the English or American reader as culture bound. The allusiveness goes inward rather than abroad, and we must start with the fact that Derrida's analysis of Genet is underwritten by a prior analysis, by local canon making or even canonization ("Saint Genet") that obliges him to meet that other Hegelian, Sartre, on common ground.

For there is a language of flowers.
For there is a sound reasoning upon all flowers.
Christopher Smart, *Jubilate Agno*

SARTRE SAW in Genet a "choix originel" or "projet existentiel" (*Glas*, 36b) maintained for thirty years and transformed into an occult religion and system of life.[4] Like Lacan in psychiatry, Sartre posits, according to Derrida, a transcendental key that might open every text or psyche, slipping "into all signifying lacunae" like a "universal phallus." But if such a key exists, adds Derrida, it is already inscribed in Genet's own text as the "verge d'acier" or "bite ailée" he calls his pen. "I was haunted by it," writes Genet. "I slept beside it because a warrior sleeps armed."

So that if there is a key, the author has locked the text and, as it were, thrown the key away—into the text. This view seems to invert Lacan's understanding of psychosis, in which the key—the "nom-du-père"—is foreclosed by being "verworfen" or expelled (through hallucination) from the symbolic order into reality. Derrida also operates another reversal on Lacan. Genet's "verge d'acier" or "steel rod"—the pen-phallus—is said to belong less to the father than to the mother: to the mother as the Virgin. The pen-penis is like a "nom-de-plume" that represents the "nom-de-mère" instead of the "nom-du-père," or what *Glas* calls "le calcul de la mère."

Derrida's interest is chiefly in this phantom mother, or her discourse, which he prefers to call a *calcul* because it is at once complex and mute. The only words we have are Genet's own and perhaps the fact so determining in Sartre's eyes, that Genet as a boy was accused of being a thief and took his identity from that. Derrida agrees that the insult, literalized, allowed the child to give himself back to his "true" mother, to identify with what is really *her* condition, that of having to draw an identity out of being abandoned. Abandoned in the absolute sense: *verworfen* or *geworfen*, without husband, father, father in heaven.

Derrida projects her image as a person without "Eigentlichkeit" and therefore also without a sense (and certainly not a bourgeois sense) of "Eigenschaften" or properties: "The mother is a thief and a beggar. She

appropriates everything because she has nothing that is her own [*en propre*]"
(170b). He makes her, wittily, a Heideggerian "Thing," even a "Ding-an-
Sich." This vastated being, however, is not filled with grace, like the Virgin,
but with ersatz; she is immaculate because she can't be stained by any gift,
wound, or word. These are mere fillers of her nonessence, decorative substitutes, votive nothings. Like certain phantoms she has the capacity of incor-
porating all the names, abusive or exalted, magnifying or mourning, her son
bestows until she becomes, in this double function of identity-vamp and
muse, what is called, untranslatably, a "bourreau berceur."

Not only, then, is Genet's work nourished by "poisoned milk," but it is
drawn ineluctably to a fantasy that transforms the Christ legend more radically
than Yeats's "Crazy Jane" poems. The mother is seen as Mary's double, just
as Mary had such a double, Mary Magdalen, who "was able to engage on an
infinite change of phallus without being changed [*detaillé*: literally, divided
up or retailed]," the ultimate phallus involving her acceptance of Christ
(*Glas*, 290b).

Even Genet's pen-phallus has a special relevance to the Christ legend.
The lilies offered to the Virgin in pictures of the Annunciation are associated
with the flower theme (*anthème*) of Genet's style ("style" being itself, since
Derrida never misses a trick, a flower term) that makes his book (*lit*, a reading)
into a bed (*lit*) of flowers resembling a floral tomb. The pen-phallus or "verge
[vierge] d'acier" reappears as the gladiolus, a name that means a little sword;
in German "sword-lily." "Through my very soul," Mary says, "A sword shall
pierce; this is my favor'd lot, / My Exaltation to Afflictions high" (Milton,
Paradise Regained II.90–92; Luke 2.34–35). Thus all of Genet's flowers of
speech are at once pure and guilty (*coupable*), like the phantom mother. His
own name is the proof of this strange purity: it derives from the plant called
"genêt" (ginestra, broom), which was his mother's, not his father's, name. He
is a flower-child, then, even a virgin's child, however *coupable* as a thief,
homosexual, and phallic being.

We understand better now the two-column structure of *Glas*. "Hegel and
the discourse of the father" is matched by "Genet and the discourse [*calcul*] of
the mother." Derrida not only brings out the "family romance" in Hegel's
thought but suggests that what Hegel leaves behind in the march of the
dialectic toward absolute knowledge is precisely the "du reste" from which
Genet seems to build the dark purity of his work. According to Derrida we
cannot reduce the coexistence of innocence and culpability in Genet's "language of flowers"—identified through Mallarmé with literariness itself—and
whose ambivalence is exactly as Freud described it at two points in *The
Interpretation of Dreams.* [5] Yet Derrida is not concerned with setting Freud or
Genet against Hegel and exposing the ambivalence of such symbols. He is
formulating a hermeneutics of indeterminacy.

In Freud the underside of symbols is necessarily sexual, even when sexuality is not what is important. Freud does not reduce dreams to sexual messages but insists rather that infantile sexual experience structures what is dreamed. Yet, for Derrida, if the phallus is always "winged," "plumy" or "disseminated," then it cannot be used in the manner of a key to lock or unlock a subject: that is, fix a person's truth or identity-theme, or found it in a drive like the libido. There is no more a Freudian than a Cartesian cogito: you cannot hypostatize a word wound as the eloquent trauma that determines all. Even in France psychoanalysis remains, according to Derrida, logocentric: a displaced religious or metaphysical discourse in search of the logos or "nom unique," of a single defining wound for which life, or else death, is the cure.

EVERY literary narrative contains another narrative: however continuous or full the one seems to be, the other is discontinuous and lacunary. Jean-Luc Nancy has called this "other" narrative the "discours de la syncope." Given that our minds tend to overestimate, even when wary or ashamed of it, fictional writing, the reader is usually forced into the position of having to recover the "discours de la syncope," that is, the precariousness of all transitions, or the undecidability of fiction's truth. Every story is like Isabel's in Melville's *Pierre*, and every authoritative title or naming should be treated on the analogy of Pierre, or The Ambiguities.

Yet this deepening sense of an endless or ungrounded or noncontinuous discourse is not purely cautionary or destructive. There is something we can take away with us: a perception similar to that offered by myths and positive interpretation. Our vision of the psyche's vulnerability broadens and intensifies; it extends into the bowels of language, from images to names and to the pathos that insistently attends the giving or calling out of a name. However different the Gothic gloom of Melville's *Pierre* and Faulkner's *Absalom, Absalom!* both novels turn on the seductive centrality of a scene of recognition—of naming and acknowledgment. The concepts of vocation, initiation, and identity run parallel yet subordinate to that central hinge that Aristotle in the *Poetics* already discerned as essential to Greek tragedy.

The desire for a "here and now," fixed image or defining word, mystic portrait or identity-imposing story, is not dissociable, according to psychiatry, from family romance: the recognition scene is always a displaced or sublimated family scene. It is no different with the Christian scandal of the "Presence of the Word" (*logos spermatikos*) in the Immaculate Conception, or more precisely, in the Annunciation. Let me, therefore, recenter these reflections on the most famous scene of nomination in our culture: the Annunciation.

There are, of course, other scenes that show the Word of God coming to earth with vocational force. But this episode is particularly relevant to Genet because it "magnifies" a woman; indeed, Mary's hymn, called the Magnificat after its Latin version, and recorded in Luke, has become part of Christian liturgy. Not only is the Presence of the Word in this scene of nomination also the Word of the Presence ("Hail, O favored one, the Lord is with you," Luke 1:28), but the transcendental signifier, as we might truly call it, issues in a Magnificat because it takes away a curse: of infertility, and more generally, in reference to woman, of impure, because infertile, menstruation. Mary's condition, moreover, could have shamed her (Matt. 1:18–20; Luke 1:24), but through the intervention of the angelic word a potential denunciation becomes an annunciation.

In Genet, profanely, the same structure holds. Denunciation is converted to Annunciation; the curse (perhaps that of being born of woman, or male seed considered as impure, as a menstrual flow, *unless* made fertile in the woman) is taken away; and the Magnificat of a convict's style results. How "you are a thief" should become functionally equivalent to the sanctifying "you are with child" is the psychic puzzle that Sartre and Derrida try to resolve.

It is not by chance that Derrida should choose to continue through Genet his critique of the "closure" imposed on thought or language by the so-called logocentric tradition. Within that closure even miracles have their limits: virgin birth or fullness (of grace) must be female. A male parthenogenesis is "inconceivable," even as miracle, except through the ultimate veil of theologic mystery. Scenes of nomination that affect men in Scripture tend in fact, as with Abraham, to be a call for child sacrifice. But Freudian pornosophy has the bad taste to raise the question of whether the artist's work is not a male childbirth, and his book a "proles sine matre nata" (Montesquieu).

"You are a thief" can only stand for "You are with child" if, at some level, Genet is trying to steal the womb itself—whereas he can at most, if we trust Ferenczi's bioanalysis, steal *into* the womb and give something to that death in order to live.[6] Genet is not successful in modifying even imaginatively the logocentric enclosure: he simply erects a subversive, symmetrical counterpart, the image of male fulness of grace, "L'annonce fait à Jean-Marie." Sound reasoning on his flowery or anthographic style must include the thought that flowers such as the lilies of the field or those associated with the Annunciation are pure in the sense that Hegel caught when he posits a nonagonistic "religion of flowers": they can grow and multiply as if by grace, without the curse of labor (cf. Gen. 3:16 ff.). The commandment, by place the first in the Bible, "Be fruitful and multiply," is death to hear, as Adam remarks in Milton's *Paradise Lost* (X.731), for it means, after the Fall, a multiplying of deaths or, as for Genet, *genitality with no grace except as it "blesses" a woman.* His family of thieves and murderers is erected in vain opposition to the survival of the "onto-theologic" model in secular society.

Genet's mirror image of the Holy Family, then, expresses a reversal rather than a transvaluation of values. Given the conservative character of the institution of language, it is doubtful that there could be transvaluation. We can reverse or trope catachretically, we can deploy all the subversive flowers in the anthology of speech, or we can reverse in another sense, by deconstruction, and expose the fallacy that every great artist's mind passes on itself—the result remains a secret recognition scene. As Genet himself has written: "The world is turned inside out like a glove. It happens that I am the glove and I understand at last that on the day of judgment God will call me with my own voice: 'Jean, Jean'" (*Glas*, 220b). Or Lacan: "The Word always subjectively includes its own reply.... The function of Language is not to inform but to evoke. What I seek in the Word is the response of the other.... In order to find him, I call him by a name which he must assume or refuse in order to reply to me." "The allocution of the subject entails an allocutor ... even if he is speaking 'off' or 'to the wings.' He addresses himself to *ce (grand) Autre* whose theoretical basis I have consolidated."[7]

Even the most deliberate counterannunciation yet conceived, Mallarmé's mirror scene in the *Herodiade,* can only use the language of flowers against itself. "Vous mentez, o fleur nue de mes lèvres." Herodiade's specular cries know they have no issue. Devoted to sterility, Herodiade is Mary's opposite in the drama of the logos that eventuates so curiously in Genet's (or Derrida's) image of the mother as "bourreau berceur." The logos as the *relève* (*Aufhebung*/fulfilment) of metaphor reifies metaphor and suppresses language fertility. Christ and Herod become co-conspirators in this Genet-ic massacre.

"VOUS MENTEZ," that denunciation so often addressed to the artist, is now, in the Nietzsche-(Wilde)-Derrida line of thinking, the only annunciation. It is addressed to language itself, "fleur nue de nos lèvres." Lacan, following Heidegger, is tempted to ground language, or the symbolic realm, in that peculiar mendacity, or error, or untruth. The second part of *Being and Time* (especially paragraphs 54–60) contains an analysis of the elusiveness of the quest for truth in terms of self-identity. Such a quest is based on a *Sich-Verhören*, a word that in German denotes at one and the same time our attempt to know the truth by taking the self into custody and interrogating it, and the failure of that attempt, since a mishearing or mistaking of what has been said is inevitable. Language gives the lie to the ego's capture of a specular identity just as it gives the lie to itself. The genuine logos is always a dia-logos; and the guardian spirit of the symbolic and differential realm is a Father barring the image's closure of dialogue, of stilling prematurely what one might call, after Hegel, the *elaboration* of the negative.

Yet to ground something in untruth is still to ground it. Is a true untruth better than an untrue truth? The dialectics become dizzying or Ibsenian. Truth (*vérité*) remains, moreover, an important word for Lacan, and Derrida objects to it, as Adorno to a Heidegger-influenced "jargon of authenticity." It might also be observed that the symbolic father (or Derrida's counterpart, the spectral mother), while a reformulation of Freud's dead primal father of *Totem and Taboo*, has no more clinical or verifiable reality than the "fair Lady of Shalott" in Tennyson's poem, who seems to be both victim and guardian of the specular capture Lacan posits. This allusion shows, however, that a *sort* of evidence exists, even if contaminated by the very realm—literature or art—being limited by scientific definition.

Derrida is very aware of this contamination, which he deconstructs rather than denies or delimits. He does not place language, by theoretical fiat, on the side of the symbolic and against the specular realm of the absolute or totalizing illusion. Language is not a "cause" that cures (a "talking cure") by drawing the mirror image into the discourse of the Other. Though Derrida views language as a School of Virtue chastening the eternally narcissistic ego, he sees no triumph of the therapeutic by means of a language that is itself infected by a sickness unto death he has labeled logo-centrism.

"I am half sick of shadows," says the Lady of Shalott, and turns from her mirror to the reality of advent. She did not know that by her avertedness, by staying within representation, she had postponed death. The most art can do, as a mirror of language, is to burn through, in its cold way, the desire for self-definition, fullness of grace, presence; simply to expose the desire to own one's own name, to inhabit it numinously in the form of "proper" noun, words, or the signatory act each poem aspires to be. Though Tennyson's Lady, unlike Mallarmé's Herodiade, "knows not what the curse may be" as she helps to weave Tennyson's language, the result is the same: a negative scene of nomination. She becomes in death what she was without knowing it in life: a floating signifier.

> Under tower and balcony,
> By garden-wall and gallery,
> A gleaming shape she floated by,
> Dead-pale between the houses high,
>   Silent into Camelot.
> Out upon the wharfs they came,
> Knight and burgher, lord and dame,
> And round the prow they read her name,
> *The Lady of Shalott.*

My reference to Tennyson suggests that a *sortie* from the textual involution of the French sphere is possible. Derrida has himself tried interpreting Poe, who is comparable to Tennyson, yet does not provide a true exit because

French commentary has been investing him since Baudelaire and Mallarmé. The trouble with Tennyson is that his poetic dream-work seems at first no work at all. It is so easy, so unlabored—deceptively "idle," to use a charged word of his own—when held beside Mallarmé's. Poem and lady remain immaculate though web, mirror, or spell may break. Such impassibility is perhaps part of the infection, an unresolved narcissism of festering lily or psyche. Yet this liaison between specular and poetic is precisely what fosters the illusion of completeness and so the attractive fetish we call a poem. For a moment the et cetera of language is absorbed into that fetish: remnant and rhyme coincide.

Derrida, however, does not allow himself even so much dallying with closure. The rhyming properties of language, the sonic rings and resonances always potentially there, are like Poe's "Bells" (cited by Derrida) and their telltale symptoms of a vertiginous *glissement* of language toward an uncontrollable echoing: a mad round of verbal associations or signifier-signifying signifiers. The anxiety roused by language *as* language is that this echoing movement cannot be economized, that it is a fluid curse, a telling that is merely that of time, whose wasting becomes a tolling: *Glas*.

His adventure is
having been *named*.
        Sartre, *Saint Genet*

. . . the difficulty begins with the name.
        Ralph Waldo Ellison, "Hidden Name and Complex Fate"

The subject too, if he can appear to be the slave of language, is all the more so of a discourse in the universal movement, in which his place is already inscribed at birth, if only by virtue of his proper name.
        Lacan, "The Agency of the Letter"

MY HYPOTHESIS, inspired by French reflections, that literature is the elaboration of a specular name, is not meant to encourage a new substantialism of the word. Since the specular name is always already a fiction—hidden or forgotten or canceled, or motivated unconsciously by a life that dies into allegory—it can determine autobiographical quests only in the manner of Plato's theory of anamnesis. The quest, as it becomes lifelong and remains indeterminate, recuperates esoteric traditions: stories about the magic of names, anagrammatic events of various kinds, scenes of nomination or annunciation, and generally, to steal the title of Karl Abraham's early essay, "the determining force of names."

Gershom Scholem has published a strange name fantasy of Walter Ben-

jamin's, written at Ibiza, Spain, in 1933.[8] It involves Paul Klee's picture
Angelus Novus (a personal icon for Benjamin, who owned it) and the ancient
tradition of the natal genius or personal angel whose name is hidden but who
represents one's true identity and secret self. Benjamin's allegory, close in
some respects to a Kafka parable and in other respects to a Baudelaire prose
poem, was deeply linked to his situation at that time: his troubled relation to
women, his Jewish ancestry, and his sense of being born under Saturn (he had
written *The Origin of German Tragic Drama* and was steeped in Baudelaire).
Scholem's beautiful and thorough interpretation has brought this out in a
definitive way, and I cannot add to what he has said.

My interest lies elsewhere; in Benjamin's fantasy as a particularly reveal-
ing example of how autobiography is determined by the idea of a hidden—
spectral or specular—name. I will quote only the opening paragraphs, which
constitute about half of this interesting document, but they suffice to show
how Benjamin verges on a complex scene of nomination: an angelus-
annunciation that turns not only on the magical force of an occult name but
also on what might happen when that name is or must be betrayed.

Agesilaus Santander

When I was born the thought came to my parents that I might perhaps
become a writer. Would it not be good, then, if not everybody noticed immediately that I was a Jew. That is why they gave me in addition to the name by
which I was called [*Rufnamen*] two further, exceptional ones, from which it
couldn't be perceived either that a Jew bore them or that they belonged to him as
first names [*Vornamen*]. Forty years ago no parents could have proved more
far-seeing. What they considered a remote possibility has come true. Except that
the precautions by which they meant to counter fate were set aside by the one
most concerned. That is to say, instead of making it public together with his
writings, he treated it as the Jews the additional name of their children which
remains secret. Indeed, they only communicate it to them when they reach
manhood. Since, however, this manhood can occur more than once in a
lifetime, and the secret name may remain the same and untransfigured only for the
pious, so to whoever is not pious the change of name might be revealed all at
once, with the onset of a new manhood. Thus with me. But it remains the name,
nevertheless, which binds together the vital forces in strictest union, and which
must be guarded against the unauthorized [*Unberufenen*].

Yet this name is not at all an enrichment of the one it names. On the contrary,
much falls away from his image when that name becomes audible. His image
loses above all the gift of appearing to be human. In the room I occupied in Berlin,
before he stepped—armed and encased—out of my name into the light, he fixed
his picture on the wall: New Angel. The Kabbala relates that in every instant [*Nu*]
God creates a numberless number of new angels, all of whom are only destined,
before they dissolve into nothing, to sing for a single moment the praise of God
before His throne. Such an angel the New one pretended to be before he would
name himself.

What emerges with startling clarity is the *aura* of being named or imaged. Benjamin also said: "Things made of glass have no 'aura'" ("Die Dinge aus Glas haben keine 'Aura'"). So the world he projects in his Romance of Being Named resists translucence or glassification: the very word "Agesilaus" strikes one as the opposite of the word "Glas"—it contains *g-l-a-s*, in fact, and becomes, as it were, its antonym. Recalling Benjamin's interest in anagrams, Scholem suggests that the title of his fantasy should be deciphered as "Der Angelus Satanas" (The Angel Satan), and he links it to the *New Angel* of Klee's picture that continued to haunt Benjamin. (See, especially, the ninth of his "Theses on the Philosophy of History," written not long before his death.) But one should add that the insistence of this picture in the writer's life is itself "demonic": it reveals a specular fixation on Benjamin's part, and seems to be transposed from German Romantic fiction or the Gothic novella. However we unriddle it, "Agesilaus Santander" remains an abracadabra phrase that aims at reviving the aura of names, or of a naming with ritual and fixative power.

I doubt, then, that this title is decipherable in a single way. The difference in sound shape, for example, between Agesilaus and Angelus (Novus) could foreground the syllable *laus*, to remind us of the Latin word for praise; if so, a relation might suggest itself between "Age"/"Ange" plus "laus" and the Kabbalistic angel whose essence is to praise God a single moment, an "*Augen*"-*blick*.

Other decipherings may be possible, but I will try only one more. Benjamin thinks of himself as a refugee: he has abandoned the orthodoxy of his fathers; he is in Spain, from which the Jews were expelled and a former home of the Kabbalists, whose mystical reflections on names was known to him through Scholem; the Nazis have come to power; and he ponders angels whose essence is not permanence but transience, whose newness is their nowness, or their flight from *Nu* to *Nichts*, as they praise and wait to be dissolved. Considering, then, that this scholar was doomed to wander, if not to flee, and that his major work had been on seventeenth-century German literature, might he not have remembered the poet of that era who took the pseudonym "Angelus Silesius" for his *Der Cherubinischer Wandersmann* (The Cherub Wanderer), a collection of epigrammatic mystical verses? "Agesilaus," though a real and not a made-up name, seems to scramble "Angelus Silesius" into a single word, and Santander could suggest the mixed Santa/Satanic quality of Benjamin the pilgrim or some desired relation to Southern (Spanish and Kabbalistic) rather than Northern spirit of place through the name of this town.

What we are given, then, is the aura of a name: "Agesilaus Santander" is the quintessence of an anagram rather than a univocally decipherable writing. The scrambling is permanent and the meanings we recover are fugitive constructions, like the "new angels" in contrast to the old. The name may even

Figure 20.   William Blake, Signature painting from *Milton*.

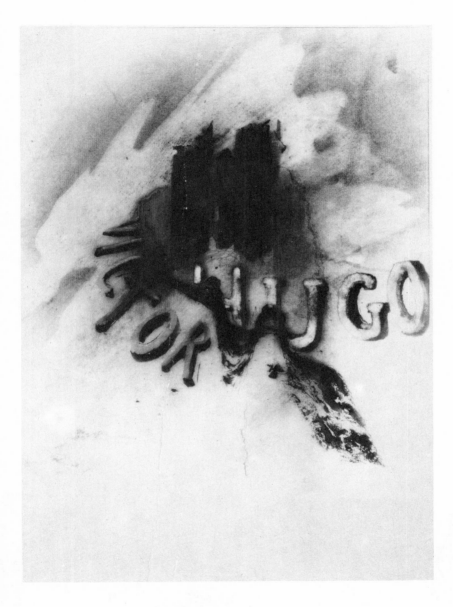

Figure 21. Victor Hugo, Signature painting. Photo Bulloz.

```
                    DANS

        FLETS           CE

            RE              MI

        LES                 ROIR

        SONT                    JE

        ME                      SUIS

        COM                         EN

        NON     Guillaume      CLOS

        ET      Apollinaire        VI

        GES                     VANT

            AN                      ET

            LES                 VRAI

            NE              COM

                GI          ME

                    MA      ON

                        I
```

Figure 22.   Guillaume Apollinaire, Name poem from *Calligrammes*.

Figure 23.   William Blake, Signature from title page to *Milton* (detail).

accuse the maker of the name: it is satanic also in that. For it stands as the product of an artificial mysticism that evokes an "aura artificiel" in the manner of Baudelaire's "paradis artificiel." It betrays a fallen aura, mere aroma of aura, the whiff of a Turkish cigarette and Eastern mysteries. Like "Xanadu" and "Kubla Khan" the name is an authentic fake, a given or proper name consumed by the imagination, the scar of a signature that belongs to no one. "Its traits had no human likeness." Benjamin's fantasy could be part of a book on hashish he meant to write. He continued to look, patiently and yet in flight, to the origin of all names in the garden God had planted eastward of Eden. Psychoanalysis: the Eden connection.

5 Words and Wounds

Hush! Caution! Echoland!

James Joyce, *Finnegans Wake*

ONCE there was a poet who wanted to be a doctor. But when he wrote his greatest poem he was already under the shadow of the tuberculosis that killed his mother and brother, and would allow him but a few years to live. Keats, writing *The Fall of Hyperion* in 1819, imagines a dream in which he confronts a High Priestess who is at once the ghost of his dead mother and the conscience of all the great poets before him who had wished for a role equal in importance to that of healing the sick. Moneta (the High Priestess) does not mince her words. She asks contemptuously:

> What benefit canst thou do, or all thy tribe
> To the great world? Thou art a dreaming thing;
> A fever of thyself . . .

Stung by the accusation, Keats tries to answer with a classic defense of poetry:

> . . . surely not all
> Those melodies sung into the world's ear
> Are useless: sure a poet is a sage;
> A humanist, Physician to all men.

Moneta then challenges him to distinguish between *dreamer* and *poet* (which is unfair, if one recalls that Keats subtitles his poem "A Dream"):

> 'Art thou not of the dreamer tribe?
> The poet and the dreamer are distinct,
> Diverse, sheer opposite, antipodes.
> The one pours out a balm upon the world,
> The other vexes it.'

The debate raises an essential question for those interested in the *value* of literature. Is there a healing power or "balm" in poetic words, or are they not

118

useless and pernicious, weakening our sense of reality, poisoning the mind with images of a world more wonderful—in terror or beauty—than the one we know? "Only the dreamer venoms all his days," is how Keats's Voice of Conscience, the High Priestess, puts it.

I began this chapter as though it were a fairy tale. For there is something naïve about raising the question of reality poisoning through the word. The fairy tale expresses a Realm of Woe or Wonder exempted by most from such a charge; and the Realm of Romance continues the fairy tale into "sophisticated" literature. Yet fairy tales, and the original folk tales, are full of the grimness of reality. Actual poisonings mingle with deadly or saving words: the mirror's reply to the queen in *Snow White*, or answers that dissolve malevolent spells. Derrida, moreover, in his essay on Plato's *Phaedrus*, shows that writing itself may be viewed as a poisoned gift.

He argues that Plato looked on writing as a drug whose effects could not be controlled: words are potentially good medicine (good letters, *bonae litterae*, cf. *Glas*, 290b, "Il est tout seul, sans aucune des bonnes lettres"), but when written down they become poison for the mind. Poison, because writing weakens memory and, correlatively, the filial nature of words, their reference back to a responsible, locatable source. The written text cannot be questioned like a speaker; it *orphans* words by depriving them of a voice that is alive and present. "The specificity of writing," Derrida alleges, "is related to the absence of the father." This absence is said to undermine the univocity of discourse by introducing words that are, at once, as weak as orphans who must be adopted and as strong as an unfathered, self-authorized voice. Derrida describes as follows the disturbing aura introduced into speech by the written sign:

> This *pharmakon* or "medicine," this philter that is at once remedy and poison . . . enters the body of discourse in all its ambivalence. This charm, virtue of fascination, power of sympathetic magic [*envoûtement*], can be—serially or simultaneously—beneficial or malign. The *pharmakon* would seem to be a *substance* featuring everything that words could imply concerning occult qualities, a cryptic depth that withholds its ambivalence from analysis and already makes room for alchemy, unless we go farther and recognize in it the antisubstance itself: that which resists every philosophical concept [*philosophème*], surplussing it indefinitely as nonidentity, nonessence, nonsubstance, and so proferring the inexhaustible adversity of its means [*fonds*] and absence of ground [*fond*].[1]

In short, with the advent of writing the very notion of substance receives a wound as incurable as that which afflicts Amfortas in *Parsifal*. But can Derrida's analysis justify a massive displacement of interest from signified to signifier? More precisely, from the conceptualization that transforms signifier into signified to those unconceptualizable qualities of the signifier that keep it unsettled in form or meaning? Is the force of the written sign such that every attributed meaning pales before the originary and residual violence of a sound that cannot be fully inscribed because as sound it is already writing or incision (German: *Riss*)?

Surely the fact that words are powerful is as important as that *written* words are powerful in a way that may be more basic still. There is a problem here, because *representation* (the realm of what is signified) and *rhetoric* (the signifying act that values oral performance) are seen as coconspirators. The rhetoric that interests Derrida derives solely from the specific power of the *written*: from texts in which language discloses its groundlessness and injures the notion of substance too well for a "cure of the ground." Traditional rhetoric, however, as the art of persuasion, relies on a smooth consensual calculus of means and ends. Specific verbal devices are isolated as if they effectively corresponded to specific mental or affectional states. (A modern version of this representational rhetoric is found in the Chicago Aristotelians.) As a highly sophisticated and teachable art this rhetoric has the same aim, if not the same lightness, as Nietzsche's *aesthetic*, which is said to keep us from a Dionysian stupor, from foundering absolutely (*zu Grunde gehen*).

For Derrida, the rhetoric of representation, especially when insisted on as a science, is a sham; it is not a science but a pragmatic and consensual exercise; one that can distract from the true cogency of speech by interposing a mechanistic model of communication. Like Heidegger, he wants to liberate language from a doctrinal effectiveness that is honorific rather than authentic, accommodating rather than awe-inspiring.

Yet that movement of liberation, that truer estimate of the way unaccommodated man uses language as something other than clothing—uses it, in fact, as anticustom or *anticouture*[2]—should not cheapen the mimetic and affectional power of words, their interpersonal impact. The Platonic dialogues are more than an exchange of words authenticated by the anticipation of Socrates' death. That death has, and has not, occurred: so it is with every author and his fictional representations. An affective and vulnerable motion of words is felt, as in novelistic encounters: between Stendhal's Lucien Leuwen and Mme de Chasteller, for example. The wrong move might spoil all; the inept word might embarrass the affair to the point of poisoning a relation that seeks a unique truth.

The problem, then, with antirepresentational theories—which try to free rhetoric from representational ends—is that they are more referential than they know: they have secretly declared what the *bad* magic is, even if they consistently and rigorously doubt that it can be remedied by the *good* word, or any word-cure whatsoever. For them the bad magic, the fatal charm, is representation itself, the very force and pathos of mimetic desire and envy.[3] These are questioned; yet writing cannot question them by means of the living voice; voice, indeed, is among the questionable charms. It has the insidious, deceptive effect of Keats's "Belle Dame sans Merci" who disarms the knight-at-arms by looking at him "as she did love / And make sweet moan." Her presence, like that subtly orgasmic sound, may be faked: Venus born of the foam, an enchantress born of words, she sings a "fairy's song" that could be the very ballad in which she appears. She leads, in any case, to absence—of voice too. "And no birds sing."

Antirepresentational modes of questioning disturb the alliance of signifier with signified by deconstructing a stable "concept" (the glue that holds them together), or by undoing the "unique" charm of particular texts: the illusion that they have a direct, even original, relation to what they represent. This second *intertextual* mode of questioning, which implicitly counters Plato's argument that writing must weaken memory (for it recalls other texts), yet affirms the argument emphasized by Derrida that writing is a sort of disaffiliation (a disclosure of the absence of a single father or unique logos)—this second mode of questioning shows that writing cannot be an antidote to anything except itself, that it questions its own representational claims by a repetition that phantomizes presence. For every voice with presence is already an inscription; already speaking from the realm of the dead, as if aware of the ancestral world, or having anticipated its own passing. Presence is thus a ghostly *effet de réalité* produced by words, and is dispelled by the same means.

Yet how good an antidote to the natural magic of representation is this repetition, or deconstructionist reversal, which claims that what seems to be a cause (*reality, presence*) is only, as in dreams too, an unfathomable effect? That when we talk of reality we are dealing with a metonymic charm, the substitution of cause for effect, or with an illusion of depth built up by the mirror-play of texts, by intertextuality?

I will try to show that the reality of the effect is inseparable, in literature, from the reality of words that conduct voice-feeling; this reality, in its discernible, empirical nearness, in its moral and mimetic impact, is the subject of "Words and Wounds." Since Derrida himself has stressed that the written sign is indefeasibly poison and cure, and that intertextuality also is radically ambivalent in that its mirror-play at once builds up the reality-effect and deconstructs it, this final chapter becomes, among other things, a counterstatement to Derrida. It is not a refutation but rather a different turn in how to state the matter. A restored theory of representation should acknowledge the deconstructionist challenge as necessary and timely, if somewhat self-involved—that is, only occasionally reflective of analogies to its own project in religious writing and especially in literary writing. A child acts, Wordsworth wrote, "As if his sole vocation / Were endless imitation"; and in Derrida there is the same strong "antitheatrical prejudice," an attempt in the name of maturity (and no longer of religion) to put away childish things, to overcome imitation. Yet the bonding involved in imitation may indeed be "endless" and therefore self-subverting. Having done my best, in previous chapters, to "translate" Derrida, by developing his exemplary contribution to literary studies, there remains, like the phenomenological *residue* Husserl sought as his certainty, this affective, reorienting issue of wounding, healing words.

To avoid the misunderstanding that mine is a "postcritical" theory like Paul Ricoeur's in *The Symbolism of Evil*, I exclude religious and magical views, though they are always implied. I am also cautionary rather than assertive about the clinical aspects of word-therapy. My aim is limited to the issue of words and wounds as imaginative literature evokes it: the poets themselves depict most clearly the power of words, their balm and venom. With the exception however, of the vital if obscure notion of "catharsis" or "purification,"[4] and Freud's exploration of the mechanism of jokes, we do not have anything useful with which to understand the tremendous impact words may have on psychic life.

Where to begin? We know something about the power of words. As Othello charms Desdemona with the "witchcraft" of speech, so Iago maddens Othello using similar means. Byron rhymes "word" and "sword" in a famous stanza of *Childe Harold* (III.97). And William Blake, in the midst of his visionary poem *Milton*, allows us to glimpse a part of its pathetic and human base:

> armed with power, to say
> The most irritating things in the midst of tears and love
> These are the stings of the Serpent!

That words can wound is a much clearer fact than their healing virtue, and Blake punctures his sublime rhetoric to make that point. Yet his poem remains the best evidence that words may redress the wound they inflict.

This brings us back to the question: what kind of a physic is literature? Shakespeare depicts madness in a faithful yet bearable manner. He does not analyze or define Ophelia's disturbance: he represents it. But in the way some illnesses are self-limiting, so with his representation of madness. The disease and the cure come together in the poet's web of words. Shakespeare has Ophelia speak a "balmy" language, one that exhibits her wound by denying it or by dressing it with the plaster of euphemistic words. How desperately her "language of flowers" evokes a realm of *simples*, that is, of herbs with a magical or medicinal effect strong enough to heal the perturbed soul:

> There's rosemary, that's for remembrance. Pray, love, remember. And there's pansies, that's for thoughts. . . . There's fennel for you, and columbines. There's rue for you, and here's some for me. We may call it herb of grace o' Sundays.
> (*Hamlet* IV.v.)

If only words were simples, like those flowers, or Ophelia's childlike tone! But they are maddeningly complex and equivocal. Literature, I surmise, moves us beyond the fallacious hope that words can heal without also wounding. They are homeopathic, curing like by like in the manner of Spenser's "myrrh sweet bleeding in the bitter wound."[5]

Hypothesis

Let me suppose, then, that words are always armed and capable of wounding: either because, expecting so much of them, looking to them as potentially definitive or clarifying, we are hurt by their equivocal nature; or because the ear, as a *psychic* organ, is at least as vulnerable as the eye. What is unclear about the first hypothesis is why we should expect so much of words. This overestimation, which may turn of course into its opposite, into contempt of talk, can suggest that words themselves caused the hurt we still feel, as we look to them for restitution or comfort. (Where there is a word cure, there must be a word-wound.) I prefer, initially, the other way of stating our hypothesis, that within the economy of the psyche the ear is peculiarly vulnerable or passes through phases of vulnerability. The "cell of Hearing, dark and blind," Wordsworth writes in *On the Power of Sound*, is an "Intricate labyrinth, more dread for thought / To enter than oracular cave."

Every literary interpreter and some psychoanalysts enter that cave when they follow the allusive character of words, their intentional or unintentional resonance. "Strict passage," Wordsworth continues, describing the auditory labyrinth, "through which sighs are brought, / And whispers for the heart, their slave. . . ." Othello's speech fills Desdemona's ear: "[She'd] with a greedy ear / Devour up my discourse." There exists a lust of the ears as strong and auspicious as the lust of the eyes about which so much has been written since Saint Augustine. The two are, doubtless, interactive: the Story of the Eye (as in George Bataille's pornosophic novella of that title) always turns out to be, also, the Story of the Ear. But whereas "the ineluctable modality of the visible" (Joyce) has been explored, especially by analysts interested in primal-scene imagery, the ineluctable ear, its ghostly, cavernous, echoic depth, has rarely been sounded with precision.

Wordsworth's phrase "strict passage" points to the "constricted" or narrowing, and therefore overdetermined, character of the sounds that make it through, but also to a moral dilemma. The ear must deal with sounds that not only cannot be refused entry, but penetrate and evoke something too powerful for any defense: Wordsworth depicts it as akin to sexual lust or the intoxication of a blood sport, "shrieks that revel in abuse / Of shivering flesh." The *percéphonic* power of poetry, song or music to undo this wounding, "warbled air, / Whose piercing sweetness can unloose / The chains of frenzy, or entice a smile / Into the ambush of despair," suggests a sweet piercing that counters or sublimates a bitter one.[6]

"Chains of frenzy" tells us how close we are to the theme of madness; "the ambush of despair," how close to depression. Moreover, to "entice a smile / Into the ambush of despair" is ambiguous, and "unloose / The chains of frenzy" has a double-negative effect that may undermine rather than reinforce the idea of a liberating cure. These phrases, like the ear itself, are constricted; and even should we attribute them to the highly condensed diction of the Pindaric ode Wordsworth is imitating, this merely rehearses the entire problem, and does not bring us a step forward. For while imitation can be therapeutic it can also be compulsive, or expressive of a word-wound that still binds the hearer. At this point, obviously, clinical material on the relation of word and wound should be adduced; not being a clinician I shall fall back on literary examples.

Names and Wounds

No wound, which warlike hand of enemy
Inflicts with dint of sword, so sore doth light
As doth the poysnous sting, which infamy
Infixeth in the name of noble wight.

So Spenser, in the sixth book of *The Faerie Queene*, alluding to the wound inflicted by the Blatant Beast, enemy to courtesy and an allegory of slander. Psychology and anthropology agree on the importance of the motif of the *wounded name*. To achieve a good name, or to maintain it, has been a motivating force in both heroic and bourgeois society. Fiction corresponds to life at least in one respect, that slander and rumor—hearsay more than sightsay—determine the drama of errors that besets reputation. A peculiar and powerful theory of what it means to redress a wounded name is developed by Jean-Paul Sartre. He speculates that his contemporary Jean Genet, a convict turned writer, fashioned his identity out of a "dizzying word" addressed to him when he was a young boy.

The word was a vocative, an insult, a common malediction like "You thief!" flung at him by a foster parent. It is said to have made Genet aware of his radically disinherited state. Genet was an illegitimate child; his mother too was a thief, or of the insulted and despised. That word, therefore, became a call, a vocation, which helped not only to establish a negative identity for Genet but redeemed that of his mother through him. A chance remark becomes, in Kierkegaard's words, "the infernal machine which sets fire to the tinder which is in every soul" (*Journals* of 1837). Genet grows up a thief, a homosexual, a powerful writer with his own magnificat and gospel: John ("Jean") becomes Saint John. The connections are very complex, and it takes Sartre a voluminous and immensely dialectical book to account for what happened.[7]

I am interested more in the elements that go into the theory than in the exact truth-value of the theory itself. What in Sartre's view wakes the child to the problem of identity is not a sight, an ocular fixation as in the famous case of Augustine's friend Alypius, but an *aural experience*. [8] Moreover, the verbal structure of what Genet hears is a vocative, and ritually it approaches an act of nomination or even annunciation. Identity is bestowed on Genet by a ghostly scene of naming, a curse that is taken to be an act of grace.

Genet, then, is word-wounded by the insult or curse, but he makes it into an identity badge by a psychic reflex, and then by a lifelong fixation. And the tinder, the inflammable material rendering him vulnerable, is the very absence of an authentic name—an absence that provokes endless fillers or substitutes.

"You thief!" while only one such filler, happens to suggest that Genet must *steal* a name if he is to own one. For "Genet" is a name that points to the absence of a proper name: it is the mother's surname, and suggests moreover a figurative origin because it is a "flower of speech." Genet, that is, takes *genêt* ("broom flower," Leopardi's *ginestra*) and turns it via his ritualistic and flower-name-laden novels into a literal figure; into something truly his own.

"Flowers of speech" is a designation for the figures or metaphors that characterize literary discourse and distinguish it from apparently straighter or more scientific kinds of writing. Genet links figurative language, or flowers of speech, with the "language of flowers," or the principle of euphemistic and courtly diction. He depicts what are criminal events in the eyes of bourgeois society by a sublime and flowery style. No one is deceived, of course: the reader sees through to the sordid wound and understands this inverse magnificat.

Yet Genet steals back his name less to magnify himself than the absent mother, or rather mother tongue. His name, elaborated, founds an artificial diction that is his only source of healing and salvation. [9] This stealing back of a name is not as naïve or exceptional as it seems, for those who have a name may also seek a more authentic and defining one. The *other* name is usually kept secret precisely because it is sacred to the individual, or numinous (*nomen numen*): as if the concentrated soul of the person lodged in it. A perilous or taboo relation may arise between the given (baptismal) name and the truly "proper" name, and then a psychic search unfolds for this hidden word under all words, this spectral name. [10] It is a quest that often leads to the adoption of pseudonyms and nicknames, and even to anonymity. So Malcolm Little erases his family name by an X curiously like the mark of the illiterate slave yet which he endows with a redemptive meaning:

> The Muslim's "X" symbolized the true African family name that he never could know. For me, my "X" replaced the white slave-master name of "Little" which some blue-eyed devil named Little had imposed upon my paternal forebears. The receipt of my "X" meant that forever after in the nation of Islam, I would be

known as Malcolm X. Mr. Muhammad taught that we would keep this "X" until God Himself returned and gave us a Holy Name from His own mouth. [11]

Twelve years later Malcolm gives himself that name, or a likeness of it from his own mouth, when he calls himself, having gone on a pilgrimage to Mecca, El-Hajj Malik El-Shabazz.

Names against Wounds

I would to God thou and I knew where a
commodity of good names were to be bought.

(1 Henry IV I.ii.80–83)

"Call me Ishmael." We don't know the original name of Melville's storyteller. Perhaps there is no original name; or it is extirpated, like Pierre's family name by the end of the novel *Pierre*. Only the act of self-naming is apparent. Yet the adopted name is not empty, of course: if not as grand as Malcolm's, it still points East, to the Orient or the Oriental tale, to a lost origin, or a compelled sympathy with exile and alien.

"Ishmael," the ending of which rhymes (at least approximately) with the first syllable of Melville's name, may evoke the homophonic word *male*. The trouble with this kind of rhyming, this illness of the ear, as W. H. Auden once defined poetry itself, is its infectiousness. What if "Melville," when heard with "Ishmael," elicits further echoes? Male(v)ill, Male Will? Or should the ear pick the assonance of *el* as the deceptive key, in its Hebrew meaning of "God" and its Arabic force as definitive article: the "the"?

Though names, then, may be medicinal, they are never simples. Yet the class of proper nouns, or names, comes closest to having the magical force of certain herbs called *simples*. Why should that be?

An observation of Saussure's on the semiotic structure of names may be relevant. Whereas ordinary nouns, *table* and *chair*, not only point to a referent in the world of things but rely on a concept of table and chair in order to signify, names seem to be pure signifiers that have only a referent (the indicated person or place) but no concept or signified. We cannot conceptualize names unless we make them into trade names (like Kodak) or type names (like calling a woman a Griselda). [12]

Naming does have a spectral dimension if we seek to perpetuate someone by calling a child after him. (It makes the child a *revenant*, Freud said). A gap opens, nevertheless, between name and meaning; and this is clearest in etymological speculation, extending from Isidore of Seville or the *Legenda*

Aurea (*Golden Legends of the Saints*) with their beautiful and fantastic elaboration of the meaning of saints' names, to Derrida's punning transformation of *Hegel* (the philosopher's name) into *aigle* (the bird's name).

This would suggest that words become magical the closer they move to the status of pure signifiers or name equivalents. Approaching the character of an "acoustical image" (Saussure), names accrue the mystery or magic of an *Open Sesame*. We can make believe that there exists a naming formula, anagram, or password to pierce the opacity of our ignorance and open the treasure house of meaning.

Perhaps the second-order discourse we call "metalanguage"—terms of art, explanatory or classifying schemes, words about words—aspires to the same magic, that of pure signification. Here Linnaeus, who established the Latin nomenclature for plants and animals in his *Systema Naturae* (1735; 10th ed., adding animals to plants, 1758), was crucial. The virtue of flowers (birds, etc.) joined with the virtue of Latin to produce a (re)naming of all creatures in a manner at once scientific and fantastic. The Latin appellation, in its very strangeness and strictness, merely succeeded in putting the vernacular name of the creatures in relief, and so induced a more complex verbal consciousness, a doubling of signifying systems: the Latinate order (itself binominal in Linnaeus) as well as the common language designation. But the wound inflicted on language, through this propagation of names, analogous to the wound inflicted by Linnaeus's discovery of sexual characteristics in plants (on which his nomenclature was partially based, and which gave a shock to the "language of flowers")—this wound proved fortunate in some respects. The new, more complex name could be used as a stronger potion for the perturbed spirit. Take Christopher Smart's liturgy, which, aware of Linnaeus, impresses the various names of the creatures as if to heal language itself after its fall from simplicity:

> Let Shallum rejoice with Mullein Tapsus barbatus good for the breast.
> For the liturgy will obtain in all languages.

> Let Johnson, house of Johnson rejoice with Omphalocarpa
> a kind of bur. God be gracious to Samuel Johnson.

> Let Adna rejoice with Gum Opopanax from the wounded root
> of a species of panace Heracleum a tall plant growing to be
> two or three yards high with many large wings of a yellowish
> green—good for old coughs and asthmas.[13]

I don't think we can know the "smart" that "Christopher" bore, except to say on the evidence of the text before us that it had to do with his sense of "existimation," a word that seems to conflate *exist*, *estimate*, and *esteem*. "For my existimation is good even among the slanderers and my memory shall arise for a sweet savor unto the Lord." The wound dressed or redressed is associated with naming, and this would not exclude, of course, the "smart" of love or the "smart" use of words to achieve or reestablish reputation.

So naming and the problem of identity cannot be dissociated. So literature and the problem of identity cannot be dissociated. Literature is at once onomatopoeic (name-making) and onomatoclastic (name-breaking). The true name of a writer is not given by his signature, but is spelled out by his entire work. The bad or empty name or nickname may be countered by the melodious or bardic magic of art:

> There is nothing in a name. The name Menschikoff, for instance, has nothing in it to my ears more human than a whisker, and it may belong to a rat. As the names of the Poles and Russians are to us, so are ours to them. It is as if they had been named by the child's rigmarole, *Iery wiery ichery van, tittle-tol-tam.* . . . At present our only true names are nicknames . . . We have a wild savage in us, and a savage name is perchance somewhere recorded as ours. . . . I seem to hear pronounced . . . [the] original wild name in some jaw-breaking or else melodious tongue. (Thoreau, *Walking*, 1862)

"Look with thine ears" (King Lear)

The motif of the wounded name, which at first seemed rather special, leads into the crucial problem of self-identity and its relation to art and writing. But let us also consider the issue from the reader's point of view.

It may prove hard to say anything definitive about the capacity of words to wound. Or about the obverse effect, their medicinal, defensive qualities. The whole theory of defenses, originated by Freud, is involved in metaphor, and becomes ever more elaborate. Moreover, we have to recognize that hearing—a receptive and, as overhearing, involuntary act—is already within the sphere of hurt. We are in bondage to our ears as to our eyes. We are all like Shakespeare's Emilia in *Othello* (V.ii) when it comes to the aggressing power of words. Emilia to Iago: "Thou has not half that power to do me harm / As I have to be hurt." That statement is itself a converted threat and suggests how much depends on hearing what is said in what is being said.

Yet this is where the study of literature enters. Reading is, or can be, an active kind of hearing. We really do "look with ears" when we read a book of some complexity. A book has the capacity to put us on the defensive, or make us envious, or inflict some other narcissistic injury. When literary critics remark of literature, "There's magic in the web," they characterize not only what distinguishes the literary from the merely verbal, but what distinguishes critical from passive kinds of reading. Critical reading, then, which almost always leads to writing, allows us to estimate words as words, to use rather than abuse their affective powers, to determine as well as be determined by them. These things are obvious, and I feel preachy repeating them; but too often we conceive of reading as a scrutiny of content or form rather than more generally of the status of words in the psyche and the environing culture.

What active reading discloses is a structure of *words within words*, a structure so deeply mediated, ghostly, and echoic that we find it hard to locate the *res* in the *verba*. The *res*, or subject matter, seems to be already words. Even images, as Freud noticed in his analysis of dreams, turn out to have the form of a *rebus*, or words (parts of words) that appear in the disguise of things. These reified verbal entities must then be translated back into the original sounds, like a charade. But words themselves, of course, may reify, by being taken too literally or absolutely. Psychoanalysis, with its emphasis on the overdetermined or ambivalent symbol, and semiotics, with its disclosure of the radical obliquity of signification, undertake to correct that abuse.

Writing and reading of the active sort are certainly homeopathic vis-à-vis the "wound" left by literalism *and* the "wound" that that literalism seeks to cure: equivocation. The search for the absolute word, or minimally for the *mot juste*, is like that for the good name. There is bound to be a noncorrespondence of demand and response: an inadequacy or lack of mutuality that relates to our drive to make words into things. However precise words may seem, there is always understatement or overstatement, and each verbal action involves itself in redressing that imbalance.

"*Nothing*" *as the* Mot Juste

Take Cordelia's famous "Nothing," which sets going one of the bloodiest of Shakespeare's plays. It is only ponderable when we think about the status of words. Cordelia exercises, of course, her power of nonreceiver, of not responding to a "Speak" that would enjoin the very words to be spoken. But within this paralegal situation her "Nothing" raises a more basic issue. Lear wants to exchange power for love; initially words of power for words of love. Cordelia's reply contains not only a judgment that the quality of love cannot be constrained but that there may be something disjunctive in language itself that makes such an exchange—or reversal, if Lear, who wants to "crawl unburdened toward death," desires a licensed regression to childhood—as unlikely as reconciling love and power in the real world. Lear's fiat, his quasi-divine command, remains naked of response, therefore; and since the original fiat in *Genesis* was answered not only by obedience ("Let there be. . . . And there was") but also by recognition and blessing ("And God saw it was good" "And God blessed. . . ."), Cordelia's "nothing" has, in its very flatness, the ring of a curse.

Lear gives all, Cordelia nothing. The disproportion is too great. In Lear's view, order itself is threatened, and his great rage is just. But order, here, is the order of words, the mutual bonding they establish. Lear is asking no more than his daughter's blessing; which is, moreover, his one guarantee in a situation where he is about to divest himself. And instead of word-issue Cordelia utters something that sounds as sterile to him ("Nothing will come of nothing") as a malediction. It is painful to recall how much of the ensuing drama is curse, rant, slander, and impotent fiat:

> Hear, Nature, hear: dear goddess, hear:
> Suspend thy purpose if thou didst intend
> To make this creature fruitful.
> Into her womb convey sterility,
> Dry up in her the organs of increase,
> And from her derogate body never spring
> A babe to honor her
>
> (I.iv.265 ff.)
>
> You nimble lightnings, dart you blinding flames
> Into her scornful eyes! Infect her beauty,
> You fensucked fogs drawn by the pow'rful sun
> To fall and blister
>
> (II.iv.160 ff)
>
> Blow, winds, and crack your cheeks! rage! blow!
>
> (III.ii.1)

Cordelia's "Nothing" proves to be sadly prophetic. It exhibits the power of words in seeming to deny them.[14] As such it may be representative of all word-wounds, given or suffered, as they approach the status of *curse* or the incapacity to *bless*. Perhaps our speculations are becoming a shade more definitive.

Curse and Blessing

"I will not let thee go, except thou bless me." And he said unto him, "What is thy name?"

Gen. 1:32.27 f

[He] in the porches of mine ears did pour
The leperous distilment

Hamlet I.v.63–64

Curse and Blessing are among the oldest types of formalized speech. Like oaths and commandments, to which they are akin, they seek to bind the

action of those to whom they are addressed, yet unlike oaths or commandments they are resorted to when legal instruments are not appropriate or have
failed. Legal codes may contain curses as a reinforcement or obversely seek to
limit a curse—but it is clear that curse and blessing have a psychological
aspect, as well as a legal or ritual role.

Supposing the psyche demands to be cursed or blessed—that it cannot be
satisfied, that it cannot even exist as a namable and conscious entity—as ego
or self—except when defined by direct speech of that kind, then we have a
situation where the absence of a blessing wounds, where the presence of a
curse also wounds, but at least defines.

Perhaps direct speech itself is the problem here, the desire for a fiat, an
absolute speech act. The evil eye, for instance, as in *The Ancient Mariner*—
the "glittering" eye or "stony eyes / That in the moon did glitter"—is surely a
curious form of that direct speech which is so condensed that *sema* is *soma*.
(Perhaps all "images" have a similar structure.) It "shoots" with as unerring an
effect as the crossbow with which Mariner killed albatross. Time is punctured
in this poem of intolerable moments of stasis, which also features as its speaker
a constricted persona. Curse is primary, blessing secondary; the one must be
drawn out of the other, like story and story time out of a negative and arresting
fiat. The very desire for a fiat is at the heart of this compulsive narrative, with
its fit-like motion.

I have inferred a verbal cause, or placed the wound in the word. But it
turns out that by *wounding* I mean principally the expectation that a self can
be defined or constituted by words, if they are direct enough, and the traumatic consequences of that expectation.[15] To quote from *Othello* once more,
". . . the bruised heart was pierced through the ear." Moreover, because the
demand to be cursed or blessed stems from the same source, and life is as
ambivalent in this regard as words are equivocal, the psyche may have to live
in perpetual tension with its desire to be worded. It may turn against as well as
toward words. The equivocations put into the mouth of Shakespeare's clowns
or fools are, thus, a babble that breaks language down because it cannot draw
a "just" or "definitive" statement out of the crying need to curse or bless or to do
both at once.

> "Do you hear *how Fury sounds her blessings forth?*"
> Aeschylus, *Eumenides*[16]

Lear opens with something like a curse, a decreating as well as a deflating
word. Ordinary language, influenced perhaps by literary stereotypes, teaches
us to think of "a father's curse" and "a mother's blessing." It is as if the action
of *Lear* strove toward "a mother's blessing" but could only attain "a father's
curse."

Shakespeare, in fact, is so puissant because he is explicit, because every-thing becomes utterable as direct speech. There is an Aeschylean and cathar-tic quality in him absent from most other poets. The defining wound is always before us, in every brazen word. And the dramatic action is as direct as the words. When Edgar, disguised as Tom o'Bedlam, meets Gloucester, his blind and beggared father, he utters a foolish cry that manages to word a terrible wound. "Bless thy sweet eyes, they bleed" (*King Lear* IV.i.54).

This outrageous pun, one of several about eyes, suggests on the basis of a link between "blessing" and "bleed" (the etymological meaning of blessing is to mark with blood in order to hallow) that *since* the eyes bleed, *therefore* are they blessed. Shakespeare moves repeatedly toward imagining the worst in the form of a divestment, a making naked, a making vulnerable, of which one symbol is this castration of the eyes. But when Shakespeare calls on that darkness, in his play's general *fiat nox*, the curse the action labors under can still generate a bearable blessing.

Blessing and curse, euphemism and slander, praise and blame under-mine statement. However neutral or objective words seem to be, there is always a tilt of this kind, produced by the very effort to speak. There are those who must curse in order to speak, and those who must bless in order to speak: some interlard their words with obscenities, some kill them with kindness expressions. These are the extreme cases that suggest how close we are to muteness: to not speaking at all unless we untangle these contrary modes. Their tension is, for the purpose of literature at least, more basic than any other; and it needs no witch doctor or psychiatrist to tell us that despite our will to bring forth unambiguous issue, words that point one way rather than the other, we remain in an atmosphere as equivocal as that of the witches' chorus in *Macbeth*: "Fair is foul and foul is fair / Hover in the fog and filthy air."

Let me also refer to Aeschylus's *Eumenides*: how, by a retrospective myth, it founds a city-state on a transfiguration of the cursing principle. The judicial process instituted by Athena is merely a breathing space or asylum in the play, like the navel stone or her idol. The real issue is the breathless rush of the Furies, unremitting, unrelenting.

> We are the everlasting children of the Night,
> Deep in the hall of Earth they call us Curses.

The final chorus, therefore, has to convert the Curses into an energy that is equal and contrary. It must honor the Furies in terms they understand, which affirms them in their onrush, their dark and eternal function:

> You great good Furies, bless the land with kindly hearts,
> you awesome Spirits, come—exult in the blazing torch,
>   exultant in our fires, journey on.
> Cry, cry in triumph, carry on the dancing on and on!

Flowers of Speech

How thoroughly the human condition is a verbal condition! The medicinal function of literature is to word a wound words have made. But if we have learned something about the limit of poet as medicine man, we have also learned something about the limit of all verbal expression. Objectivity in language is always a form of "You great good Furies": a neutralizing or musicalizing of badmouthing. The very production of speech may depend on a disentangling of blessing and curse, on the outwitting of that eternal complex. Everything we say has to bind the Furies in the fetters of benevolence. Flowers of speech, as Baudelaire made explicit (laying the ground for Genet), are also flowers of evil. These equivocal flowers or figures characterize the literary use of language.

I give two examples of how a great writer outwits the intolerable tension of curse and blessing, and founds a language of his own that enables, and sometimes disables, ours.[17]

In *Finnegans Wake* James Joyce's (or Jeems Joker's, as he signed himself) hero is HCE. This acronym, though given various interpretations, may be a truncated reversal of E-C-H-O, reinforcing HCE's name of "Earwicker." The ear does become ineluctable in this book, which is the extended ballad of *Perce-Oreille*. Joyce methodically exposes the vulnerable ear by showing the unvirginal or contaminated state of language. In his "mamafesta" no phrase remains simple. Sexual innuendo subverts or thickens every sentence, as it often does in Shakespeare. Words *are* jokes: they betray their compound or compoundable nature; they are not from eternity but rather created and adulterated, of equivocal generation, beautiful in corruption. "In the name of Annah the Allmaziful, the Everliving, the Bringer of Plurabilities, haloed be her eve, her singtime sung, her rill be run, unhemmed as it is uneven!"

Yet here the wounded name is joyfully plural. Language has suffered a fortunate fall ("O fortunous casualitas"). Blasphemy is reconciled with good humor, and lust sings in obscene echoes that perpetually hollow and hallow this prose, as in the following "joycing" of the language of flowers:

> Bulbul, bulbulone! I will shally. Thou shalt willy. You wouldnt should as youd rememser. I hypnot. 'Tis golden sickle's hour. Holy moon priestess, we'd love our grappes of mistellose! Moths the matter? Pschtt! Tabarins comes. To fell our fairest. O gui, O gui! Salam, salms, salaum! Carolus! . . . I soared from the peach and Missmolly showed her pear too, onto three and away. Whet the bee as to deflowret greendy grassies yellowhorse. Kematitis, cele our erdours! Did you aye, did you eye, did you everysee suchaway, suchawhy, eeriewhigg airywhugger?

An ancient belief held that there was in nature a "general balm" (John Donne, "A Nocturnal upon St. Lucie's Day") with the virtue of sealing all wounds. A related group of superstitions considered excretions like sweat or blood or even excrement as therapeutic. Joyce releases into language a "Thinking of the Body" that would be unthinkable but for a "language of flowers." Literature sweats balm, and heals the wound words help to produce.

My second example is an episode from *King Lear*. In act IV, scene vi, Lear enters "fantastically dressed with wild flowers." The scene is marked by ear-piercing puns as well as moments of terrible pathos. At one point Lear's rambling language, itself tricked with wild figures, culminates in the dialogue:

> *Lear.* . . . Give the word.
> *Edgar.* Sweet marjoram.
> *Lear.* Pass.

What is being reenacted by Lear in his traumatized and defenseless condition is a type-scene of defense: getting past sentinel or guard. Also being reenacted is the first scene of the tragedy, his command to Cordelia, the "Speak" that led to "Nothing." But Edgar plays along, and the password he gives is taken from a language of flowers close to the mother tongue. "Sweet marjoram." Literature, as figurative language, extends that password.

The Language Exchange

> The stutter is the plot
>
> Charles Olson, on Melville's *Billy Budd*

Edgar's word *recognizes* the game Lear plays; its meaning resides in this act of recognition rather than in its semantic appropriateness. It is not quite a nonsense word, but almost any word would have done. That it is drawn from the language of flowers converts the royal, now all-too-human, challenge into a childlike game, like riddle or charade. Infancy is close: the king still leads, but as "His Majesty, the child." That "marjoram" is a near-palindrome, related to vernacular feelings or beliefs, aids this sense of a redemptive word that has retained a link with childhood. To keep talking, in this situation, is not only to allow Lear to keep up appearances but to maintain a trust in words themselves. *La séance continue.*

Such speech acts remind us how much responsibility is on the respondent, on the interpreter. Dialogue itself is at stake, and the medium becomes the meaning at this crucial point. Literary speech, quite obviously, is not eloquent for the sake of eloquence; if eloquence plays a part it is because mutism, the failure to speak or to trust in speech, is never far from the deceptive flow of words. Every strong instance of verbal condensation is as much a stutterance as an utterance and skirts aphasia, like a riddle.

A word, then, on riddles. Do they provoke a response or silence? Riddles divide into a silent and pointed part (the presumed answer) and a periphrastic and expressed part. They have been called a simple form (A. Jolles), but they are rarely found except as components of developed and complex literary structures. Lear's "Give the word" is like the demand of the sphinx, and yet very unlike, since the implied riddle is so general (life as the mystery, Lear's fate as the mystery) that any word of recognition, of response, might do. We realize that even in less pathetic circumstances this contradiction between word as meaning and word as act of speech prevails. For do we not address many situations with words that are essentially passwords: signs of obeisance or identity or mutual recognition? When Lear tests Cordelia and her sisters, the word he demands, the giving of it, seems all too easy. A verbal satisfaction is necessary, as in a rite of passage; and the link between survival and readiness of speech is publicly affirmed.

Wit, the presence of mind in words, is the opposite of a failure to speak. Yet wit, pointed or periphrastic, is often felt as a wounding of language, of "natural" language. Wit is called for in moments when words might fail as meanings: when the code is unknown, or when it is in such danger of devaluation that it must be rescued by surcharge. Love produces such dangerous moments. It beggars words, as Cordelia knows, yet it continues to demand them. The language of love can become, therefore, a cliché, as in the periphrastic language of flowers; or it can fall pointedly silent.

Goethe's commentary on his own *West-East Divan* (imitations of Oriental poetry) includes a section entitled "Exchange of flowers-and-signs" ("*Blumen- und Zeichenwechsel*"). The flowery diction associated with Oriental style is shown to be a necessity rather than a luxury. It brings things and words into a single system of signs, and so facilitates the exchange of feelings. The diction, or lover's discourse, is established in the following way. The lover sends a gift to the beloved who must pronounce its name and figure out which among the rhymes of the word designating the received object completes the message and solves the riddle. "*Amarante: Ich sah und brannte*" ("Amaranth: I saw and burnt"). "*Jasmin: Nimm mich hin*" ("Jasmin: Take me with you"). "*Seide: Ich leide*" ("Silk: I suffer").

It is not possible—though Goethe refuses to say so openly—to guarantee this private code, for the code is always in the process of being established. It depends on a twofold gift: that of flower or precious object, and of responsive word ("Give the word"). Thus the skill or will of the interpreter is essential: his skill in playing, his will to find or else to impose a meaning. Goethe calls this literary game a "passionate divination." It brings ear and wit into play and may occasionally create a short novel by the establishing of a "correspondence"—Goethe means, probably, of word and thing, of word and rhyming word, as well as of the feelings of the lovers in a letterlike exchange.

There are analogies here to the interpretive situation generally. Emily Dickinson could call her poems "my letter to the world"; so the literary text or artifact is a gift for which the interpreter must find words, both to recognize the gift, and then to allow it to create a reciprocating dialogue, one that might overcome the embarrassment inspired by art's riddling strength.

Goethe does not develop these analogies; nor does he explore an important contradiction. Each exchange of things-and-words involves a private language that at its limit is intuited; and each exchange involves the contrary, a public and highly stylized word-system. He simply apposes these two aspects. In the next section of his commentary on the *Divan*, entitled "Codes" ("*Chiffer*," literally "Ciphers"), he reports how in Germany around 1770 the Bible was so crammed into educated youth that many were able to use it wittily to "consume Holy Writ in conversation." It was possible, therefore, to "make a date with a book" ("*ein Buch verabreden*"), that is, by a ciphered system of allusions to make it the textual intermediary to a secret rather than open exchange of thoughts. This conversion of a public system of signs into a sort of *trobar clus* also enters Goethe's section on the exchange of flowers and words, for Goethe suggests there that the "passionate divination" he has described could return to the speechlessness in which it began: the silence not of embarrassment, concealment, or evasion, but of perfect divinatory understanding. "Lovers go on a pleasure trip of several miles and spend a happy day together; returning home they amuse themselves with charades. Not only will each guess immediately what is intended as soon as it is spoken, but finally even the word that the other has in mind, and intends to cast into the form of a verbal puzzle, will be anticipated and pronounced by immediate divination."

How much Goethe takes for granted! That love needs secrecy and a code, or a special system for exchanging tokens and thoughts, is not explicitly related by him to any psychic or social condition (to the danger of persecution, for example, or the sense of self-esteem). He describes what is, not the reason for it, since this Eastern phenomenon is understandable in the West, and has its own parallels there. Goethe is valuing established genres as archetypes or primal phenomena. He does not wish to repristinate or orientalize what is current in the West, because his understanding can intuit the same pattern there without an explanatory or analytic scheme. He sees the genre in the idea of it.

Yet this intuitive procedure (Goethe sometimes called it *Anschauung*) papers over the problematic breach between private and public language, as between intuition and expression. It is necessary to reflect that the happiness associated with being intuitive, with the intimacy of understanding or being understood, may be the obverse of not being understood, or of having been understood and betrayed. Betrayal, breach of promise, breach of trust, misunderstanding, misinterpretation, persecution—these are equal realities. The more intimacy, the more potential misery. Goethe's "correspondence"—the exchange and the system of meaning built on it—cannot be guaranteed, intellectually or socially. It is always a dangerous liaison.

One should not talk of understanding, therefore, as if it were a matter of rules or techniques that become intuitive and quasi-silent. There is, of course, an internalization; but the life-situation of the interpreter has to deal with riddles as well as puzzles: what is sought is often the readiness to take and give words in trust, rather than the answer to a problem. "Language," Iris Murdoch writes, summarizing Sartre, "is that aspect of me which, in laying me open to interpretation, gives me away." Troth rather than truth: the ability to exchange thoughts in the form of words; to recognize words of the other; or to trust in the words to be exchanged. One breaks words with the other as one breaks bread. What is guaranteed by recognition, in the political sphere too, is the language exchange itself.

The art of divination Goethe describes can indeed be cultivated by parlor games whose purpose is to diminish shyness or strangeness. But this parleying aspires to recognition and not to absolute knowledge; and indeed, there is much to be said against being known by others. The other's words, which may be riddling—inherently so, if words are not subject to pure anticipated cognition—these words are allowed to create a value by means of our own reception, by our formal willingness to interpret them. Each transaction consists of exchanging words for words as well as sounding out the words in words.

Partial knowledge is the *normal* condition, then, of living in the context of words. Words themselves help us tolerate that state: recognition must precede as well as follow cognition. To put the entire emphasis on the cognitive function (*connaissance*) will damage the recognitive function (*réconnaissance*) and the language exchange as a whole. Values continue to be created that may seem purely ritual, or not entirely perspicuous. Even when art represents a movement from ignorance to knowledge, it is not for the sake of clearing up a simple misunderstanding or emending the human mind in an absolute manner. Tragedy, for instance, hinges on a mistake that questions the very possibility of language exchange: in the case of Oedipus, a human understanding mistakes the language of the gods. Oedipus is faced with an oracular statement that forces interpretation to go blind, to stumble along by means of tense, stichomythic exchanges, "epitaphic comments, conflictingly spoken or thought" (cf. Melville, *The Confidence Man*, chap. 2). The oracular allows no development, no capacious response.

Or tragedy flows from a scene of nonrecognition, deliberate rather than the result of ignorance or mischance. In Faulkner's *Absalom, Absalom!*, Sutpen (unlike King David, who laments aloud over his estranged son, calling him by name) refuses to recognize a son of mixed blood, to accord him the honor of the family name. That nonrecognition may expose its victim to the elements, to a position outside the law. The very possibility of having one's words regarded may then be lost.

Simple misunderstandings are not the proper topic for comedy, either, and barely for jokes. Jokes based on mistaking the sense of words produce a forced laughter; to be effective they must be deliberate and dangerous *jests*, and so they skirt tragedy again. Therefore, in *Love's Labour's Lost*, Berowne is sentenced by his lady Rosaline to a year's jesting in a hospital ("To move wild laughter in the throat of death"), so that his indiscriminate mockery, his "wounding flouts," may heal instead of hurt, or proving impotent will be self-cured. In a jest the laughter is ultimately on words: at the expense of language that can't and must be trusted.

Trusting and words: there is a scene of passionate divination in Tolstoi's *Anna Karenina* (part 4, chap. 13). Levin is together with Kitty, who had rejected him at the time she was in love with Vronsky. Their conversation turns on the vanity of arguments and what causes them to end so suddenly. Levin explains his theory to Kitty who "completely grasped and found the right expression for his badly expressed thought. Levin smiled joyfully: he was so struck by the change from the confused wordy dispute with his brother and Pestov to this laconic, clear and almost wordless communication of a very complex ideal." Kitty then goes to a table covered by a green cloth in preparation for a game of cards and begins drawing on it in chalk. Levin wants to propose to her a second time, and is afraid to do so in so many words; yet he must find the words. A private game follows in which he chalks on the same cloth the initials of the words he wishes to utter; she divines them and answers with initials of her own. He takes the lead, but Kitty overtakes him; and though the initials are a kind of stutter, because of Kitty's intuitiveness the potentially hurtful words are twice-born, and the language exchange is restored:

> He sat down and wrote out a long sentence [in the code]. She understood it all, and without asking if she was right, took the chalk and wrote the answer at once. For a long time he could not make out what she meant, and he often looked up in her eyes. He was dazed with happiness. He could not find the words she meant at all; but in her beautiful eyes, radiant with joy, he saw all that he wanted to know. And he wrote down three letters. But before he had finished writing she read it under his hand, finished the sentence herself, and wrote the answer: "Yes."[18]

Interpretation

... je m'immisce à de sa confuse intimité
Mallarmé

What I have called, conscious of the metaphor, a word-wound has so far been discussed under two aspects. The word-wound may be real, in the sense of being a wounding word that is actually experienced or fantasied. Lacan launched the clinical myth of a mirror phase or specular image; and I have argued that there exists also the fantasy of a specular or spectral name, which is at once degraded and recalled by the wounding word, its "negative" force of characterization. But there is a second aspect of the word-wound that does not lend itself to empirical evidence, or to the creation of a clinical myth that seems to uncover that evidence. Language itself, in the extruded form of words, their equivocal, fallible, tricky nature, exposes us to continual psychic hurt. There is no pure intuition: the interpreted words remain to be interpreted. There is no complete internalization: words cannot be whited out by truth, because understanding cannot take place without trust or troth. But these are as fragile as the words that commit us to them.

Interpretation, in short, is not only intuitive, it is also counterintuitive. It is not difficult to appreciate this after the advent of psychoanalysis: the analyst may find the "wrong" word or meaning for the gift (dream or artifact) brought by the other.[19] In one contemporary theory, that of Harold Bloom, reading is therefore viewed as misreading and analyzed into a number of richly perverse conformations of text and reader. Interpretation has the same kind of "error" for its subject as tragedy or comedy: not a simple error that can be corrected (though this error also exists), but an inevitable error, whether deliberate or unconscious, arising from an ideal of communication that seeks absolute intimacy.

Kitty's reading of Levin is highly intuitive. Interpretation and intuition converge to produce an exceptional intimacy. But the result is that words become mere tokens. The lovers exchange glances as well as words, and the context points to something beyond speech. Here, as the language exchange is restituted, words are paradoxically left behind.

The reason may be that for Tolstoi there is a religious as well as an erotic intimacy, which bases capable understanding on a preunderstanding associated with benevolence; and between this benevolence and human love there is, ideally, no fissure. (That is why the relation between Anna and Vronsky is so disturbing, so obtrusive: *their* love cannot, does not, remain in the sphere of benevolence.) Levin is shown to be Kitty's scholar from the beginning of the chapter, when he joins the conversation in the drawing room by fulfilling "the promise he had made her, of thinking well of and always liking everybody." Or, to quote from 1 Corinthians 13, "Charity thinketh no evil."

That basic principle of Christian hermeneutics appears dramatically in the opening pages of Melville's *The Confidence-Man*. A mute stranger holds the Corinthian sentence up, chalking it on a slate in its various Pauline versions. He exhibits it adjacent to a placard "offering a reward for the capture of a mysterious impostor, supposed to have recently arrived from the East." A further contrast is furnished by "a gaudy sort of illuminated pasteboard sign" hung up by a barber and reading "NO TRUST."

The Pauline doctrine in 1 Corinthians 13 and 14 contrasts speaking in tongues with prophesying. The former uses unknown languages, perhaps divine, the latter uses a language, equally divine, but addressed to the human understanding. Paul seeks to regulate the speaking in tongues rather than to repress it utterly. The problem is put as one of housekeeping or churchkeeping: order, decency, avoiding confusion, building the community are stressed. No tragic epistemic division is suggested between human and divine in terms of language; tongues are known or unknown, and the known is preferred to the unknown because it is "edifying" in its effect. The charity Paul considers more important than speaking in tongues—the charity that, indeed, makes Christian interpretation possible—is applied to the gift of tongues itself.

But in Melville a tragicomic question arises, because there are many tongues and no interpreter. The appearance of the mute stranger and potential interpreter takes place on April Fool's Day, and close to Pentecost. True, the tongues we hear in those opening pages are not tongues precisely in the Pauline sense, but that all speak in a known character is only a semblance, for within it a split has widened to become Babel. Having no interpreter means now the lack of a communitarian or edifying principle. Even the Pauline hermeneutic of charity or benevolence is but one tongue, idiolect, or sociolect. Melville mocks the interpretive and religious principle of charity by having a "gentleman" propose a Society, called The World's Charity, which might levy "one grand benevolence tax upon all mankind" in order to do away with the present system of promiscuous contribution. It sounds like a parody of Tolstoi before Tolstoi—though not before Emerson.

The opposition between Basic Trust (Charity, Benevolence) and No Trust is like that between Blessing and Curse, and it seems unresolvable in a world where imposture is rife. So ambiguity prevails, and all sorts of inscriptions or extruded words jostle each other. The author is no longer Prophet or Interpreter, but the place where this confusion of tongues becomes conscious.

In Tolstoi there is a greater, an almost musical feeling of Basic Trust, which suffers and absorbs contraries and does not worry excessively about the imposture at the very heart of things. It is no accident that the conversation Levin joins concerns itself with communal systems and the "choral principle." The dream of community and the dream of communication are closely linked; perhaps as closely as words and music; yet words are often more jarring, and so Levin remarks, moving toward Kitty and away from the controversy: "What I miss in the country [is] music." The recurrence of music as theme or metaphor (Levin will later find a deeper music in the country) reminds us that interpretation is not an argument that resolves arguments or dissolves words. It brings understanding without agreement, or charts the very space between understanding and agreement.

The Conscious Ear

. . . semel emissit volat irrevocabile verbum
                              Horace

                              I wake
To caress propriety with odd words
                              Geoffrey Hill

It would take me too far to discuss the different consequences for literature of intuitive and counterintuitive concepts of interpretation. The religious tradition would have to be brought in: both the contemporary developments in hermeneutics and such older issues as inspiration and accommodation. We seem to have no settled concept, at present, of Interpreter or Critic. The Interpreter was often defined as one who translated strange or unknown tongues into an edifying idiom, or one who could bring contradictory words and aspects of a text into harmony. The Critic was often defined as one who distinguished the authentic text from the inauthentic, or authentic from inauthentic in a text. What has happened is that those who call themselves interpreters now claim an edifying or reconciling function even when the language of the text is well-known; while the critics adopt a methodically suspicious or doubtful attitude toward the value of every text, secular or sacred. These functions, moreover, mingle confusingly within the same person. At best, as I have suggested, critical readers resist the intuitive and accommodating approach, and chart the space between understanding and agreement: they defer the identification of agreement with truth by disclosing how extensively understanding is indebted to preunderstanding.

If critical reading becomes self-reflective, and explores this area of preunderstanding, an embarrassing question arises. Why can't we look into ourselves without the the detour of a text? Why does pure self-analysis seem beyond our competence? Some philosophers, including the Heidegger of *Being and Time*, who contributed greatly to defining preunderstanding, actually think it is possible, that there is self-exegesis. But Heidegger saw that even without a text there would be a text, that is, our own reflections in written or writeable form; and this suggests, then, that to look into ourselves is always to "look with ears."

To put it differently: critical reading is not only the reception (*Rezeption*) of a text, but also its conception (*Empfängnis*) through the ear. No doubt the crossover from silent eye to reactivated ear is partly inspired, partly necessitated, by print culture: Andrew Marvell, celebrating (in imitation of Brebeuf and Lucan) the invention of writing, calls it the ingenious art of "lending an ear to eyes"; Rilke imagines "yeux sonores" in one of his French lyrics. The idea of a conception through the ear counterbalances that of the immediacy of the eye, suggesting an antiocular internalization or transformation: "O Orpheus singt! O hoher Baum im Ohr!" ("O Orpheus sings! O high tree in the ear!" Rilke, *Sonnets to Orpheus*).

So we substitute one mode of intuition for another. Yet reading, especially in a print culture, is often used to blind the ear. In principle, the gospel injunction "He that has ears to hear, let him hear" should be facilitated by reading as dissemination (a word I prefer to the evangelical notion of "proclamation" or *Verkündigung*), but the sowing of words by means of the written page seems often to harden the ear, as if indeed "when they have heard, Satan comes immediately and takes away the word that was sown in their hearts" (Mark 4:3–20). And that is why poetry makes its curious alliance with critical reading, in order to reactivate the ear. Both are auscultations that have the capacity of putting us on the alert toward the silence in us: the wrongly silenced words as well as the noisy words that get in their way and prevent thoughtfulness. The words of a text, in their silence, are but divining rods to disclose other words, perhaps words of the other.

This movement of discovery is not for the sake of discovery alone, as if a source—a secret source—could magically satisfy the act of reading. There *is* a secret, but it amounts to the fact that words have interiority, that there is always a *sermo interior*; and critical reading allows us to describe that interiority, to estimate words as words, to see them as living in and off us.

Let me concentrate on this recovery of words in their silence. It is by no means a resolving or transcending of the word as wound. The hurtful element in words cannot be removed, because it is at once potential and potentiated: that is, intrinsically associated with an ear that cannot chose but hear, and with *some* actual experience of wounding words. It may be possible to discover the very words, but it is not necessary to do so; what *is* necessary is the assumption that the experience of a word-wound is inevitable and will affect our relation to words generally. Reading, from this point of view, is an activity full of suspense, seeking yet avoiding a penetrating word, a definitive *de te fabula narratur*. The suspense provided by a good plot satisfies that need openly: our wish to find that which is (not) to be heard.

That which is (not) to be heard is a secret. But this secret, in literature, is a formal assumption, even a device to be motivated. The secret as lost object, grail, primal scene, spectral and identifying name, seductive charm, becomes from the aspect of a literary reconstitution of language an *a priori* or intentional rather than imitated object. It has the status of an anticipation, something known yet not as a direct object; something known as if always already forgotten, and therefore present only preconsciously, absentmindedly. In a psychologistic era, of course, it is tempting to suspect a compulsive or infantile element in the *a priori* secret. Formalization, moreover, does not help to remove so just a suspicion. For the insistent verbal play, the acrostic, alliterative, cipherlike hide-and-seek that intrigues us in literary texts (the gradation, for example, of O/Orpheus/O/hoher/Ohr in Rilke's verse) provokes an erection of the ear (Rilke's *"Tempel im Gehör"*) by means of nonsensical or spectral sounds.

If like causes like, then words are caused by words, or by something "like" words. Yet a theory of literature cannot simply point to the multiplication and interelaboration of texts. The literary word is a language-sensitive word; and so the question arises what this language-sensitivity may be. Here I return to my initial hypothesis, that the ear is vulnerable, or passes through phases of vulnerability. Its vulnerability is linked—the actual causes being obscure—to real or fantasied words, to an ear-fear connected with overhearing; or to the word as inherently untrustworthy, equivocal, betraying its promise of immediacy or intimacy.

When these two types of vulnerability converge the effect is especially traumatic, and the ear becomes intolerably conscious. This happens, for instance, when a solecism is thought to have occurred. A specific phrase becomes the focus, one that shocks or shames, and at the same time the very hope of acceptance and intimacy is compromised.

The fear of committing a solecism is probably worse than the fact, but it should not be dismissed because it is so trivial a cause for language-sensitivity. Walter Pater reports in his essay on Prosper Mérimée: "Gossiping friends, indeed, linked what was constitutional in him and in the age with an incident of his earliest years. Corrected for some childish fault, in passionate distress, he overhears a half-pitying laugh at his expense, and has determined, in a moment, never again to give credit—to be for ever on his guard. . . ." (*Miscellaneous Studies*). The collocation of gossip, overhearing, a (perhaps) imagined slight or embarrassment, is very distressing: the reaction seems so extreme, and one wonders why *Pater* gave credit to it. Was it really the solecism or a similar fault, a mere *faux pas*, that explains it?

Geoffrey Hill's *King Log* (1968) contains a cycle of poems attributed to an apocryphal Spanish poet, "Sebastian Arrurruz: 1868–1922," who is said to have abandoned society after a solecism was discovered in his first publication. Well, if Pater can choose a French surrogate, Hill can choose a Spanish one; but it may be too easy a way out to characterize as an English disease this "anxiety about *faux pas*, the perpetration of 'howlers,' grammatical solecisms, mis-statements of fact, misquotations, improper attribution."[20] That a national identity is specified is the important fact: it may be a displaced identity but it confirms that a particular language-centered culture rather than a general sense of honor is involved. The writer's sense for language is so exquisite, so care-ful, that we think he is dealing not with language but with a virginal or sacred object. Henry James had the very same sense of adjacency, in words, of *faux pas* and fatal step.

Style may be a *continued* solecism. The language-sensitive writer makes the transgression habitual. His cryptic or idiosyncratic manner is an expressive mask. Publication itself is a sort of public self-exposure, fraught with danger to oneself and others. "Infection in the sentence breeds." "Could mortal lip divine / The undeveloped Freight / Of a delivered syllable / 'Twould crumble with the weight" (Emily Dickinson). The casual phrase may contain a carnal blunder. Certain authors, like Coleridge or Flaubert, exhibit a related or parallel anxiety: that of an uncontrollable stream of consciousness, as in the compulsion to confess or a nervous seizure. "One feels images escaping like spurts of blood," Flaubert wrote in his letters. When this attack takes the form of words, does it resemble the phenomenon of "speaking in tongues"?

The word is only "like" a word in these situations: it is divinely stupid or a ghostly sound. It is, precisely, a word that does *not* contain other words, that therefore cannot be translated, interpreted, and enter the language exchange. The structure of words within words, while complicating the process of understanding, also founds the possibility of interpretation or of exchanging word for word. To this process, however, there is no bottom, and so no truth in the ordinary sense. Writing goes on and on, and always at risk. "I write, write, write," said Mme. Blavatsky, "as the Wandering Jew walks, walks, walks."

One tries to find ways, of course, to allay this infinitude; and these ways constitute what is called "closure." But there is also a foreclosure, this glossolalia, that takes words away before they can be profaned by the language exchange. They are withdrawn from circulation as soon as uttered; they are at once elliptic and epileptic. They suggest an intransitive intimacy, or the wish to encrypt in oneself the womb—the maternal (paternal) source—of verbalization. If that is so, we understand better the importance of inner dialogue, of chatter and babble developing into verbal thought. But verbal thought remains a precarious self-probing, as in Gertrude Stein's prose, so close to a beginning that never ends, to an insistently euphemistic and cryptic style that is both a continued solecism and inviolably retiring: "Always then from the beginning there was in me always increasing a conscious feeling loving repeating being, learning to know repeating in every one, hearing the whole being of anyone always repeating in that one every minute of their living. There was then always in me as a bottom nature to me an earthy resisting slow understanding, loving repeating being" (*The Making of Americans*). In the beginning was the Word, and the Word was the loving repeating being, the ticking of the watchful heart, the soft namings of a maternal voice.

Soft Names

I have been half in love with easeful Death,
Call'd him soft names in many a mused rhyme.

Keats

In the fairy tale *Dornröschen* (*Sleeping Beauty*), the language of flowers triumphs explicitly over a curse, yet the curse can only be deferred or temporized. Story and story time are drawn out of a deadly, arresting fiat. The death of the princess is commuted into a hundred-year sleep; and time itself—the shock of puberty perhaps—is becalmed into a continuation of dormancy, the end of which is the kiss of a prince instead of a deadly prick. The wound that makes the girl a woman also makes her into a rose to be plucked despite potentially dangerous obstacles and defenses. Whether the wounding event is puberty, the death of a child or childhood, or lies in the imagination itself that cannot stop brooding over such passage moments (child/woman, life/death), stories like these allow time—rather, our consciousness of it—to recover its "rosy fingers" after a traumatic interruption. The "soft name," when temporalized, becomes a "repetition in a finer tone."

The principle of euphemism, then, can be extended into other literary areas. But is there a contradiction in the fact that Modernism has stressed the demythologizing and demystifying force of literature? How can irony, say, be understood as a "soft name"?

Modernism, it is now generally recognized, was a movement that tried to bring together, in a mutual and saving compact, myth and irony, visionary figures of speech and verbal refinement, the rhetorical aspect of art and discriminating tonal values. Paradox, ambiguity, irony, dramaticity—these were the tough sinews, the inner iron, of a poetics that gave up nothing of literature's bardic daring despite the doubts and subversions of enlightened thought. Romanticism, it is now also recognized, was a greater Modernism, or its fountainhead: a place where this compact was still struggled for and not yet a formalism.

It is not surprising, then, that flowery poems from the *Roman de la Rose* to the odes of Keats, or Blake's and Shelley's extensions of the language of flowers—*The Sensitive Plant* could be described as a flower fabliau—have gradually been valued as more than adolescent fantasies; and that the inner, indefeasible relation of pastoralism to poetry continues. It may be good to view even irony as a varietal and sophisticated sort of blessing, enabling the poet to speak. Irony, in this sense, is a counter-genre to satire, which is explicitly cursing, castigating, corrosive.

Yet satire itself may be a reduced form within the history of laughter, within a "destructive humor" not directed simply against isolated aspects of life but against all reality, against the finite world as such (see Mikhail

Bakhtin, *Rabelais and His World*). As we read Bakhtin on Rabelais we become aware of the lawlessness of a laughter that finds its nourishment and its victims anywhere. The laughing truth degrades power by curses, abusive words, ridicule, obscenities, grotesqueries, the carnival spirit. The opening of Melville's *The Confidence-Man* (see also above), though not funny in the conventional sense, seems to participate in "Easter laughter" (the *risus paschalis*). It is social satire, of course, but recalls, like the later Joyce, "the disintegration of popular laughter, after its flowering in Renaissance literature." What Bakhtin labels as "genres of reduced laughter"—humor, irony, sarcasm—develop into stylistic components of serious literature, and especially of the novel. Bakhtin states explicitly that the most extensive form of reduced laughter after Romanticism is irony; and that contemporary analyses have not respected its link to the culture of folk humor, or unreduced, revolutionary laughter.

The whole question of our modern seriousness—that Matthew Arnold, for example, would doubt Chaucer's greatness because of his lack of "high seriousness," or that Nietzsche, who reinvented the "feast of the ass" in *Zarathustra*, could never quite manage more than a strained or manic gaiety—that question threatens to bracket the period of approximately 1740 to 1920 as neoclassical, often despite itself. Laughter survives, of course, but chiefly in censored, oppositional or popular forms. "In the new official culture" that Bakhtin says arises with French Classicism and the absolute monarchy, and extends into the Enlightenment, "there prevails a tendency toward the stability and completion of being, toward one single meaning, one single tone of seriousness. The ambivalence of the grotesque can no longer be admitted."

Irony seems a Lilliputian device against the background of satire and popular, picaresque, revolutionary laughter. But what Bakhtin mostly regrets is, I believe, the purging vigor of the vernaculars, as they come into their own as literary and developed tongues. In Melville and Mark Twain we still feel some of that vigor; and even in some contemporary writers, in Joyce, Beckett, and Pynchon. Irony, no doubt, does develop an alternate tradition, less dependent on "mother wit" or sheer language libido. But this does not mean that irony is less radical than radical laughter. When a language has stabilized it develops a different kind of elasticity, perhaps more subversive than the self-enriching mutability of the developing vernaculars. Irony, as Kierkegaard saw, is like a "secret trap door through which one is suddenly hurled downward," not to a definite depth but uncertainly, infinitely. It comes so close to a silencing truth that the very possibility of comic catharsis is put in doubt.[21] Language can give the lie to everything, but if it gives the lie to itself, can it survive as its own anatomy?

Irony as language giving the lie to itself yet still relishing its power can be illustrated by a series of modern examples. Consider first how soft-naming does not cancel the cruelty of Blake's "The tender maggot, emblem of immortality." Consider next Mallarmé's *"la faute idéale de roses"* (from "L'Après-midi d'un faune"), so vibrant a disappearance of the thorn or thorn-inflicted wound it may refer to that these become indeed more ideal than real, and the fault is transferred to a language that can achieve such a delusive and provoking effect. As the thorn is removed from the rose it becomes a thorn absent from all flowers, and wounds imagination by its very absence. Imagination itself seems to need that potentiated thorn or that symbolic wound. The irony here is not a property of phrase or periphrasis, but of the rhetorical consciousness[22] that subverts creatively the link between poetry and euphemism, between poetry and the language of flowers. As a final example, take Wordsworth's famous brief lyric:

> A slumber did my spirit seal;
> I had no human fears;
> She was a thing that could not feel
> The touch of earthly years.
>
> No motion has she now, no force;
> She neither hears nor sees;
> Rolled round in earth's diurnal course,
> With rocks, and stones, and trees.

No flowers here; and language itself barely speaks. But the very subject of the first stanza is an inward, unconscious power of idealization that deludes the poet into thinking Lucy is immortal. That delusion is named a "sweet dream" and "Nature's gentlest boon" in the opening poem of the Lucy cycle; it is present here not in the form of flower and star imagery, or other soft namings, but as a spontaneous, proleptic movement of the mind. Proleptic, because it forestalls the opposite thought, the thought of death, one that emerges—but again curiously forestalled—in the second stanza. The poet-slumberer (himself the *Dornröschen*) wakes into the consciousness of death, but instead of pity or terror or the human fear that had been elided, his recognition expresses an irony: now indeed Lucy cannot feel "The touch of earthly years." She is what she seemed to be. His image of her has come true, but as a curse he may have laid on himself unawares.

Yet is it a curse? This *Kindertotenlied*, this lyric about a child who dies before womanhood is confirmed, recalls Rilke's Eurydice, always already lost. *"Sei immer tot in Eurydice"* ("Be always dead in Eurydice," *Sonnets to Orpheus*). Rilke invents a new branching of lament and praise; really a new poetic eloquence; but Wordsworth quiets language till myth is present only in "unheard" form and irony is the point-zero between curse and blessing. Wordsworth's second stanza, as if a new sealing had taken place, is tonally unreadable, leaving consciousness where it was, strangely intact like Lucy herself. Irony leans toward silence. The language of flowers recedes into a language of nature too deep for tears but also too deep for ears. It does not cry or cry out: there is no "final finding of the ear" (Wallace Stevens). This muteness, however, is close to a mutilation, a "blinding" of the ear and an ultimate defense against the unquiet imagination.

Closure

Thy firmness makes my circle just
And makes me end where I begunne.

John Donne

Ein jeder Geist sieht nicht weiter als in seine Mutter, daraus er seinen Urkund hat und darinnen er steht; denn es ist keinem Geist möglich, in eigener natürlicher Macht in ein ander Prinzip zu sehen und das zu schauen, er werde denn darinnen wiedergeboren.

Jakob Boehme[23]

Wordsworth's lyric rescues itself from silence. It borders on silence because, giving death its due, not wishing to curse or to bless, it is tempted to say nothing rather than something, and because, in saying something, it seals the wounded spirit in its own way. The issue of how words have a healing effect returns at this point; and even if terms like "heal" and "wound" seem too literal the experience encompassed by them is clear enough.

Perhaps we should adopt Wordsworth's expression "seal." For we can give a modest description of the healing influence of words by associating the latter with the sense of closure. Something is resolved; impulses are assuaged; haunting persons, words, or images are rememorated until we are calmed and refreshed rather than exhausted. The line between this calm that seals and renews, and apathy or vacancy of spirit, remains precariously indeterminate—in Wordsworth too. His lyric, I have said, may induce the thought of a muteness close to mutilation. Yet aesthetic concepts from catharsis to objectification, from harmony and balance to integration and defensive mastery, stress the recreative power of art. The history of art, moreover, shows that certain forms have had the virtue of inducing closure; of allowing the mind something to rest on. A happy end or a luminous meaning emerges; disagreeables evaporate; things are unified; above all, the eye is quieted like an ear, "by the power of harmony."

Yet who has succeeded in going from closure understood formalistically (how poems end, how we know a sentence is complete, how the universal shines through, how sound echoes rather than exceeds or subverts sense) to art in its immediacy? Closure remains a relatively bloodless notion; and placing it in a historical field that includes concepts of harmony, identity, and reconciliation is correct rather than enlightening.[24] Precisely at this juncture the impotence of aesthetic theory is felt: we are tempted to become associative and metaphorical, asserting, for instance, that the feeling of closure conveyed by Wordsworth's "A slumber" is due to his converting a wounding thought of death into a beautiful irony.

Our best critics have always demystified this turn to beauty. In *The Philosophy of Literary Form* Kenneth Burke insists that beauty is accompanied by an "element of *discomfort* (actual or threatened) for which the poetry is 'medicine'"; even more plainly, that "threat is the basis of beauty." He thinks his way back to the eighteenth-century distinction between the beautiful and the sublime, which he diagnoses as a falsification intended to save beauty from threat or terror, qualities now assigned to the sublime. Beauty for him is simply an effect that points to the "medicinal" or "symbolic" action of art.

Burke's interpretive readings erode forms of closure in art and concepts of beauty in aesthetic theory: he exhibits their illusory or purely conventional force and opens a text so much that to close it again may seem impossible.[25] Must the aesthetic charm, then, gradually disappear from the interpreted work of art, and leave us but an intellectual construct, one with a fascinating, fallacious, teasingly evasive mode of being?

We have two problems now. One we started with: can the feeling of closure be related not only to the formal structure of art, but also to art as essential human experience? The other deals with the pressure of criticism on art, and on itself.

Criticism in the past was able to invent new types of closure to stem the drive toward endless interpretation. That drive is dangerous because it suggests that the interpreted object (Scripture, and now art) is but a means to reflection and might be replaced by pure mind or pure ideology. So plain-sense theories counter allegoresis; and concepts of organic form or Classicist distinctions between genres and media prevent limitless experimentation or the intellectual erosion of art and its internal differences. Nietzsche's Apollonian "gaiety" or "levity" also intends to save the illusion of beauty from a groundless truth. Today we retain an interest in the "aesthetic" dimension of art, however undefinable it may be; we also tolerate presentational and often meretricious devices that restore immediacy, though not always beauty, to art: the spectacular new setting of a play, the transposition of one medium into another, at times the invention of new media. Given our broadened historical perspective, however, there is now more helplessness about interpretation as it stretches toward an infinity of statements and contaminates art itself.

The recent emphasis on intertextuality may even disable the question of how closure is possible. Nothing, according to this theory, not even meaning, closes writing off; the spirit cannot master the letter. Words disclose words as well as meanings, and the insistence of the "letter" in the "spiritual force" of any structure that makes a claim of truth on us is a scandal as great as the psychoanalytic plague. It may indeed be a version of the latter, though stimulated not only by Freud's clinical findings but also by the "scene of writing" that his restless, self-revising works exhibit.

I can say little about the loss of innocence that has afflicted interpretation and the melancholy of a mind that cannot find satisfaction unless closure takes the form of verifiable truth. I have sometimes thought that design perception and interpretive brooding were separate gifts, and that we have genuine criticism only when interpretation reinforces perception or does not erode it. The ideal act of criticism would circle back, in that case, to the design (the partial or complete object) that stimulated it; and this circling would take on a form of its own, closed enough to be recognizable as a form, open enough to be extended. In this manner the form of interpretation rather than a positive content would respect the sense of closure associated with art.

Let me leave aside the problem of closure in criticism. I am principally concerned with the relation of closure to the undefined, therapeutic element in art. Closure is a sealing with healing effect. Yet Freud showed in his analysis of mourning that there is psychic "work" to be done before the healing closure can take effect. (To call it "work" does not necessarily imply it is against nature but that it takes time and that psychic energies are spent in ways not immediately scrutable.) Is the "work" of art similar to the work of mourning, though bordering on the area designated by Freud as melancholy rather than mourning; where the lost object cannot be fathomed with certainty, and the possibility of closure is therefore threatened?

I have presupposed a word-wound, one that has to be imagined rather than positively identified by the "work" of art. A convergence of Freud's special theory of mourning with a general theory of literature suggests that the affective power of the word itself is what is enclosed by the literary work. The circle of art, like that of interpretation described above, limits the word as the subject of an endless brooding. Closure formally seals that brooding (whether it is in the service of separation or recuperation); it sets a limit to brooding, or makes that limit coincide with imagining it.

Closure as positive negation—as setting a limit through imagination to imagination—is not, of course, a punctual act, as when one writes THE END. It includes that moment, but in significant art there is a generalized sensitivity to premature closure, one that delays or multiplies endings and creates limits that prove to be liminal. In poetry this "sense of an ending" embraces rhythm, rhyme, and caesura: what happens toward the end of a line, or rhythmically within the line, until lineation itself is affected. The compounding or tmetic disjoining of words is also involved. Other literary features, the creation of personae, the use of metaphor and allusion, could also be viewed as playing a larger sense of closure against its punctual forms: *fuis . . . la pointe assassine* has more implications than even Verlaine could give it.

Take, as an important case, the personae of art: they raise the question of who is speaking and to whom, where the words now put on stage or page have started, whether a person speaks in his own person or is a *porte-parole*—the question raised equally by dreams, and by Lacan's reflection on a "discours de l'Autre." On the one hand, there is no word without a bearer of that word; whose word it is makes a difference and helps to potentiate it. On the other hand, words survive their speakers and reappear in and even usurp other speakers by a process of transference similar to metaphor. Every speaker is potentially a *bouche d'ombre*, like Moneta; for the same reason ghostly, schizoid, or supernatural themes are natural to art; and anonymous words, such as writing on the wall, graffiti, oracles—which have some affinity with the "impersonality" or "indeterminacy" of art—rouse the fear (a thrilling fear) of the abyss in all words whose resonance haunts us and must be appeased.

Having come this far I feel that everything remains to be explained. If there is always a haunting word or voice—"What can that music be?"—is it "in principle" that of the mother, as Boehme suggests? How literally are we to understand that "primal knowledge" or "principle" (*In principio* is the Vulgate's version of the Bible's first words, "*In the beginning* God created the heavens and the earth")? Wordsworth is more cagey than Boehme when he describes in "Tintern Abbey" a "serene and blessed mood" in which "we see into the life of things." Even should we construe "the life of things" as a periphrasis, gentle and expansive, for a continuing maternal presence—a presence celebrated in the "Blessed Babe" passage of the second book of *The Prelude* as the primal, nurturing bond of all imaginative development and growth of mind—the periphrasis itself, words for words, not only words in words, would need pondering.[26]

Boehme is right to this extent: as "natural beings in the strength of Nature" (*The Prelude*, book 3) we cannot see beyond the mother, only into her. Yet this "into," at once insight and penetration, also compels us to look beyond the mother/nature identity. For too much is anchored in the mother as beginning and end, womb and ultimate repose, principle and limitary horizon. Closure, inspired by her, could become idealized incest, claustrophobic vision.

If we repose in the mother, or "stand" in her (to use Boehme's expression), how is this related to closure in art? Is closure a mimetic residue of the inland murmur of enclosing breast and heart? Or does it emanate from verbal as well as preverbal, from the mother-softened "music" of words that the child probably associates with the mother's face? "The mother's face, the purpose of the poem, fills the room" (Wallace Stevens). It is a room, then, even if claustral. How rich and complicated this relation between voice and visage can be is shown when Keats describes Moneta.

Terrified by robes and veils that "curtain'd her in mysteries," Keats is more terrified by Moneta unveiled: "deathwards progressing toward no death was that visage." Terror of enclosure is replaced by terror of separation: of the mother from life or from death; of Keats from the mother; but more purely than either, of face from face. The humanity of this face is about to be lost, as we approach a face without closure, one that "happy death / Can put no end to"—a death mask changing, laboring, like the mortal-immortal moon.

How do we read that face? Insofar as it labors it suggests a new birth, a new coming; insofar as it separates itself from itself it betrays the *father's* face, that "other" and sterner principle that demands a change of perspective tantamount to rebirth. What I wish to stress, however, is not Keats's Boehmian insight but Moneta's radical ambivalence of expression.

For that expression reminds us, who cannot leave natural perception behind, of an ecstasy close to the primal moments of labor *and* orgasm. If the father-principle emerges, it is still within this maternal sphere. "My power," Moneta says to the poet-dreamer, "Shall be to thee a wonder. . . . Free from all pain, if wonder pain thee not." But this wonder does pain; the wonder of the human face in which, at these moments—moments that exceed the child's capacity for interpretation, though not his memory—signs of agony and joy, of death and life, mix ambivalently.

Perhaps we can think of art as a binding or closure of such ambivalence, such wondrous pain: as a holding onto the human face. The natural image of such a binding would be a smile so subtle that it betrays nothing yet knows everything, as in Leonardo's *Mona Lisa* or *St. John the Baptist*, or as in Nietzsche's famous lines from *Thus Spoke Zarathustra*: "We do not converse with each other, because we know too much—; we exchange silences; we smile at each other through our knowledge."

But closure may itself be part of the problem: it cannot rest purely within a maternal or paternal sphere. The former would result in a stilling that is absolute, the latter in a fixity that is absolute. Keats envisages, through the *Hyperions*, a "happy death" rather than the astonishing-stonying of a face. What are the gods except alienated faces, silenced faces, to the point that they are no longer human but death masks, "sculpture builded up upon the grave / Of their own power"?

The remarkableness of Moneta is that her face is traveling, travailing; it cannot fix itself as mortal or immortal; it is eloquently mute; in fact, what it progresses toward is a resolved voice. Voice is always about to dissolve face, to make it too human, or else so ghostly that it cannot be laid. But images lay voice; Monet's visage "dubs" her own or the poet's voice. It may be true that

voice and visage, "dreaming mouth" and "speaking eyes," cannot be ultimately distinguished; yet here the haunting face, and other images too, take
over from voice. The mother's voice is featured, visualized, through the silent
sound of images that try at once to render and to still that voice. Are not these
silent yet speaking images the "signs" that constitute the matter of semiotics,
and which cannot resolve themselves entirely into unambivalent, unvoiced
images?

Let me turn to a very different poem, also complex, yet more familiar and
graspable. My first epigraph comes from Donne's well-known "Valediction:
Forbidding Mourning." I conclude with some thoughts on this poem, which
like Wordsworth's "Slumber" and Keats's *Hyperion*, also begins close to silence: Donne's actual plea is "Let us part and make no noise."

Donne not only analogizes, gently enough, parting and death, but uses
the occasion—as both lover and preacher—to limit mourning now, perhaps
in view of the greater parting to come. The most commented-on stanzas are
the last, which contain the famous compass image:

> If they be two, they are two so
>   As stiffe twin compasses are two,
> Thy soule the fixt foot, makes no show
>   To move, but doth, if th'other doe.
>
> And though it in the center sit,
>   Yet when the other far doth rome,
> It leanes, and hearkens after it,
>   And growes erect, as that comes home.
>
> Such wilt thou be to mee, who must
>   Like th'other foot, obliquely runne;
> Thy firmnes makes my circle just,
>   And makes me end, where I begunne.

Donne ends with two uses of the same image, as if a double coda, a
double act of sealing, were required. The doubling increases our awareness
that the image is only an image, the emblematic product of an imaginative
faith. It is perishable and may need further shoring up. The ending, unabsolute, provides a simulacrum of faith, just as parting is a simulacrum of death.
When we recall the initial stanza, which hangs the evidence of life on a word,
on less than a word, on a vocal inflection or quantity, the difference between
"now" and "no"—

> As virtuous men passe mildly away,
>   And whisper to their soules, to goe,
> Whilst some of their sad friends doe say,
>   The breath goes now, and some say, no:

—then this tandem image is a whisper finely extended, airy despite its solidity.

It is only as affecting and perishable as all words that are breath. And it reflects another doubling, one that transposes this duality onto the level of language as such: there is, throughout the poem, a Latinate dimension that recalls an authoritative and ideally stable diction, still felt in the term "valediction"; and there is Donne's virtuoso use of the developing everyday language, the *materna lingua* that blends with the *sermo patrius* and frees Donne's poem from a rigor (almost a *rigor mortis*) that lingers as an overtone in its final, eternizing emblem.

The questions we are left with are not different from those raised by Wordsworth and Keats. Is closure in the sphere of the father or the mother? Does Donne promise the woman, and himself, a return to a "center" that is the woman? Is the circle he describes the line drawn by passionate love, which undermines all thought of death except love-death? Or does the poet forbid mourning in the name of a "masculine persuasive force" based on the pre-rogative of his sex, which is itself based on a patriarchal morality? Enough of the idiot questioner: the closure—though one might prefer to say the binding, the *re-ligio*—that emerges is mediated here by words that can only be received if the lover's ear play its part. Donne mingles harsh and sweet, blends the mother- and the father-tongue, and suggests a persuasion, or a language of persuasion, so finely mixed that the two are one.

Retrospect

There is a tender empiricism [*zarte Empirie*] that identifies
with its subject-matter and only through that becomes a theory.

Goethe

I do not want to conclude this book without a thought on method. I have tried to recover a sense of "the wound in the word" in relation to "the word in the word." The contemporary emphasis on semiotics has influenced the direction I have taken; semiotics, even when it contributes to psychoanalysis, as in the work of Lacan, may produce an unfeeling language of description. Lacan deals with this anesthetic tendency by adopting an aggressive style that punctures equanimity; yet that style is often self-defeating, because it makes us think of the analyst as a frustrated prophet who cannot heal himself.

I have wished to describe rather than explain; and I have used mainly literary examples. I cannot find it in myself to worry the question of the relation of empirical evidence to theory and, in particular, to the hypothesis of a primal word-wound. I always slip back to a historical or psychological starting point mediated by literature. My field of inquiry is bounded by language and its intricate relation to human development. The category of curse or blessing is fundamental only from a literary or historical perspective always convertible into the psychopathology of everyday life.

Goethe's "tender empiricism" suggests an affectionate sort of theorizing, on the unlikely pattern of a conversation, not excluding carnal conversation. "Tender" means unwounding; theory, or our search for intelligibility and evidence, should not impose or lacerate but allow in others—in the world itself—an unconstrained response. That theory could take such a form is too good to be true; yet the ideal is not only a Romantic one. A contemporary philosopher, developing Wittgenstein's *Philosophical Investigations*, has written:

> Empirical statements that claim truth depend upon evidence; statements that claim truthfulness depend upon our acceptance of them. My acceptance is the way I respond to them, and not everyone is capable of the response, or willing for it. I put this by saying that a true statement is something we know or do not know; a truthful statement is one we must acknowledge or fail or refuse to acknowledge.[27]

What is here called acknowledgment I have called recognition: a recognition without the benefit of a great or startling discovery except, possibly, that of the mediacy of words. Yet there is some danger in insisting on a tender rather than exact (as in the "exact sciences") theorizing, and its preference for "ordinary language" terms. Let me explain.

To bring words back from their metaphysical to their everyday use (*Philosophical Investigations* I.116) involves, according to Wittgenstein, an investigation of them that cannot premise logical purity of a crystalline or clear-cut sort (I.105 ff.). It gives that up, yet does not give it up, for "where there is sense there must be perfect order.—So there must be perfect order even in the vaguest sentence" (I.98). What is to be done, then, with the *terrible crystal* of logic, something that is *prior* to all experience, yet must run through all experience? "No empirical cloudiness or uncertainty can be allowed to affect it—It must rather be of the purest crystal. But this crystal does not appear as an abstraction; but as something concrete, indeed, as the most concrete, as it were the *hardest* thing there is" (I.97).

It may be an illusion to try to grasp the "incomparable essence" of language or thought. To do so produces pseudo-problems that feed rather than dispel a certain pathos (I.110). Neither pure logic nor a cloudy empiricism can get hold of "the workings of our language"—indeed, it is the latter that must solve the philosophical problems posed by the former. But how can these workings be described, and in such a way as to make philosophy a battle against the bewitchment of the intellect? (I.109)

To talk about language without falling into illusory problems about the essence of language means to "talk about it as we do about the pieces in chess when we are stating the rules of the game, not describing their physical properties. The question 'What is a word really?' is analogous to 'What is a piece in chess?'" (I.108). This is the famous notion of the language-game. But the game of words in real life ("we are talking about the spatial and temporal phenomenon of language, not about some non-spatial, non-temporal phantasm") is not only a game and not only a description of rules. A violation of the rules may be terrible in its effect, precisely because language is not "unique," but also a social game with often implacable penalties. These penalties themselves, of course, may reflect a bewitchment or superstition: that there is only one (proper) way of playing. Logic comes back in its crystalline, hard, exigent character. Wittgenstein's "dialogue of one" blunts the issues (probably related) of solecism and of the high, queer, or extraordinary style. Is an everyday metaphysical style a possibility?

Here I find Heidegger to the point. There is a danger, even in Wittgenstein, of talking things to death. His is never, of course, mere talk, what Heidegger calls *Gerede*, which manifests despite itself the crystalline silence it compulsively breaks. Wittgenstein achieves a style that is surely more than ordinary: a blend of rigor and vacillation, at times close to Kafkaesque in its hammering out of the paradox that "*thought* can be of what is *not* the case" (I.95).

But Heidegger adopts a style more severe, and a mode of analysis that threatens ordinary language by its very care for the extraordinariness of the ordinary (cf. *Philosophical Investigations* I.97, 98, 108). There must always be a tension, correctly interpreted or not, between the ordinary and the extraordinary expression. Perhaps, then, style (we can now drop "high")—its apparent deviation from natural speech or what passes for such—is itself the sword that hangs over every thinker who is language-sensitive. To write without style, to write unseen, would be, at once, to reduce visibility and vulnerability, or to be purposive without purpose. A pointless pattern speaks to us, yet it may be Philomela's speaking picture, her "voice of the shuttle." The words are the wounds that are always, again, words. In this everyday metaphysical style—which may simply be how prose should be defined—the difference between high and low subject matters becomes questionable: one can take up the oracle that overshadows the life of Oedipus *or* a threat uttered by an anonymous voice over the telephone. But one cannot deny a word-wound, the thread of such a threat.

At the end (of this book at least) is the omen, and its relation to naming, the nomen. Oracle or anonymous voice: they are both insidious and affecting. Who knows what they are motivated by? Who can discern their intent? Is it vengeance, malice, chance, or an obscure and fateful justice? Whose voice is it?

The dread of a threat lies in its deferred fulfillment: the threat hangs over us, and unless strictly delimited, even lifted, by ritual or legal action, it is hard to see what could purge it from the now conscious ear. This ear-fear is fundamental; Nietzsche associates it with the intolerable music of Dionysus in *The Birth of Tragedy out of the Spirit of Music*; and by such haunting rhymes as "Weh spricht: Vergeh" he suggests that the ear tries to clear its fear by this action on itself called rhyme, or other forms of a repeated and compulsive tonality.

My very desire to know or to imitate—as in this essay—is also an "aesthetic" maneuver to master an intolerable ear-fear, to convert it into an act of will that strives, particularly after Socrates, to establish the ideal of science as pure cognition or disinterested knowledge. That all human beings desire knowledge, in the form of *theoria* or *imitatio*, and that these are intrinsically pleasurable, Nietzsche transvalues as a Maian postulate, the matrix of a healing and necessary illusion. The truth-value of such a postulate is subverted by the very desire for truth, one that seeks the quietus in logic, not logic itself.

I return to language in its relation to the conscious ear. Threats can be subsumed under the category of curse; but more important is that their resonance is linked to our difficulty in receiving words whose echo in the mind cannot be economized. We cannot *not* heed threat or oracle, yet should we take them literally? To take them literally is, in a way, to bring them about, to live under their sway, or else to wish for a partial fulfillment that might be interpreted as satisfying, and so averting, them.[28] But this fulfillment is really not literal at all: it negates the temporal insistence of the threat by a closure invented as a counterdeferral. By equivocation or figurative action we substitute for the dread words another meaning, in effect another set of words.

What if these words too are "anonymous" in the sense of conveying a powerful impression of impersonal origination or autonomous being? "A poem nearly anonymous" is how J. C. Ransom honors Milton's "Lycidas." The literary or aesthetic effect proper is often described in similar terms. When this effect is present we "shudder" for the same reason as when we are wounded through the ear. Words have been found that close the path to the original words. This absolute closure is what we respond to, this appearance of definitive detachment and substitution. The words themselves block the way. There is no going back, no stumbling through ghostly or psychoanalytic vaults: the "dread Voice" exists as the poem or not at all.

Notes

Chapter 1

1. I start with this epigraph not only to indicate a vein of similarity between Coleridge and Derrida when it comes to using words in a speculative manner, but also to broach the subject of *cultural translation:* how to convey, in an English text-milieu, what Derrida is about. I take courage from Dryden, who remarks in the "Dedication" to his translation of the *Aeneid:* "If sounding words are not of our growth and manufacture, who shall hinder me to import them from a foreign country? I carry not out the treasure of the nation which is never to return, but what I bring from Italy I spend in England. Here it remains and here it circulates, for, if the coin be good, it will pass from one hand to another. I trade both with the living and the dead, for the enrichment of our native language." This more hopeful aspect of my effort should not disguise either Coleridge's or Derrida's aggressive undoing of the univocal, cleanly, or "proper" sense of words.

2. *La voix et le phénomène,* p. 117.

3. Ibid.

4. For the critique of the concept *book* in the light of the concept *écriture*, see also Derrida, *Writing and Difference*, pp. 10–13 and 294 f. Also *Of Grammatology*, chap. 1; and *La dissémination*, pp. 51 ff. Additionally, Paul Zumthor, "La généalogie du livre," in *Langue, texte, enigme*. Other essays of interest that touch the issue of *écriture* and *book* are: Paul de Man, "The Rhetoric of Blindness: Jacques Derrida's Reading of Rousseau," in *Blindness and Insight*; and Edward Said, "Abecedarium Culturae: Structuralism, Absence, Writing," in *Modern French Criticism*, ed. John K. Simon.

5. In "La crise de l'esprit" (1919), first published by *Athenaeum* in an English version.

6. Not an academic question, if we think first of Croce, then of the importance of Kojève's mediation of Hegel.

7. Now available in translation as *Words Upon Words*.

8. Genet's piece on Rembrandt is found in the fourth volume of his *Oeuvres complètes*. The phrase "se divise en deux" has, therefore, as its simplest reference, the presentation of the text in Genet. Derrida had split the page into uneven columns in his essay "Tympan" (*Marges de la philosophie*). There the subject is the labyrinthine ear; here it seems to be the "eery" (labyrinthine) connection between "coup d'oeil" and castration. Bataille may also be present through his conception of painting as putrefaction: see "Soleil pourri" in *Documents* (1930), *Oeuvres complètes*, vol. 1.

9. Georges Bataille, whose works are now fully published by Gallimard, and whose essays on Genet and on the language of flowers, as well as the poem entitled "Glas" are quoted by Derrida in *Glas*, is the subject of an illuminating book by Denis Hollier, *La prise de la concorde*. Bataille can be said to have launched a new phase of Nietzsche studies with his *Nietzsche: volonté de chance*. Derrida's essay on Nietzsche, "La question du style," is found in *Nietzsche aujourd'hui*, vol. 1. Maurice Blanchot has been writing criticism and novelistic *récits* since the late 1930s. His influence on Derrida, Foucault, and others has been considerable; his criticism is beginning to be translated. Derrida devotes an essay to Blanchot in *Deconstruction and Criticism*.

10. Now in *La vérité en peinture*.

11. *Sa*[3] might be "S.A.," abbreviation for *Société Anonyme* (in English, *Inc.*, for "Incorporated"). That opens the question of what role the legal fiction of the incorporated person plays in Hegel or in philosophy's "impersonifications." Who speaks? What "subject"? By what authority? Derrida's "Coming into One's Own" in *Psychoanalysis and the Question of the Text* (ed. G. H. Hartman) addresses the shiftiness of person and persona(e) and the eternizing or, more soberly, the institutionalizing force of texts.

12. Lacan's influential essay on the mirror phase has been translated by Alan Sheridan in *Ecrits: A Selection*. On the movement of French criticism in a Lacanian direction, consult Jeffrey Mehlman, *A Structural Study of Autobiography: Proust, Leiris, Sartre, Lévi-Strauss*.

13. At one point (220b) *Glas* reveals, through Genet, something of that ultimate machine by which Jean thinks to rag Jean and shred not only what Lacan calls the "imago du corps propre" but also the "imago du nom propre."

Chapter 2

1. See *Positions*, p. 58. In a recent essay Derrida paragraphs by using a rectangular quotation mark open at the angle and enclosing the unprinted rather than than the printed space. On "Painting/Writing" see also the fine issue of *Triquarterly* 20 (1971), and essays by Michel Butor, especially in *Répertoire 3*.

2. *De la grammatologie*, p. 49. *Of Grammatology*, trans. G. Spivak, pp. 32–33.

3. See, in addition to Genet's "*ce qui est resté d'un Rembrandt déchiré . . . ,*" Derrida's "Tympan" in *Marges de la philosophie*. The *Ersatzbeziehung* between eye and penis in castration anxiety is, of course, discussed by Freud in *Das Unheimliche*. On the relation of wounded *ear* and *coupure*, Bataille is once again an important source through his "Mutilation sacrificielle et l'oreille coupée de Vincent van Gogh," in *Documents*.

4. "Behove this sound of Irish sense. Really? Here English might be seen. Royally? One sovereign punned to petery pence. Regally? The silence speaks the scene. Fake! So This is Dyoubelong? Hush! Caution! Echoland!" (*Finnegans Wake*).

5. *Vorschule der Aesthetik*, para. 54: "*Notwendigkeit deutscher witzigen Kultur.*" The *Vorschule* has been translated by Margaret Hale as *Horn of Oberon*.

6. But see "*La double séance*" in *La dissémination* for Derrida's subtlest, if still

subversive, valuing of history writing: "Entre Platon et Mallarmé, dont les noms propres, ici encore, ne sont pas des références réelles mais des indications de commodité et de première analyse, une histoire a eu lieu" (p. 209).

7. See my *Criticism in the Wilderness*, pp. 143–47.

8. See especially *The Anxiety of Influence*.

9. In a remarkable essay on Kant's Third Critique, Derrida argues that Kant's treatment of the nonaesthetic, or the opposite of *taste* ("*dégout*," "*Eckel*," "*je m'eckel*"!), still serves to maintain the association of representability with pleasure that goes back to Aristotle's understanding of mimesis. Kant is said to admit (however ambivalently) the representability of an "X *dégoutant*" or "*le vomi*" in order to save philosophy's "economy" (which is auto-affective and logo-centric) from an unidentifiable "*exclu absolu*" beyond naming or the "parergoric" remedy of speech. Hence the title of Derrida's essay "Economimesis" in *Mimesis: des articulations*. On the relation of *nom propre* and *non-propre*, see also Spivak's introduction to her translation of Derrida's *Of Grammatology*. About this X, cf. Heidegger, *Kant and the Problem of Metaphysics*, p. 127: "The X [as transcendental object] is 'something' of which we can know nothing."

10. In "La double séance" ("double science") Derrida therefore extends Freud's understanding of the antithetical character of primal words to all possible syntactic units: "On peut reconnaître une certaine loi de série à ces lieux de pivotement indéfini: ils marquent les points de ce qui ne se laisse jamais maîtriser, relever, dialectiser par *Erinnerung* et *Aufhebung*. Est-ce par hasard que tous ces effets de jeu, ces 'mots' qui échappent à la maîtrise philosophique, ont . . . un rapport très singulier à l'écriture?" (*La dissémination*, p. 250). On *écriture* (and *différance*) conceived as the *Aufhebung* of *Aufhebung*, cf. *Positions*, pp. 54 ff.

Chapter 3

1. The reference numbers are those of paragraphs in the A. V. Miller translation of *Hegel's Phenomenology of Spirit*. When quoting, I have sometimes slightly modified this translation. The play on read/reap comes from I. A. Richards himself, in *How to Read a Page*.

2. From "Sketches and Thoughts" of spring 1871, associated with *The Birth of Tragedy*.

3. The last column on p. 290 of *Glas* (far left) dramatizes the "machine" (291b) of printing and publishing, that is, questions of owning, dating, counting, accountability, which appose ironically the insistence on property rights with this movement away from the proper name. Books qua books, are still too proper.

4. An attempted translation might run: "Hypothesis apotheosis of the father in himself not being there." Cf. *Glas*, 122b. The allusion is to the last paragraph (787) in Hegel's account of "Revealed Religion" and refers to Genet's quasi-religious fantasy. (The relevant phrase in Hegel is "just as the individual divine Man has a father in principle and only an actual mother" [*ansichseiende Vater und nur eine wirkliche Mutter*].) Or to Nietzsche's riddle at the beginning of *Ecce Homo*, touching on a similar fantasy: "As my own father I am already dead, as my own mother I still live and grow old."

5. "*Aphanisis* of the subject . . . when the subject appears somewhere as meaning, he is manifested elsewhere as 'fading,' as disappearance." See *The Four Fundamental Concepts of Psychoanalysis*, trans. Alan Sheridan, p. 218.

6. "Wir dürfen keinen Abgrund der Betrachtung scheuen, um die Tragödie bei ihren Müttern aufzufinden: diese Mütter sind Wille, Wahn, Wehe." A note from the time of *The Birth of Tragedy*, dated 22 September 1870. Cf. *The Birth of Tragedy*, section 20.

7. Francis Ponge, "The Sun as a Spinning Top, II," in *The Sun Placed in the Abyss*, trans. Serge Gavronsky.

8. Emile Littré, *Dictionnaire de la langue française*; Edition intégrale; Walther von Wartburg, *Französisches etymologisches Wörterbuch*. But see Leo Spitzer's critique of Wartburg (and Meyer-Lübke) for neglecting the learned or religious aspects of words in favor of the *lingua del pane*: "in [Wartburg's] article *Forma*, for example, he fails to deal with the concept of 'form' as developed by the Greeks, Romans, and Christians, preferring rather to list all the dialectal words referring to varieties of material forms: forms of pastry, of hats, of cheeses. . . . Not to deal with the meaning of learned words means simply to shy away from the whole semantic content of our civilization" (*Essays in Historical Semantics*, pp. 4–5).

9. See Jean Starobinski, ed., *Les mots sous les mots: les anagrammes de Ferdinand de Saussure*. Now translated as *Words Upon Words*.

10. From Derrida's "Le parergon" (1974). Now in *La vérité en peinture*. This is one of Derrida's essays on Kant, which uses ⌊ and ⌐ as a typographical "*pointure*" enclosing an empty space, as if "le manque formait le cadre de la théorie . . . Arête/manque."

11. Or "Ruminates . . . its shadow," since *remord(s)* can also be French for "remorse," comparable to the Old English *Agenbit*. Through this multidimensional writing, the architectural metaphor (a picture-writing hinting at the earliest, "symbolic" stage of the spirit, when colossal funerary monuments were built) betrays also a temporal theme, related either to the course of Apollo—sun or sundial—or to the fact that Time is introduced into Hegel's dialectic through the *act* of writing "Now is Night" (*Phenomenology*, para. 95). Hegel begins the subversive march of the dialectic by emptying the concept of "sense-certainty": the shadow introduced by the simple act of writing-and-thinking (i.e., dialectic) has to disappear before "self-certainty" (i.e., the subject "sûr de soi") can reappear at a higher level. But at the end of *Glas* we remain at the beginning of *Glas*, for what has disappeared is still the subject (the grammatical subject introducing the sentence "Remord lentement son ombre") and everything seems as labored and funerary as ever. The hand that writes is like the hand of the clock itself, going round and round, unable to purge death knell or shadow. Writing the "Now" ("Quoi du reste, maintenant") at once realizes and unrealizes the writer's presence, like obelisk or sepulchral monument.

12. A substantial portion of Derrida's Hegel commentary rehearses what the *Encyclopedia* and the *Philosophy of Law* say about the relation of father, mother, sister, etc. to the family and of the family to the state. It may be unfair to name this important topic a second plot, but its relevance to *Glas* as a whole is connected to the way Hegel's bourgeois family romance contrasts with the ghostly and transgressive "presence" of the family in Genet's fiction.

13. Note the way the column that follows (*Glas*, 113b) is arranged to go from

"surnoms" to "noms," the latter word "coupé" by the page's edge, like "Notre" in the first line.

14. *Les mots anglais* (1877), is quoted from the Pléiade edition of Mallarmé's *Oeuvres complètes*, ed. Henri Mondor and G. Jean-Aubry.

15. This negative *éc-stase*, linked perhaps to Genet's homosexuality, is understood by Derrida along a very broad meditation on gender. It contrasts the maleness-oriented *Je m'éc/Je mec* with the femaleness-oriented *IC*. Genet's fantasy is that of an *Immeculée Conception*.

16. *Of Grammatology*, p. 112. Derrida's "vocatif absolu" displaces Hegel's "savoir absolu": I have preferred to translate the phrase as "absolute vocative."

17. Starobinski, *Les mots sous les mots*, p. 152.

Chapter 4

1. Cf. Sherry Turkle, *Psychoanalytic Politics: Freud's French Revolution*.

2. I quote from Lacan's "Discours de Rome" or "The Agency of the Letter in the Unconscious or Reason since Freud." Anthony Wilden's *The Language of the Self* is a fully annotated version of the "Discours." A fine Lacanian study that should be mentioned here, because it is directly focused on literature and relevant to *Glas*, is Laplanche's *Hölderlin et la question du père*.

3. On wounding and naming, see Leslie Brisman, "'At Thy Word': A Reading of *Romeo and Juliet*," pp. 21–35; also Norman Holland, "A Touching of Literary and Psychiatric Education," pp. 287–99. On the psychic import of names, the following sources may prove interesting: Sir J. G. Frazer, *The Golden Bough*, vol. 3, "Tabooed Words"; Sigmund Freud, *Totem and Taboo*, chap. 4, the section "Nominalist Theories"; Karl Abraham's short essay of 1911, "Über die determinierende Kraft des Namens"; and Jean Starobinski, *Words Upon Words*. See also Derrida, *Of Grammatology*, "The Battle of Proper Names," pp. 107–18. Additionally, A. Dwight Culler, *Tennyson*, chap. 1, "Tennyson, Tennyson, Tennyson." The amphibious relations between proper and common nouns are deepened by the work of Nicolas Abraham and Maria Torok on cryptonomy in *Cryptonomie: le verbier de l'homme aux loups*. This is preceded by "Fors," an essay by Derrida translated in *Georgia Review* 31 (1977): 64–120. On "personality" and naming, see Geertz, *The Interpretation of Cultures*, pp. 368 ff. On nicknames, endearments, and naming in private or mystical moments that could restrict "The Language Exchange" (see my chap. 5), cf. the remarkably humane book by Ernst Leisi, *Paar und Sprache*, esp. pp. 17–33. On negative or "poisonous" nicknames, see e.g. Heine's *Memoirs*.

4. Sartre's book on Genet, originally published in 1952, is translated by Bernard Frechtman as *Saint Genet: Actor and Martyr*. I refer chiefly to the section "A Dizzying Word" in book 1, which contains the story of Genet's "specular capture" (Lacan's, not Sartre's, phrase) by the identity-imposing words "You are a thief."

5. Freud's remarks on the "language of flowers" in *The Interpretation of Dreams* are found in the Standard Edition of *The Complete Psychological Works* 4: 319–25 and 5: 652; see also pp. 374–77.

6. Sándor Ferenczi's bioanalysis is his *Thalassa: Toward a Theory of Genitality*, first published in German in 1924. An important step in the French reception of the book was Nicolas Abraham's edition for the Petite Bibliothèque Payot in 1962.

7. See Anthony Wilden, *The Language of the Self*, pp. 20, 62–63.

8. Gershom Scholem's "Walter Benjamin und sein Engel," containing the *Agesilaus Santander* text in its two versions, is found in *Zur Aktualität Walter Benjamins*, ed. Siegfried Unseld. I quote the second version of Benjamin's text and have modified the translation by W. J. Dannhauser in *Denver Quarterly* 9 (1974): 9–12. There is some wordplay that cannot be rendered in translation; it includes perhaps an allusion to the fact that as a name "Walter Benjamin" seems to contain two first names. The German word for first name, *Vorname*, is homophonous with *Vornahme*, that is "project" or "resolution." Benjamin's concept of the "aura" is described at length in *The Work of Art in the Age of Mechanical Reproduction*, originally published in 1936.

Chapter 5

1. "La pharmacie de Platon," in *La dissémination*. In the "Genet" column of *Glas*, especially toward the end (p. 290), the question is raised what kind of "milk" (*lait/legs*) writing was for Genet; a writing characterized by the literal absence of the father, but also by the ambivalent absence/presence ("Lait de deuil cacheté") of the mother.

2. Cf. my *Criticism in the Wilderness*, pp. 150–52, for the importance of the clothes metaphor in Carlyle, and the convergence of "custom" and "costume."

3. Cf. René Girard, *Deceit, Desire, and the Novel*, for a subtle argument concerning the mimetic and mediated character of desire. It may not be an accident that Girard's later work, typified by *Violence and the Sacred*, uses the notion of *pharmakos*, but in the sense of "scapegoat," to build up an aggressively referential theory of myth and signification.

4. Paul Ricoeur explores the "bond, so fundamental for the history of our culture, between defilement, purification, and philosophy," and which requires a "*symbolic language.*" See his chapter, "Defilement," in *The Symbolism of Evil*; and cf. my *Criticism in the Wilderness*, chap. 6, "Purification and Danger 2: Critical Style."

5. *The Faerie Queene* I.i.9. While "sweet" and "bitter" stand in an allopathic relation, the idea of a curative "bleeding" into or from within the "wound" carries the homeopathic idea. I mention later the ancient notion of healing excretions: myrrh, balsam, and the like exude their unguents, sometimes through cuts in the bark. They are "wounded" in order to release a sweet or healing "blood": resin. It was natural to associate this phenomenon with the efficacy of Christ's blood. Cf. Lynn Thorndike, *A History of Magic and Experimental Science*, I.xvi.

6. Wordsworth's lines are themselves already allusive: they echo the ending of Milton's *L'Allegro*, the "Cheerful Man," which is paired with the poem of *Il Penseroso*, the "Melancholy Man." On "*le nom tout à la fois floral et souterrain de*

Perséphone [*percé-phone*]" (Michel Leiris), see Jacques Derrida's "Tympaniser—la philosophie," the overture to his *Marges de la philosophie.*

7. See J.-P. Sartre, *Saint Genet: Actor and Martyr,* trans. B. Frechtman. See also above, chap. 4. The obverse theme, that of a "speaking wound," becomes therefore the literary conceit par excellence: it at once offers and negates the possibility of muteness. See Julia's address to Eusebio in Calderón's *Devoción de la Cruz,* or Northumberland's speech to Morton in the second part of *Henry IV* (I.iii).

8. Alypius succumbs to a spectacle in the Circus: "As soon as he saw that blood, he drank down savageness with it; he did not turn away but fixed his eye and drank in frenzy unawares, delighted with the guilty combat, intoxicated with the bloody sport," *Confessions,* book 6, chap. 8. It is significant, however, that his eyes open when he hears the crowd shout. Augustine's own conversion was initiated by a voice, or the aural event *"tolle, lege."* See also Hans Robert Jauss, *Aesthetische Erfahrung und literarische Hermeneutik,* pp. 136–60, which defines Alypius's experience as a perverted form of *compassio* (sympathetic identification) and connects it with the role of catharsis in aesthetic experience.

9. Cf. above, chap. 4. A remarkable (true or not) account of the rejection and countercreation of a mother tongue is found in Louis Wolfson, *Le schizo et les langues.* Kenneth Burke's criticism abounds in speculations on the psycholiterary role of proper names: see, e.g., the remarks on "Thomas" Eliot, and on a character in one of his own stories, in *Attitudes Toward History* 1: 109–11 and 2: 108–10.

10. I develop the idea of a spectral name more fully in chap. 4, "Psychoanalysis: The French Connection." In applying the idea to Genet I owe a debt to Derrida's *Glas.* Concerning the relation of spectral to "absent" name, cf. Lacan: "The neurotic has been subjected to imaginary castration from the beginning; it is castration that sustains the strong ego, so strong, one might say, that its proper name is an inconvenience for it, since the neurotic is really Nameless." *Ecrits,* p. 323.

11. From *The Autobiography of Malcom X* (as told to Alex Haley), chap. 12.

12. The point can be made in different ways, with different implications. Bertrand Russell says "Only such proper names as are derived from concepts by means of *the* can be said to have meaning, and such words as *John* merely indicate without meaning." Leo Spitzer remarks in an essay on Villon that (I translate) "there is a poetry inherent to proper nouns... one can enjoy a name as *matière sonante,* as the material basis for reverie." Cf. Roland Barthes, "Proust et les noms," in *To Honor Roman Jakobson.*

13. I excerpt from W. H. Bond's edition of *Jubilate Agno.* To go into the aetiology of Smart's disturbance would mean to go beyond the boundary of what is empirical— as Freud did, toward the end of *Totem and Taboo,* a book as deeply concerned as Smart's poem with the "primal deed" or "primal wound" from which culture may have sprung, and which may still echo in feelings of guilt and ambivalence.

14. Cf. Theodor Reik on psychoanalysis, which "reveals the power of the word and the power of withholding the word, of keeping silent." "Die psychologische Bedeutung des Schweigens" (1926) in *Wie Man Psychologe Wird.* Reik's essay is a short yet remarkably comprehensive analysis of the emotional interdependence of "Sprechen" (speaking) and "Schweigen" (keeping silent), and raises the possibility that silence is always, to some degree, deathlike.

15. What is more effective with regard to self-definition, curse, or blessing? *The*

Ancient Mariner shows a man still laboring under a curse, yet promulgating a message of blessing, a good spell. Set against the "merry din" of a marriage feast, the poem seems to affirm, almost as a blessing, our *manque à être*: the peculiarly human sense of incompleteness, of ontic lack and separation from "bird and beast," together with the desire for completion, or rejoining the community of creatures. Perhaps, as Freud surmised, too much of human development takes place outside the womb, so we feel intrinsically premature, untimely separated from sustaining nature.

16. All renderings of Aeschylus are from the Robert Fagles translation of *The Oresteia* (Harmondsworth: Penguin, 1977).

17. The cycle of words-and-wounds continues, because great writers so often reduce us to muteness, or else require us to echo them deviously. The creative way in which this "curse" of the precursor's greatness weighs on later poets is the subject of Harold Bloom's work on the "anxiety of influence." I should also pay tribute here to Kenneth Burke's concern throughout *The Philosophy of Literary Form* with the connection of art to homeopathic "medicine." The quotations from Joyce's *Finnegans Wake* that follow in the next paragraphs are taken from the definitive eighth edition (New York: Viking, 1958), pp. 44, 175, 104, 360.

18. In quoting Tolstoi I use the Louise and Aylmer Maude translation.

19. See, for example, Freud's sexual interpretation of a dream about flowers, with the result that "the dreamer quite lost her liking for this pretty dream after it had been interpreted." *The Interpretation of Dreams*, chap. 6D.

20. Geoffrey Hill, "Poetry as 'Menace' and 'Atonement'," pp. 72–73. Cf. Christopher Ricks in *Keats and Embarrassment*: "Is embarrassment not only a nineteenth-century sentiment but a narrowly English one?" Ricks describes the poet's closeness to a heightened consciousness whose effects seem physiological but whose cause is not a specifically social "offense." How this "offense" should be defined involves the imagination as it reveals or risks itself in a conventional circle. See Thomas M. Greene, "*Il Cortegiano* and the Choice of a Game," pp. 173–86. The ideal, as Greene states it, is that "nothing will be said . . . which the resilience of this circle [the particular social group] will not contain." Other courtesy books, especially Gracian's *Il Discreto*, also contain hints that these trivia are not trivia: Gracian has a remarkable conversation on the good listener.

While Trilling in "Manners, Morals, and the Novel" (*The Liberal Imagination*) does not deal directly with solecism and only passingly with social offense, he states the subject of the modern novel as the conflict between "solid" reality and "artificial" manners. In a symposium devoted to him, moreover, the question of social offense surfaces in a way that makes Trilling observe: "Is the true self in some sense a product of your imaginative reflection on the offense you've given or the forgiveness you've received?" (*Salmagundi* 41 [Spring 1978], 92) Forgiveness, of course, as in Dostoievski, can itself, when religiously public and fervent, act as a social offense, an insult thrown back at "manners."

Part of the attraction of adopting Basic English as a universal language, C. K. Ogden argues, is that it will reduce to a minimum the "'fear of committing the slightest breach of etiquette' (like the average Englishman when he stumbles over the eccentricities of French gender)." But the subject remains relatively unexplored, even in social history. An exception is J. M. Cuddihy's *The Ordeal of Civility*, which proposes that a revisionist perspective on culture like Freud's is not only *received* as a solecism on a grand scale, but may have been *based* on Freud's own experience of social offense—on the situation of a Jew among Gentiles. Cf. also Leisi on code disturbances in *Paar und Sprache*, pp. 119–32.

On the relation of the (family) name to "honor" and the social code, cf. Walter Benjamin, *The Origin of German Tragic Drama*, p. 87. In Ballanche's *L'homme sans nom* (1820), the regicide-executioner of Louis XIV seeks to expiate his guilt by withdrawing into a state of namelessness.

Cuddihy's view may bear some relation to Van Wyck Brooks's *The Ordeal of Mark Twain*, a book that helped to rescue a "bitter" Twain for American studies. Brooks himself was so mortified by a sense of American cultural inferiority that he was relieved to discover that Tolstoi's birthplace, Yasnaya Polyana, was but the equivalent of Plainfield, the name of his New Jersey hometown. Also of interest is Erving Goffman's *Stigma*, which emphasizes *visual* or *public* traits, although the effect is the same as the one here discussed: "an individual who might have been received easily in ordinary social intercourse possesses a trait that can obtrude itself upon attention and turn those of whom he meets away from him, breaking the claim that his other attributes have on us. He possesses a stigma, an undesired differentness from what we had anticipated" (p. 5). His analysis of "passing" (pp. 73 ff.) suggests that the desire to be accepted, to go from marked to unmarked status, extends over a very large range of relatively normal experiences. This desire, moreover, often complicates life as if it were an intricate novel. So the stutterer dodges certain words, "substituting non-feared words in their places or hastily shifting . . . thought until the continuity of . . . speech becomes as involved as a plate of spaghetti" (cited, p. 89).

Friedrich Schlegel asks laconically, in one of the *Athenaeum* fragments (I translate): "Why is one thing always absent from all fashionable listings of basic moral principles: the Ridiculous [*das Ridicüle*]? Is it because this principle has general validity only in experience [*in der Praxis*]?" That Schlegel uses a Gallicism, "*das Ridicüle*," perhaps better rendered as "the Outlandish," indicates that we are dealing with social error: with false wit, malapropism, an unconscious or affected breach of decorum. The tyranny of neoclassical ideals intensified the possibility of ridicule and embarrassment: in Heinrich von Kleist's "On the Marionette Theater" a vulgar art form is praised as exhibiting a type of physical grace that is infinitely beyond a beauty easily marred by embarrassment. A young man is said to have lost his "innocence" before the narrator's "very eyes" because of a remark that made him self-conscious, so that he could not recover the classical grace of posture he had sought to emulate. How hardy and healthy is Shakespearean comedy, which both releases wit from shame by allowing its outrage, its discountenancing of everyone, and makes it serviceable by the kind of labor Rosaline imposes on Berowne in *Love's Labour's Lost*. In this play, Don Adriano de Armado, called a "fantastical Spaniard," can be considered as the extravagant obverse of Geoffrey Hill's Arrurruz.

21. Kierkegaard, *The Concept of Irony*, trans. Lee M. Capel, pp. 63–64 and 271–73. Kierkegaard attributes to irony the very universality Bakhtin reserves for laughter in *Rabelais and His World*. "Irony in the eminent sense directs itself not against this or that particular existence but against the whole given actuality of a certain time and situation." Unlike satire and ridicule "it does not destroy vanity, it is not what punitive justice is in relation to vice, nor does it have the power of reconciliation within itself as does the comic."

22. At the limit, then, irony is not a surface feature but coextensive with literariness. (See Beda Allemann, "Ironie als literarisches Prinzip" in *Ironie und Dichtung,* ed. Albert Schaefer, for the best description of this device without properties, "where the cues are lacking, where this lack of cues even becomes the conditio sine qua non of the highest reaches of irony" and where, therefore, "purely formal analysis must fail.") To understand the elimination of the surface/depth distinction that irony achieves we must imagine the possibility of speaking *through* a face (per-sona) without distorting it into mask or grimace; or, obversely, a face that can listen to what is said without being discountenanced, or *dévisagé.* Irony limits *being known*—being defined or betrayed by words, or by the very assumption that there is a nuclear and intuitable essence to our being, a naming that coincides with an "I am." For a little satyr play on this question, see *Love's Labour's Lost* V.ii.590 ff.

23. "The individual spirit cannot see further than into its own mother, from which it derives its knowledge of origins and in which it stands; for it is impossible that this individual spirit should by its own natural power see into another principle and to behold it, unless born again within it." Jakob Boehme, chap. 7 of *Die drei Principien göttlichen Wesens* (*The Three Principles of Divine Being*). My translation perforce remains rough; and Boehme, it should be cautioned, uses "*Mutter*" as a quasi-alchemical term. But the anthropomorphic and psychological connotation is unavoidable.

24. Two exceptional studies should be mentioned, however. The relation of closure to rhythm or "haunting melody" (Theodor Reik), and to Romantic and Nietzschean speculations on music, is taken up in a suggestive essay by Phillippe Lacoue-Labarthe, "L'Echo du sujet," in *Le sujet de la philosophie.* Barbara Herrnstein Smith's *Poetic Closure* is a study of the formal endings of poems, which leads to important observations on the concept of closure generally.

25. His notorious reading of Keats's "Beauty Is Truth, Truth Beauty" as "Body Is Turd, Turd Body" is only an extreme case of counterstatement still linked to the question of beauty's truth. There is always, according to Burke, something more to know.

26. Differentiating speech from music, Theodor Adorno insists that music "innervates the intentions [meanings] that flash up, without losing itself to them, or binding them." Taking up in his own way certain ideas of Benjamin's, he views music as aiming at "intentionless speech," or "a demythologized kind of prayer, freed from the magic of efficacy, from the always frustrated human attempt to name the Name itself." In *Musikalische Schriften,* vol. 2.

27. Stanley Cavell, "The Acknowledgment of Silence," in *The World Viewed.* On recognition as a mutual act, see also Hegel, *Phenomenology of Spirit,* IV.A. For conversation as the ideal for style and understanding, cf. Hans-Georg Gadamer, *Truth and Method,* 340 ff.; and "Purification and Danger: Critical Style" in my *Criticism in the Wilderness.*

28. This would lead into the area explored by Reik, who follows up Freud's theory of trauma and repetition-compulsion. There are implications here for both secular and religious systems of law. See esp. Reik on shock, affrightedness, and deathly fear (*Todesangst*): "The defended ego has suddenly come to feel the threatening might of fatality, of a paternal edict [*Vatersatz*]." *Der Schrecken,* p. 24.

Bibiliography of Cited Works

Abraham, Karl. "Über die determinierende Kraft des Namens" (1911). In *Psychoanalytische Studien zur Charakterbildung und andere Schriften.* Edited by Johannes Cremerius. Frankfort: S. Fischer Verlag, 1969.

Abraham, Nicolas, and Torok, Maria. *Cryptonomie: le verbier de l'homme aux loups.* With a prefatory essay, "Fors," by Jacques Derrida. Paris: Aubier-Flammarion, 1976.

Adorno, Theodor W. *Eingriffe: Neun kritische Modelle.* Frankfort: Suhrkamp Verlag, 1963.

———. *Musikalische Schriften.* 3 vols. Frankfort: Suhrkamp Verlag, 1978. Vol. 2 first appeared in 1962.

Aeschylus. *The Oresteia.* Translated by Robert Fagles. Harmondsworth: Penguin, 1977.

Allemann, Beda. "Ironie als literarisches Prinzip." In *Ironie und Dichtung.* Edited by Albert Schaefer. Munich: Beck, 1970.

Althusser, Louis, and Balibar, Etienne. *Reading Capital.* Translated by Ben Brewster. London: NLB, 1970. First published in French in 1965.

Bachelard, Gaston. *Le droit du rêve.* Paris: Presses Universitaires de France, 1970. [*The Right to Dream.* Translated by J. A. Underwood. New York: Grossman, 1971.]

———. "Instant poétique et instant métaphysique" (1939). In *L'intuition de l'instant.* Edited by Jean Lescure. Paris: Gonthier, 1966.

Bakhtin, Mikhail. *Rabelais and His World.* Translated by Helene Iswolsky. Cambridge, Mass.: MIT Press, 1968. Written in Russian in 1940, but not published till 1965.

Barfield, Owen. *Saving the Appearances: A Study in Idolatry.* London: Faber & Faber, 1957.

Barthes, Roland. "Proust et les noms." In *To Honor Roman Jakobson: Essays on the Occasion of His Seventieth Birthday.* 3 vols. The Hague: Mouton, 1967. Vol. 1, pp. 150–58.

———. *S/Z.* Translated by Richard Miller and with a Preface by Richard Howard. New York: Hill & Wang, 1974. First published in French in 1970.

Bataille, Georges. *Oeuvres complètes.* 6 vols. Paris: Gallimard, 1970–73.

———. *Histoire de l'oeil,* vol. 1, pp. 13–69 [*Story of the Eye.* Translated by Joachim Neugroschel. New York: Urizen, 1977].

————. "La mutilation sacrificielle et l'oreille coupée de Vincent van Gogh," vol. I, pp. 258–70.

————. *Sur Nietzsche: volonté de chance*, vol. 6, pp. 11–205.

Benjamin, Walter. *The Origin of German Tragic Drama*. Translated by John Osborne. London: NLB, 1977. First published in German in 1927.

Blake, William. *The Poetry and Prose of William Blake*. Edited by David V. Erdman. Commentary by Harold Bloom. Garden City, N.Y.: Doubleday Anchor, 1965.

Blanchot, Maurice. *Le dernier homme; récit*. 3d ed. Paris: Gallimard, 1957.

————. *L'entretien infini*. Paris: Gallimard, 1969.

Bloom, Harold. *The Anxiety of Influence: A Theory of Poetry*. New York: Oxford University Press, 1973.

Boehme, Jakob. *Jakob Böhmes Sämtliche Werke*. 7 vols. Edited by K. W. Schiebler. Leipzig: J. A. Barth, 1831–47. Vol. 3, *Die drei Principien göttlichen Wesens* (1619).

Brisman, Leslie. "'At Thy Word': A Reading of *Romeo and Juliet*." *Bulletin of the Midwest MLA* 8 (1975): 21–35.

Brooks, Van Wyck. *The Ordeal of Mark Twain*. New York: E. P. Dutton, 1920.

Brown, Norman O. *Closing Time*. New York: Random House, 1973.

Burke, Kenneth. *Attitudes Toward History*. 2 vols. New York: New Republic Press, 1937.

————. *The Philosophy of Literary Form*. 3d ed. Berkeley and Los Angeles: University of California Press, 1973. First published in 1941.

Butor, Michel. *Répertoire: études et conférences*. 4 vols. Paris: Editions de Minuit, 1960–74. Vol. 3 was published in 1968.

Cavell, Stanley. *The World Viewed: Reflections on the Ontology of Film*. New York: Viking, 1971.

Coleridge, Samuel Taylor. *The Notebooks of Samuel Taylor Coleridge*. 3 vols. Edited by Kathleen Coburn. New York: Pantheon Books, 1957–61.

Cuddihy, J. M. *The Ordeal of Civility: Freud, Marx, Lévi-Strauss, and the Jewish Struggle with Modernity*. New York: Basic Books, 1974.

Culler, A. Dwight. *Tennyson*. New Haven: Yale University Press, 1977.

De Man, Paul. *Blindness and Insight: Essays in the Rhetoric of Contemporary Criticism*. New York: Oxford University Press, 1971.

Derrida, Jacques. *La carte postale de Socrate à Freud et au-delà*. Paris: Flammarion, 1980.

————. *De la grammatologie*. Paris: Editions de Minuit, 1967. [*Of Grammatology*. Translated by Gayatri Spivak. Baltimore: Johns Hopkins University Press, 1976.]

————. *La dissémination*. Paris: Editions du Seuil, 1972.

————. "Economimesis." In *Mimesis des articulations*. By Sylviane Agacinski et al. Paris: Aubier-Flammarion, 1975.

————. *L'écriture et la différence*. Paris: Editions du Seuil, 1967. [*Writing and Difference*. Translated by Alan Bass. Chicago: University of Chicago Press, 1978.]

————. "Fors." Translated by Barbara Johnson. *Georgia Review* 31 (1977): 64–120.

———. *Glas.* Paris: Galilée, 1974.

———. *Marges de la philosophie.* Paris: Editions de Minuit, 1972.

———. *L'origine de la géométrie.* A partial translation of Husserl's *Die Krisis der europäischen Wissenschaften und die transzendentale Phänomenologie.* With an Introduction. 2d ed. Paris: Presses Universitaires de France, 1974.

———. *Positions; entretiens avec Henri Ronse, Julia Kristeva, Jean-Louis Houdebine, Guy Scarpetta.* Paris: Editions de Minuit, 1972.

———. "The Purveyor of Truth." *Graphesis* (*Yale French Studies* 52). Edited by Marie-Rose Logan.

———. "La question du style." In *Nietzsche aujourd'hui?* 2 vols. Paris: Union Générale d'Editions, 1973. A selection from Derrida's essay has been trans-alted by Ruben Berezdivin. In *The New Nietzsche: Contemporary Styles of Interpretation,* pp. 176–89. Edited by David B. Allison. New York: Delta, 1977.

———. "Signéponge." *Digraphe* 8 (1976): 17–39.

———. *Spurs: Nietzsche's Styles/Eperons: les styles de Nietzsche.* Bilingual edition. Translated by Barbara Harlow. Chicago: University of Chicago Press, 1978.

———. "Structure, Sign, and Play in the Discourse of the Human Sciences." In *The Structuralist Controversy: The Languages of Criticism and the Sciences of Man,* pp. 247–72. Edited by Richard Macksey and Eugenio Donato. Baltimore: Johns Hopkins University Press, 1972. Also in *Writing and Difference.*

———. *La vérité en peinture.* Paris: Aubier-Flammarion, 1978.

———. *La voix et le phénomène: introduction au problème du signe dans la phénoménologie de Husserl.* Paris: Presses Universitaires de France, 1967. [*Speech and Phenomenon.* Translated by David B. Allison. Evanston: Northwestern University Press, 1973.]

———. "White Mythology: Metaphor in the Text of Philosophy." Translated by F.C.T. Moore. *New Literary History* 6 (Fall 1974): 5–74. First published in 1971, now in *Marges de la philosophie.*

Donoghue, Denis. *Thieves of Fire.* New York: Oxford University Press, 1974.

Ellison, Ralph Waldo. *Shadow and Act.* New York: Random House, 1964.

Felman, Shoshana. *La folie et la chose littéraire.* Paris: Editions du Seuil, 1978.

Ferenczi, Sándor. *Thalassa: A Theory of Genitality.* Translated by Henry A. Bunker. New York: W. W. Norton, 1968. Originally published in German as *Versuch einer Genitaltheorie* in 1924.

Frazer, Sir James G. *The Golden Bough.* 8 vols. London: Macmillan, 1911. First published in a shorter version in 1890.

Freud, Sigmund. *The Standard Edition of the Complete Psychological Works of Sigmund Freud.* Under the general editorship of James Strachey. 24 vols. London: Hogarth Press, 1953–74. Vols. 4 and 5, *The Interpretation of Dreams* (1900). Vol. 13, *Totem and Taboo* (1913). Vol. 23, *Moses and Monotheism* (1939).

Gadamer, Hans-Georg. *Truth and Method.* Translation edited by Garret Barden and John Cummings. New York: Seabury Press, 1975. First published in German in 1960.

Geertz, Clifford. *The Interpretation of Cultures: Selected Essays*. New York: Basic Books, 1973.

Genet, Jean. *L'atelier d'Alberto Giacometti*. Isère: Décines, 1958.

———. *Journal du voleur*. 2d ed. Paris: Gallimard, 1949. First published in a limited edition, probably 1948. [*The Thief's Journal*. Translated by Bernard Frechtman. With a Foreword by Jean-Paul Sartre. New York: Grove Press, 1964.]

———. *Oeuvres complètes*. 4 vols. Paris: Gallimard, 1951–68. The essay on Rembrandt, "Ce qui est resté d'un Rembrandt déchiré . . . ," is included in vol. 4.

Girard, René. *Deceit, Desire, and the Novel: Self and Other in Literary Structure*. Translated by Yvonne Freccero. Baltimore: Johns Hopkins Press, 1965. First published in French in 1961 as *Mensonge romantique et vérité romanesque*.

Goethe, Johann Wolfgang von. *West oestlicher Divan* (1819). Edited by Hans Albert Maier. Tübingen: Max Niemeyer, 1965.

Goffman, Erving. *Stigma: Notes on the Management of Spoiled Identity*. Englewood Cliffs, N.J.: Prentice-Hall, 1963.

Greene, Thomas M. "*Il Cortegiano* and the Choice of a Game." *Renaissance Quarterly* 32 (1979): 173–86.

Hartman, Geoffrey H. *Criticism in the Wilderness: The Study of Literature Today*. New Haven: Yale University Press, 1980.

———. *The Fate of Reading and Other Essays*. Chicago: University of Chicago Press, 1975.

Hegel, G. W. F. *Sämtliche Werke*. *Jubiläumsausgabe*. 20 vols. Edited by Hermann Glockner. Stuttgart: Frommann, 1927–30. Vol. 2, *Phänomenologie des Geistes*. [*Phenomenology of Spirit*. Translated by A. V. Miller. Oxford: Clarendon Press, 1977]. Vol. 6, *Enzyklopädie der philosophischen Wissenschaften im Grundrisse*. [*Encyclopedia of Philosophy*. Translated by Gustav E. Mueller. New York: Philosophical Library, 1959]. Vols. 12–14, *Vorlesungen über die Aesthetik*.

Heidegger, Martin. *Holzwege*. Frankfort: Klostermann, 1950.

———. *Kant and the Problem of Metaphysics*. Translated by J. S. Churchill. Bloomington: Indiana University Press, 1962. First published in German in 1929.

———. *Sein und Zeit*. 7th ed. Tübingen: Niemeyer, 1953. First published in 1927. [*Being and Time*. Translated by John Macquarrie and Edward Robinson. New York: Harper & Row, 1962.]

Hill, Geoffrey. *King Log*. London: A. Deutsch, 1968.

———. "Poetry as 'Menace' and 'Atonement.'" *University of Leeds Review* 21 (1978): 72–73.

Holland, Norman. "A Touching of Literary and Psychiatric Education." *Seminars in Psychiatry* 5 (1973): 287–99.

Hollier, Denis. *La prise de la concorde: essais sur Georges Bataille*. Paris: Gallimard, 1974.

Husserl, Edmund. *Ideen zu einer reinen Phänomenologie und phänomenologischen Philosophie*. Halle: Max Niemeyer, 1913. [*Ideas: General Introduction to Pure*

Phenomenology. Translated by W. R. Boyce Gibson. London and New York: Macmillan, 1931.]

Jabès, Edmond. *Le livre des questions.* Paris: Gallimard, 1963.

Jameson, Fredric. *The Prison-House of Language: A Critical Account of Structuralism and Russian Formalism.* Princeton: Princeton University Press, 1972.

Jauss, Hans Robert. *Aesthetische Erfahrungen und literarische Hermeneutik: Versuche im Feld der aesthetischen Erfahrung.* Munich: Fink, 1977.

Jolles, André. *Einfache Formen: Legende, Sage, Mythe, Rätsel, Spruch, Kasus, Memorabile, Märchen, Witz.* Halle: Max Niemeyer, 1930.

Joyce, James. *Finnegans Wake.* Eighth Printing. With the author's corrections incorporated in the text. New York: Viking Press, 1958. First published in 1939.

Kierkegaard, Søren. *The Concept of Irony.* Translated by Lee M. Capel. Bloomington: Indiana University Press, 1968. First published in Danish in 1841.

———. *Søren Kierkegaard's Journals and Papers.* 7 vols. Edited and translated by Howard V. Hong and Edna H. Hong. Bloomington: Indiana University Press, 1967–78.

Lacan, Jacques. *Ecrits.* 2 vols. Paris: Editions du Seuil, Collection "Points," 1970–71. First published in 1966. Several of these essays have been translated by Alan Sheridan. In *Ecrits: A Selection.* New York: W. W. Norton, 1977.

———. *The Four Fundamental Concepts of Psychoanalysis.* Translated by Alan Sheridan. London: Hogarth Press, 1977.

———. "Seminar on *The Purloined Letter.*" *French Freud (Yale French Studies* 48). Edited by Jeffrey Mehlman.

Lacoue-Labarthe, Phillippe. *Le sujet de la philosophie: typographies I.* Paris: Aubier-Flammarion, 1979.

Laplanche, J. *Hölderlin et la question du père.* Paris: Presses Universitaires de France, 1961.

Leisi, Ernst. *Paar und Sprache: Linguistische Aspekte der Zweierbeziehung.* Heidelberg: Quelle & Meyer, 1978.

Levinas, Emmanuel. *Totality and Infinity: An Essay on Exteriority.* Translated by Alphonso Lingis. Pittsburgh: Duquesne University Press, 1969. First published in French in 1961.

Littré, Emile. *Dictionnaire de la langue française* (1874). Edition intégrale. Paris: Gallimard/Hachette, 1962–69.

Mallarmé, Stéphane. *Oeuvres complètes.* Edited by Henri Mondor and G. Jean-Aubry. Paris: Pléiade, 1945.

Mann, Thomas. "Freud and the Future." In *Essays.* Translated by H. T. Lowe-Porter. New York: Alfred A. Knopf, 1957. First published in German in 1936.

Marx, Karl. *The Eighteenth Brumaire of Louis Bonaparte.* New York: International Publishers, 1963. First published in German in 1852.

Mehlman, Jeffrey. *A Structural Study of Autobiography: Proust, Leiris, Sartre, Lévi-Strauss.* Ithaca: Cornell University Press, 1974.

Murdoch, Iris. *Sartre: Romantic Rationalist.* New Haven: Yale University Press, 1953.

Nancy, Jean-Luc. *Le discours de la syncope.* Paris: Aubier-Flammarion, 1976.

Nietzsche, Friedrich. *The Birth of Tragedy* (1872). Translated by Walter Kaufmann. New York: Vintage Books, 1966.
_____. *Ecce Homo* (written 1888, but first published 1908). Translated by Walter Kaufmann. New York: Vintage Books, 1968. Published with *On the Genealogy of Morals* (1887).
_____. *The Gay Science* (1882). Translated by Walter Kaufmann. New York: Vintage Books, 1974.
_____. *Gesammelte Werke, Musarionausgabe.* 23 vols. Edited by R. Oehler, M. Oehler, and F. C. Würzbach. Munich: Musarion Verlag, 1920–29.
_____. *Thus Spoke Zarathustra: A Book for All and None* (written 1883–85; first complete edition, 1892). Translated by Walter Kaufmann. New York: Vintage Books, 1966.
Ogden, C. K. *Debabelization.* London: Kegan Paul, Trench, Trubner & Co., 1931.
Olson, Charles. *Call Me Ishmael.* New York: Reynal & Hitchcock, 1947.
Pater, Walter. *Miscellaneous Studies.* London: Macmillan, 1895.
_____. *The Renaissance: Studies in Art and Poetry.* 3d ed. London: Macmillan, 1888. First published in 1873.
Ponge, Francis. *The Sun Placed in the Abyss.* Translated by Serge Gavronsky. New York: Sun Press, 1977.
Reik, Theodor. *The Haunting Melody: Psychoanalytic Experiences in Life and Music.* New York: Farrar, Straus & Young, 1953.
_____. *Der Schrecken und andere psychoanalytische Studien.* Vienna: Psychoanalytischer Verlag, 1929.
_____. *Wie Man Psychologe Wird.* Leipzig, Vienna, Zurich: Psychoanalytischer Verlag, 1927.
Richards, I. A. *How to Read a Page: A Course in Effective Reading.* New York: W. W. Norton, 1942.
Richter, Jean Paul. *Vorschule der Aesthetik.* In *Sämmtliche Werke.* 33 vols. Berlin: G. Reimer, 1840–42. Vols. 18 and 19. [*Horn of Oberon.* Translated by Margaret Hale. Detroit: Wayne State University Press, 1973.]
Ricks, Christopher. *Keats and Embarrassment.* Oxford: Clarendon Press, 1974.
Ricoeur, Paul. *The Symbolism of Evil.* Translated by Emerson Buchanan. New York: Harper & Row, 1967. Originally the second part of Ricoeur's *Finitude et culpabilité.* Paris: Aubier, 1960.
Rosenzweig, Franz. *Der Stern der Erlösung.* Third unaltered printing. Heidelberg: Lambert Schneider Verlag, 1954. First edition, 1921. [*The Star of Redemption.* Translated from the second edition of 1930 by William W. Hallo. New York: Holt, Rinehart & Winston, 1971.]
Said, Edward. "Abecedarium Culturae: Structuralism, Absence, Writing." In *Modern French Criticism: From Proust and Valéry to Structuralism.* Edited by John K. Simon. Chicago: University of Chicago Press, 1972.
Sartre, Jean-Paul. *Saint Genet: Comédien et Martyr.* Paris: Gallimard, 1952. [*Saint Genet: Actor and Martyr.* Translated by Bernard Frechtman. New York: George Braziller, 1963.]
Saussure, Ferdinand de. *Course in General Linguistics.* Edited by C. Bally,

A. Sechehaye, and A. Riedlinger. Translated by Wade Baskin. New York: McGraw-Hill, 1959. First published in French in 1916.

Schlegel, Friedrich. *Athenaeum*. Eine Zeitschrift von A. W. Schlegel und F. Schlegel. Berlin: Bey F. Vieweg, 1798–1800.

————. *Dialogue on Poetry and Literary Aphorisms*. Translated by Ernst Behler and Roman Strue. University Park: Pennsylvania State University Press, 1968.

Scholem, Gershom. "Walter Benjamin und sein Engel." In *Zur Aktualität Walter Benjamins*. Edited by Siegfried Unseld. Frankfort: Suhrkamp, 1972. [Translated by W. J. Dannhauser in *Denver Quarterly* 9 (Fall 1974): 1–45.]

Smart, Christopher. *Jubilate Agno*. Edited by W. H. Bond. Cambridge, Mass.: Harvard University Press, 1954.

Smith, Barbara Herrnstein. *Poetic Closure: A Study of How Poems End*. Chicago: University of Chicago Press, 1968.

Sollers, Philippe. *Logiques*. Paris: Editions du Seuil, 1968.

Spitzer, Leo. *Essays in Historical Semantics*. New York: S. F. Vanni, 1948.

Starobinski, Jean, ed. *Les mots sous les mots: les anagrammes de Ferdinand de Saussure*. Paris: Gallimard, 1971. [*Words Upon Words: The Anagrams of Ferdinand de Saussure*. Translated by Olivia Emmet. New Haven: Yale University Press, 1979.]

Stein, Gertrude. *The Making of Americans: Being a History of a Family's Progress*. Paris: Contact Editions, 1925.

Thoreau, Henry David. "Walking" (1862). In *The Selected Works of Thoreau*. Cambridge Edition. Edited by Walter Harding. Boston: Houghton Mifflin, 1975.

Thorndike, Lynn. *A History of Magic and Experimental Science*. 8 vols. New York: Macmillan, 1923–58.

Tolstoi, Leo. *Anna Karenina*. Translated by Louise and Aylmer Maude. New York and London: Oxford University Press, 1926. Now available as a Norton Critical Edition.

Trilling, Lionel. *The Liberal Imagination: Essays on Literature and Society*. New York: Viking, 1950.

Turkle, Sherry. *Psychoanalytic Politics: Freud's French Revolution*. New York: Basic Books, 1978.

Valéry, Paul. "The Crisis of the Mind." In *History and Politics* (vol. 10 of *The Collected Works of Paul Valéry*). Translated by Denise Folliot and Jackson Mathews. Princeton: Princeton University Press, 1962. First published in English in 1919.

————. *Oeuvres de Paul Valéry*. 2 vols. Edited by Jean Hytier. Paris: Gallimard, 1957–60.

Wartburg, Walther von. *Französisches etymologisches Wörterbuch*. Bonn: Fritz Klopp, 1928–69.

Wilden, Anthony. *The Language of the Self: The Function of Language in Psychoanalysis*. Baltimore: Johns Hopkins Press, 1968. A fully annotated translation of Lacan's "Fonction et champ de la parole et du langage en psychanalyse" (1956).

Wittgenstein, Ludwig. *Philosophical Investigations*. 3d English ed. Translated by G.

E. M. Anscombe. New York: Macmillan, 1968. First published in English in 1953.

———. *Zettel*. Edited by G. E. M. Anscombe and G. H. von Wright. Translated by G. E. M. Anscombe. Oxford: Basil Blackwell, 1967.

Wolfson, Louis. *Le schizo et les langues*. Preface by Gilles Deleuze. Paris: Gallimard, 1970.

Zumthor, Paul. *Langue, texte, enigme*. Paris: Editions du Seuil, 1975.

Index of Names

Abraham, Karl, 111, 162 n.3
Abraham, Nicolas, 162 n.3, 163 n.6
Adami, Valerio, 17, 33, 35, 43, 62
Adorno, Theodor W., 110, 167 n.26
Aeschylus, 132, 165 n.16; *Eumenides*, 132, quoted, 131
Allemann, Beda, 167 n.22
Althusser, Louis, xix–xx, xxv; *Reading Capital*, xix
Ammann, Jost, 52
Antigone, 89–90
Antonioni, Michelangelo, xxi
Apollinaire, Guillaume, 35, 43
Arendt, Hannah, 63
Aristotle, xv, 160 n.9; *Poetics*, 107
Arnold, Matthew, 146
Artaud, Antonin, 52
Auden, W. H., 126
Augustine, St., 123, 125, 164 n.8

Bachelard, Gaston, 17
Bakhtin, Mikhail, 145–46, 166 n.21
Ballanche, Pierre-Simon, 166 n.20
Balzac, Honoré de, 65
Barfield, Owen, 8
Barthes, Roland, xxv, 16, 164 n.12
Bataille, Georges, xxv, 16, 22, 25, 123, 158 n.8, 159 nn.9 and 3
Baudelaire, Charles, xxvi, 72, 111–12, 117, 133
Beckett, Samuel, xxiv, 146
Benjamin, Walter, xvii, 47, 111–17, 163 n.8, 167 n.26; "Agesilaus Santander" fantasy, 112–13, 117; *The Origin of German Tragic Drama*, 112, 166 n.20; "Theses on the Philosophy of History," 113
Bergson, Henri, xx

Bewick, Thomas, 43
Blake, William, 7, 24, 26, 48, 52, 65–66, 145, 147; and dissemination, 50–51; *The Four Zoas*, 23–24, 50–51; *Milton*, 122
Blanchot, Maurice, xxv, 16, 63, 90, 159 n.9; quoted, 6, 7, 24, 63
Bloom, Harold, 56, 139, 160 n.8, 165 n.17
Boehme, Jakob, 151, 167 n.23; quoted, 148
Boullée, Etienne-Louis, 35, 41, 42
Brisman, Leslie, 162 n.3
Brissot, Jacques Pierre, 52
Brooks, Van Wyck, 166 n.20
Brown, Norman O., 63
Buber, Martin, 64
Burke, Kenneth, 15, 49, 51, 149, 164 n.9, 167 n.25; *The Philosophy of Literary Form*, 149, 165 n.17
Butor, Michel, 159 n.1
Byron, Lord (George Gordon), 122

Calderón de la Barca, Pedro, 164 n.7
Camus, Albert, 63
Carlyle, Thomas, 163 n.2
Cavafy, Constantin, xvi
Cavell, Stanley, xvi, 155, 167 n.27
Cervantes, Miguel de, 47
Chardin, Jean Baptiste, 17
Chaucer, Geoffrey, 146
Chicago Aristotelians, 120
Cicero, Marcus Tullius, 26
Claudel, Paul, 6
Coleridge, Samuel Taylor, xix, xxiii, 1, 4, 45, 144, 158 n.1; *The Ancient Mariner*, 131, 164–65 n.15
Crane, Hart, "The Broken Tower," quoted, 77, 87
Croce, Benedetto, 158 n.6

Cuddihy, J. M., 165–66 n.20
Culler, A. Dwight, 162 n.3

Dante Alighieri, quoted, 82
Da Vinci, Leonardo, 152
Deleuze, Gilles, xxv
De Man, Paul, 158 n.4
Derrida, Jacques, xv–xxvii passim, 1–32
passim, 33–66 passim, 67–95 passim,
96–98, 100, 101–7, 108–11, 119–22; *La
carte postale*, xxvi; "Coming into One's
Own," 159 n.11; *Derrière le miroir* essay (on
Adami), 17, 45; *La dissémination*, 4, 6, 21,
47, 158 n.4, 159 n.6, 163 n.1; "La double
séance," 160 n.10; "Economimesis," 160
n.9; "Fors," 162 n.3; *Glas*, xv–xxvii passim,
1–32 passim, 33–66 passim, 67–95 passim,
101–7; *Of Grammatology*, 90, 92, 103,
158 n.4, 162 nn.16 and 3, quoted, 43, 93;
Marges de la philosophie, 158 n.8, 159 n.2,
163–64 n.6, quoted, 86; "Le parergon," 161
n.10; "La pharmacie de Platon," 119, 163
n.1; *Positions*, 45, 159 n.1, 160 n.10,
quoted, 35, 52, 59; "La question du style,"
159 n.9; *Spurs*, xxii–xxiii; *La vérité en peinture*, 159 n.10, 161 n.10; *La voix et le
phénomène*, 5–6, 158 nn.2 and 3; *Writing
and Difference*, 158 n.4
Descartes, René, xv, xix, 1, 97
Dickinson, Emily, 135–36, 144
Diderot, Denis, 47
Donne, John, 50, 52, 133; "Lecture upon a
Shadow," 81; "A Valediction: Forbidding
Mourning," 153–54, quoted, 26, 148
Donoghue, Denis, 60
Dostoievski, Fyodor, 165 n.20
Dryden, John, 30, 158 n.1
Duchamp, Marcel, 22, 35

Eliot, T. S., xvi, xx, 5, 164 n.9
Ellison, Ralph Waldo, 111
Emerson, Ralph Waldo, 140
Empson, William, 22–23
Erasmus, Desiderius, 49

Faulkner, William, 107, 137–38
Ferenczi, Sándor, 108, 163 n.6

Feuerbach, Ludwig, 25
Flaubert, Gustave, 144
Foucault, Michel, xxv, 159 n.9
Frazer, Sir James George, 162 n.3
Freud, Anna, 27
Freud, Sigmund, xxvi–xxvii, 8, 20, 22, 24,
26–28, 35, 45, 61, 96, 104, 106–7, 108,
110, 122, 126, 128–29, 150, 159 n.3, 160
n.10, 164 n.13, 165 n.15, 165–66 n.20,
167 n.28; *Interpretation of Dreams*, 44,
106–7, 162 n.5, 165 n.19; and Lacan,
98–99; *Moses and Monotheism*, 58; quoted,
134; *Totem and Taboo*, 162 n.3; and wit, 48
Frye, Northrop, 49, 56

Gadamer, Hans-Georg, 167 n.27
Gautier, Théophile, quoted, 31
Geertz, Clifford, xxv, 162 n.3
Genet, Jean, 16–18, 22, 31, 44, 58–59, 61,
67, 73–76, 79, 82–83, 91–92, 97, 101–2,
104–6, 124–25, 133, 158 n.8, 159 n.3,
160 n.4, 161 n.12, 162 nn.15 and 4, 163
n.1, 164 n.10; and the Annunciation,
108–9; *L'atelier d'Alberto Giacometti*,
quoted, 91; neoclassical style and lost
mother tongue, 51
Giacometti, Alberto, 91
Girard, René, 163 n.3
Goethe, Johann Wolfgang von, 135–37,
154–55; *West-East Divan*, 135–36
Goffmann, Erving, 166 n.20
Gracian, 165 n.20
Greene, Thomas M., 165 n.20

Hegel, Georg Wilhelm Friedrich, xvii–xx,
4–32 passim, 35–49 passim, 61–66 passim,
67–94 passim, 97, 101–2, 104–6, 108–9,
158 n.6, 159 n.11, 167 n.27; *Encyclopedia
of the Philosophical Sciences*, 43–44, 161
n.12; *Phenomenology of Spirit*, 9, 14–15,
67, 73–74, 86, 160 nn.1 and 4, 161 n.11,
quoted, 78; *Philosophy of Law*, 161 n.12
Heidegger, Martin, xviii–xix, xxiv–xxvii, 2,
4–5, 14–15, 19, 21–22, 64, 66, 90–91, 96,
106, 110, 120, 141, 160 n.9; *Being and
Time*, xviii, xxvi, 4, 109, 141; and Wittgenstein, 156

Heine, Heinrich: *Memoirs*, 162 n.3; quoted, 78

Hill, Geoffrey, 143–44, 165–66 n.20; quoted, 141, 143

Hiltensperger, Johann Kaspar, 52

Hölderlin, Friedrich, 64, 101

Holland, Norman, 162 n.3

Hollier, Denis, 159 n.9

Homer, 24, 49

Hopkins, Gerard Manley, "The Windhover," 31–32

Horace, 46; quoted, 83, 141

Husserl, Edmund, xvi, 1, 5–6, 14, 16, 122

Ibsen, Henrik, 110

Isidore of Seville, 126

Jabès, Edmond, quoted, 64

James, Henry, 144

Jauss, Hans Robert, 164 n.8

Johnson, Samuel, 48

Jolles, André, 135

Joyce, James, xix, 15, 22–23, 44–45, 52, 64–65, 80, 146; *Finnegans Wake*, 2, 79, 133–34, quoted, 45, 118, 159 n.4, 165 n.17; *Portrait of the Artist as a Young Man*, 57, 63; *Ulysses*, quoted, 123

Jung, Karl, 51

Kafka, Franz, 62–63, 112, 156

Kant, Immanuel, 85–86, 87, 93, 160 n.9, 161 n.10

Keats, John, 145, 152–54, 167 n.25; *The Fall of Hyperion*, 118–19, 152–53; *Hyperion*, 152–53; "La Belle Dame sans Merci," 120–21

Kierkegaard, Søren, 124, 146, 166 n.21

Klee, Paul, 35, 112–13

Kleist, Heinrich von, 82, 166 n.20

Kojève, Alexandre, 158 n.6

Lacan, Jacques, xxv–xxvi, 21, 26–28, 45, 61–62, 66, 81, 96–101, 103–5, 109–10, 139, 151, 154, 159 n.13, 164 n.10; "The Agency of the Letter," quoted, 98, 109, 111, 162 nn. 2 and 4; and Derrida, 18, 31, 77–78; *Four Fundamental Concepts*, quoted, 161 n.5; on self-identity, 58, 74

Lacoue-Labarthe, Phillippe, 167 n.24

Laplanche, J., 162 n.2

Legenda Aurea, 126–27

Leiris, Michel, 52, 163–64 n.6

Leisi, Ernst, 162 n.3, 166 n.20

Leopardi, Giacomo, 125

Levinas, Emmanuel, xvii, xxv

Linnaeus, 19, 127

Little, Malcolm (Malcolm X), 125–26, 164 n.11

Littré, Emile, 82–83, 161 n.8

Lombardo, Bill, 35

Loyola, St. Ignatius, 50

Luther, Martin, 50

Magritte, René, 35

Malherbe, François, 65

Mallarmé, Stéphane, xvii, xxv, xxvii, 6, 9, 21, 25, 32, 45, 49, 51, 66, 77, 106, 110–11; "L'Après-midi d'un faune," 87, 147; "Cantique de Saint Jean," 21; "Crayonné au Théâtre," 21; *Herodiade*, 109–10; "Mimique," 59; *Les mots anglais*, 87–89, 162 n.14; "Prose pour des Esseintes," 21

Mann, Thomas, 27

Marinetti, Emilio Filippo Tommaso, 35

Marvell, Andrew, 46, 142

Marx, Karl, xx, 22, 25; *The Eighteenth Brumaire*, 63

McLuhan, Marshall, 56

Mehlmann, Jeffrey, 159 n.12

Melville, Herman, 57, 126, 146; *The Confidence-Man*, 90, 137, 139–40, 146; *Moby-Dick*, 126, quoted, 57; *Pierre, or The Ambiguities*, 107, 126

Mérimée, Prosper, 143

Merleau-Ponty, Maurice, 6

Milton, John, 8, 44, 56, 66, 163 n.6; *Lycidas*, 52, 157; *Paradise Lost*, 108; *Paradise Regained*, quoted, 106

Murdoch, Iris, quoted, 137

Nancy, Jean-Luc, 107

Nerval, Gerard de, 103

New Criticism, xxi

Nietzsche, Friedrich, xxiv, 22, 24–25, 27–32 passim, 47, 49, 67, 78, 80–81, 84–85, 109, 120, 146, 149, 157, 159 n.9, 167 n.24; and asceticism, xxvi, 56; *Birth of Tragedy*, 67, 157, 160 n.2, 161 n.6; *Ecce Homo*, 67, 160 n.4; *Gay Science*, quoted, 129–30; *Genealogy of Morals*, xxiv; quoted, 26, 72–73, 95; on *Schein* (illusion), 4, 25, 30, 47, 149, 157; *Thus Spoke Zarathustra*, 29, 80, 146, 152
Novalis (Friedrich von Hardenberg), 47

Ogden, C. K., 165 n.20
Oldenberg, Claes, 35
Olson, Charles, 56–57; quoted, 57, 134

Parsifal (Wagner), 119
Pascal, Blaise, 48
Pater, Walter, 32, 67, 72, 84, 143
Paul, St., 139–40
Philo Judaeus, 51
Piaget, Jean, 100
Plato, xxvi, 4, 49, 66, 120–21; Derrida on, 119
Poe, Edgar Allan, xviii, 31, 110–11; "The Bells," 35, 111
Ponge, Francis, 2, 81, 161 n.7
Pound, Ezra, 43, 56
Proudhon, Pierre, quoted, 7, 92
Proust, Marcel, 72
Pynchon, Thomas, 146

Rabelais, François, 49, 146
Ransom, John Crowe, 157
Reik, Theodor, 164 n.14, 167 nn.24 and 28
Rembrandt van Rijn, 16–18, 58, 91
Resnais, Alain, *Last Year at Marienbad*, 100
Richards, I. A., 160 n.1
Richter, Jean Paul, 47–48, 50, 159 n.5
Ricks, Christopher, 165 n.20
Ricoeur, Paul, 122, 163 n.4
Rilke, Rainer Maria, 2, 26, 142–43, 147
Rimbaud, Arthur, 100
Robbe-Grillet, Alain, 35, 77
Ronsard, Pierre de, 49
Rosenzweig, Franz, xvii–xviii, 64

Rousseau, Jean Jacques, 4, 22, 87, 91
Roussel, Raymond, 52
Ruskin, John, 72
Russell, Bertrand, 164 n.12

Sade, Marquis de, 22
Said, Edward, 158 n.4
Saint-Simon, Henri de, 98
Santayana, George, 49
Sartre, Jean-Paul, 22, 25, 44, 90, 99, 103, 108, 124–25, 137; on Genet, 105, 124–25; *Saint Genet*, quoted, 111, 162 n.4, 164 n.7
Saussure, Ferdinand de, 15, 20, 43–44, 61, 83, 94, 104, 126–27, 158 n.7, 161 n.9
Schelling, Friedrich Wilhelm Joseph von, xix
Schlegel, Friedrich, 47, 52, 166 n.20
Scholem, Gershom, 111–13, 163 n.8
Schopenhauer, Arthur, 28
Schwitters, Kurt, 35
Shakespeare, William, 47, 52, 91, 131–33; *Hamlet*, 59, 122, quoted, 130; *1 Henry IV*, quoted, 126; *2 Henry IV*, 164 n.7; *King Lear*, 129–30, 131–32, 134–35; *Love's Labour's Lost*, 138, 166 n.20, 167 n.22; *Macbeth*, quoted, 132; *Othello*, 122–23, 128, 131; *Romeo and Juliet*, quoted, 101; *Troilus and Cressida*, quoted, 59, 96; *The Winter's Tale*, xxii
Shelley, Percy Bysshe, 31, 145
Silesius, Angelus, *Der Cherubinischer Wandersmann*, 113
Skelton, John, quoted, 92
Sleeping Beauty (Dornröschen), 145
Smart, Christopher, 50, 52, 62, 82, 127–28; quoted, 8, 48, 105, 127, 164 n.13
Smith, Barbara Herrnstein, 167 n.24
Snow White, 102, 119
Socrates, xxii, xxvi, 26, 120, 157
Sollers, Philippe, xxv, 52
Spenser, Edmund, 2, 123, 124, 163 n.5
Spitzer, Leo, 161 n.8, 164 n.12
Spivak, Gayatri, 160 n.9
Starobinski, Jean, 15, 158 n.7, 161 n.9, 162 nn.17 and 3
Stendhal (H. M. Beyle), 120
Sterne, Laurence, *Tristram Shandy*, 47
Stevens, Wallace, xxiv, 74, 80; quoted, 2, 148, 151–52
Swift, Jonathan, 52

Tennyson, Alfred, Lord, 111; "The Lady of Shalott," 97, 110–11
Thoreau, Henry David, 22; *Walking*, quoted, 128
Thorndike, Lynn, 163 n.5
Tolstoi, Leo, 138–39, 140–41, 166 n.20; *Anna Karenina*, 138–39, 165 n.18
Torok, Maria, 162 n.3
Trilling, Lionel, 165 n.20
Turkle, Sherry, 162 n.1
Twain, Mark (Samuel Clemens), 146

Valéry, Paul, xxii–xxiii, xxv, 14, 65; "The Crisis of the European Mind," xv–xvi, 9, 158 n.5; *Eupalinos*, xxii–xxiii, xxv, 7; "Fragments du Narcisse," quoted, 100; quoted, 25
Vergil, *Georgics*, 49–50
Verlaine, Paul, 151
Vico, Giambattista, xv, 63

Wartburg, Walther von, 19, 82–83, 85, 161 n.8
Wilde, Oscar, 56, 109
Wilden, Anthony, 162 n.2, 163 n.7
Winckelmann, Johann Joachim, 72, 83–85, 90
Wittgenstein, Ludwig, xvi, xxvii, 28–29, 155–56; *Philosophical Investigations*, 28, 155–56; *Zettel*, 28
Wolfson, Louis, 164 n.9
Wordsworth, William, 1, 57, 121, 153–54, 163 n.6; *On the Power of Sound*, 123–24; *The Prelude*, 151; "A Slumber Did My Spirit Seal," 147–48, 149, 153; "Tintern Abbey," 151

Yeats, William Butler, 106

Zumthor, Paul, 158 n.4

Index of Subjects

Allegoresis, xxv, 51, 149

Ancestors, precursors, *maiores*, xvi, xviii, 67, 72, 80, 160 n.4, 167 n.28; as *bouche d'ombre*, 151

Aphasia (stutterance), 134; muteness, 57, 148; word-loss, 59

Aphorism, 2, 63; aphoristic energy, 2, 4, 28. *See also* Epigram

Apollo, Apollonian, xix, 25, 27, 30, 72–74, 79, 80–81, 93–94, 149, 161 n.11

Aufhebung, 16, 18, 30, 31, 77, 89, 92, 109, 160 n.10; as "elation," 24, 29, 32, 74

Autobiography: and spectral name, 112–17

Bible, 24, 30, 50, 56, 63, 136, 149, 151; Abraham story, 18, 47; Corinthians, Letter to, 6, 139–40; Genesis, 49, 65–66, 129, quoted, 130; Job, Book of, 57; Luke, 108; Mark, quoted, 142; Matthew, 108, quoted, 57

Blessing, 99, 108, 129–33, 164–65 n.15; and irony, 145–48

Book, xvi, xxvi, 2, 90, 158 n.4; of the Creatures, 6, 19, 127; *Glas* as farce or satura, 63; *Glas* as nonbook, xvi, 2, 18–19, 79; printed page as *carré/cadre*, 16, 35, 45, 85–86, 159 n.1

Castration, 18, 21, 30–31, 83, 100, 159 n.3, 164 n.10

Chiasmus, 18, 28, 33, 45, 62; X factor, 89

Christianity, 31; anti-Christ, 67; and asceticism, 56; kenosis (Hegel), 78

Classicism, 48, 87, 149; as Apollonianism, 83; French, 82, 146; Hellenism, xix–xx, xxii, 17–18, 84; and separation of genres, 63

Closure, 16, 48, 109, 144, 148–54, 157; glossolalia as foreclosure, 144, 167 n.24

Commentary, literary: as genre, xv–xx, 79–80; interstitial thinking, 1, 3, 66

Correspondence, xxvi, 72, 135–38

Coup/coupure/cut, 18–19, 22, 29, 31, 59, 72

Crosswording, 62, 73. *See also* Equivocation

Curse, 110, 125, 129–33, 145, 147, 154, 157, 164–65 n.15; and Furies, 132–33

Deconstruction, 7, 23, 24, 28, 35, 51, 61, 109, 110, 121

Dionysus, Dionysian, xix, 27, 67, 72–76, 78–81, 93–95, 120, 157

Dissemination, 17–18, 19, 20, 48–51, 56, 63, 76, 79, 81, 103; and cultural translation, 49, 65, 158 n.1; in Renaissance, 49–50; in Romanticism, 50

Ear: blinding of, 148; ear-fear, 143, 157; Gothic groping of, 57; mishearing/mistaking, 109; overhearing, 128, 142–43; spectral sounds, xxii, 143, 151, 157; wounded, 44, 57–59, 123, 128, 133, 159 n.3

Empiricism, 154–55

Enlightenment, 146

Epigram, 12, 35, 113. *See also* Aphorism

Equivocation, xvi, xxiii, 14, 19, 21, 22, 23, 44–45, 60–61, 79, 98, 123, 133; in Shakespeare, 131–32, 139, 143, 157. *See also* Crosswording; Word play

Euphemism, 122, 125, 133, 145–48; and "soft names," 145, 147. *See also* Blessing; Curse; Language: flowers of language/language of flowers

Eye, 44, 123; and ear, 46, 59, 142; the look (*regard, coup d'oeil, Augenblick, Glanz,* glance), 6, 16–18, 20, 44, 113, 158 n.8. *See also* Image

Face, 152–53; mask (per-sona), 167 n.22
Family, 18, 89, 100, 161 n.12; family romance, 102, 106, 107, 109
Figures of speech. *See* Language: flowers of language/language of flowers

Heiterkeit (gaiety), 24
Hermeneutics: Christian, 139–40; of hope, 62
History, 28, 63–64, 66, 76, 113, 154–55; Ancients and Moderns, 8, 56; in dictionaries, 82–83; historicism, xix–xx; literary, 48, 51, 56, 159 n.6; and textuality, 30
Homosexuality, 108–9, 162 n.15

Image, 3, 18, 100–101, 152–53; picture-thinking, 86; picture-writing, 43; as puncturing, 97, 131, 164 n.8; speaking picture, 35–36; speaking silence, 58
Impersonality, xx, xxv, 6, 72, 76, 77, 159 n.11
Indeterminacy, xx, 1–2, 14, 21, 46, 98, 106–7, 151; "abysmation," xxii, 20, 52; infinitizing, 23, 103, 144; interminable analysis, xv, 22, 28, 149; mirror-play, 121; unbottoming, 66
Internalization (*Er-innerung,* inscription), 5, 73, 75–77, 80, 86, 139
Interpretation, 60, 134–41, 149–50; and charity, 139–40
Irony, 145–48, 166 n.21, 167 n.22; Romantic, 47; Socratic, 24

Jewishness (Hebraism), xix–xx, 17–19, 63, 95, 112–13
Jokes and jests, 133, 138; earnest jesting (*serio ludere*), 22, 24, 29

Kabbalah, 56, 113

Language: anagrams, 102, 113; babble, 144; charades, 136, 138; cognitive, recognitive, 137; contamination/purification, 15,

49–51, 65, 82, 87–88; discourse of the Other, 16, 109, 110, 142, 151; echo-nature of, 60–62, 111; economy of, 59, 90–93; English, 89; flowers of language/language of flowers, 19, 46, 79, 94, 105, 106, 109, 122, 125, 127, 133–34, 145, 162 n.5; and "free-play," 22, 25, 90; French, 87, 89; "good" and " bad" letters, 119–20; heterogeneity of discourse, 90; and law, 62–63; and libido, 48, 87; logic and, 155–56; love-hate of, 4; *materna lingua/sermo patrius,* 154; and maternal "calculus," 75–78, 98, 105–6; matrix, 82–83; meta-, 99, 127; *mot juste,* 129–30; mother tongue (vernacular), 48, 50, 52, 125, 134, 146, 154, 164 n.9; ordinary and extraordinary, 152; originary violence of, 92, 119; and play, 5; private and public, 136–37; and psyche, 96–117 passim; radically metaphoric, 4, 46, 109; rebus, 43, 59, 83, 102; riddle, 134–35; slip/slippage/slipperiness of, 8, 19–20, 62, 64, 82, 111; Wittgenstein on, 155–56; womanly speech (Discours d'Elle), 82–83, 87, 89, 99; word-therapy, 122, 128; written sign, 35–44, 119–21. *See also* Logos
Language Exchange, 134–38
Logos, xix, xxii, 5–8, 19, 48, 56, 92, 101, 103, 107, 109, 121, 144; logocentrism, 5, 6, 101, 110

Madness, 48, 52, 122, 124
Mannerism, 35
Mimesis (imitation), xx, xxvi, 48–51, 120–21, 124, 157, 160 n.9, 163 n.3; and dissemination, 49–50; and translation, 64, 65, 158 n.1
Modernism, 145
Monument, monumentalism, 5–7, 25, 27, 33–35, 89, 104, 161 n.11; equilibrium/disequilibrium, 83–86; mirror, statue, automaton, 27–28, 82; residue (debris, *le reste*), xxiv, 14–32 passim, 60, 75, 79, 84, 106; Ruins of Time, 7; "symbolic" architecture, 80
Morcellation (*corps morcelé*), 96, 100–101
Mother tongue. *See* Language

Nachträglichkeit (Freud), 8–9
Name: act of naming, 62, 67; and Annuncia-

tion, 107–9; antonomasia, 81; fading of, 73–75, 102, 103; of the father, 57, 105–6; hypogram, 15, 83, 94; imago of proper name, 20, 97, 101; and Linnaeus, 127; of the mother, 76, 81, 83, 105–6; nicknames, 125, 128, 162 n.3; onomatoclastic, 16, 80, 97, 128; as proper noun, 5, 15, 18, 20, 32, 33, 59–60, 64, 77, 79, 86, 93–94, 106, 117, 133, 163 n.8, 164 n.9; scene of nomination, 62, 101–2, 111–12; spectral, 62, 125–26, 164 n.10; specular, 101–2, 111–17; wounding of, 59–60, 95, 101, 117, 124–28, 162 n.3. See also Signature

Narcissism, 4, 74, 100, 102, 111, 128

Nausea, 44–45, 83, 92

Negative theology, xvii, 7, 57

Nihilism, xxiv, 56; "nothing," xvii, 129–30

Nonbeing, xviii; forgetting of being (Seinsvergessenheit), xix, xxiii

Painting, as ecriture, 16–17, 33–35

Phallus: differentiating, 100; pen-phallus, 105–7; as signifier, 99; as "transcendental key," 18, 105

Philosophy: and art, 67–68, 90; and death, xvii–xviii, 26–27; as heterology, 16; in language, 23, 46; Western, 96; will to knowledge (truth), 31, 47

Poet/writer: as medicine man, 20, 97, 118–19, 133, 149, 165 n.17

Presence, xx, xxv, 3, 4, 65, 74, 92; and absolute knowledge, 97; and aura, 60, 113; directness of speech, 96–97, 130; ecstatic identification, 27, 58, 104, 106; face to face, 97, 151–52; and fiat, 92, 131; glassification, 28, 113; ici, maintenant, 14–32 passim, 61–62, 107; and image, 16, 18, 131; and Immaculate Conception, 31, 61, 103–4; immediacy, 15, 97; magnificat/magnification, 101–2, 108; maternal/musical, 151; metaphysics of, 18, 26, 61; nunc stans, 21; presence of word/word of presence, 107–8; presentness, 15, 97; prestige of origins, 51–52, 121, 157; proper/propre, 4, 53–54, 83, 93, 99, 106, 110; and recognition scene, 62–63, 107, 109, 167 n.27; and translucence, xvi, xix, 17. See also Monument, monumentalism

Prose, 9, 45, 66, 87, 152

Psychoanalysis, xviii, 27–28, 45, 60, 97–117

passim, 123, 129, 157; and catharsis, 122, 132, 148; defenses, 27, 128; ego psychology, 27, 99; Marienbad complex, 100; metapsychology, 26; mirror phase, 24, 26, 100, 101, 139; and theology, 99; traumatic interruption, 145; work of mourning, 30, 103, 150, 153

Quotation, 9, 14–15, 18, 63. See also Language; Words within words

Reading, xix–xx, 29, 50, 52–53, 85, 128–29, 141–42

Religion of Art, 67, 72, 79, 84

Representation, xxv, 17, 48, 59, 100, 119–22, 160 n.9; nonrepresentational art, 86

Reserve: "Hegelianism without reserve," 16; and mute letter, 14, 46; and style, 23, 29

Rhetoric, 120

Romanticism, Romantics, xx, 47–51, 113, 145–46, 155, 167 n.24

Satire: in the history of laughter, 145–46

Saving the appearances, xv, xxi

Savoir absolu/absolute knowledge (Hegel), 4–5, 15, 29, 72, 102; and non-savoir (unknowingness), 16, 52

Semiotics, xxii, 5, 43–44, 99, 126–27, 129, 153, 154; "semidiotic," 21

Signature, 4, 19, 32, 33, 59–62, 80, 95, 103; and style, 16–17, 128

Silence, xvi–xvii, 31, 46, 58, 81, 136, 142, 147–48, 164 n.14

Solecism: and language-sensitivity, 143–44; and social offence, 165 n.20; and style, 144, 156

Speaking in tongues (glossolalia), 140, 144

Style, xxii–xxiii, 4, 22, 28, 51, 65, 106, 156; bifide, 45, 51; as continued solecism, 144; Greek/Asiatic, 16; neoclassical, xix, 22, 25, 51

Subject (sujet, self-identity), xxi, 5–6, 19–20, 58, 62, 65, 75, 94, 97, 102, 107, 109, 128, 159 n.11; and anamnesis, 62–63; aphanisis of, 77–78, 161 n.5, 161 n.11; ego/echo, 9; in Lacan, 26–27, 58; natal genius, 112; negative identity, 124; self and other, 99, 110. See also Psychoanalysis

Techne, xxv–xxvi, 48; sound machine, 27, 159 n.13; word-, 45, 160 n.3; writing machine, 27, 159 n.13

Text, textuality, xix, xxv, 3–4, 7–8, 15, 29, 52, 59, 66, 83, 102, 141; antisubstance, 3, 19, 64–66, 119; and conceptual knowledge, 24, 29; errands of, 35, 51–52; intertextuality, 25, 29, 105, 121, 149; literary text and trust, xxi, 137; and psyche, 58

Thanatopraxis (economy of death), xxv–xxvi, 26

Theft (discourse of), 91–93, 94, 98; bricolage, xxiii, xxv, 65, 95

Thing (res, chose), 21, 32–33, 46, 66, 81, 83, 86, 90, 106, 129

Totality, xvi–xvii, 4, 110

Tragedy, 107, 137

Voice, voices, xviii, xxii, 5–7, 57, 119, 121, 151–53, 156, 157; absolute vocative, 93–94; image of voice (imago vocis), xxii, 35; impersonification, 6; orphic power of, 44, 151; sermo interior, 192

Will to write, xxiv

Wit (esprit), 24, 35–48, 50, 135; mother-wit, 50, 146; and Romantic irony, 47; as wound, 46

Word-divination, 135–38

Word play: anglais/anglé, 87; Argo/argot, 93; ça/cas/cas-tration, 13, 18, 21, 53, 74–75, 83; coin/coin, 85; EC/IC, 9, 61; Ecke/Ekel, 85, 93; elle/aile/L, 87; encre/ancre, xxiii, 73; Fall/phallus, 75; Fall/Falle (of words), 3, 13; fort (gone)/fort (strong), 33, 45; genet/genêt, 92; Hegel/aigle, 9, 94, 127; IC/ici/ich/chi, 61–62; "joycing," 5, 133; L'a/la/là, 87, 90; L/elle, 75–77; legs/lait, 77, 163 n.1; lis/lit/lit, 19, 106; lui/luire, 73; qui/chi (chiasmus), 33, 45; res/reste, 66; réséda/res, 95; Sa/ça, 20–21, 31, 60–61; sans/sens, 79, 85; savoir/s'avoir, 92; seing/sein/Sein (sign), 81, 104; voie/voix, 5; vol/vol, 93; Winckel-mann (Angle-man)/Kant, 85. See also Equivocation

Words within words, 129, 142, 144, 151, 154

Word-wound, xxii, 60, 118–21, 123, 138–39, 142, 154, 156; speaking wound, 164 n.7. See also Name: wounding of

Writing (ecriture), xviii–xx, 4, 8, 16–19, 22, 24–25, 35, 86–87, 159 n.4, 161 n.11; aniconic, xix, 17; and Aufhebung, 160 n.10; deconstructs Latinity, 25; destabilizes meanings or words, xxi–xxii; and nonbeing, xix–xx; in Plato, 119; primal scene of, 14; as stored speech, xx, 43

The Johns Hopkins University Press

This book was set in VIP Electra by The Composing Room of Michigan Inc. from a design by Charles West. It was printed on 50-lb. Eggshell Offset Cream paper and bound by Universal Lithographers, Inc.